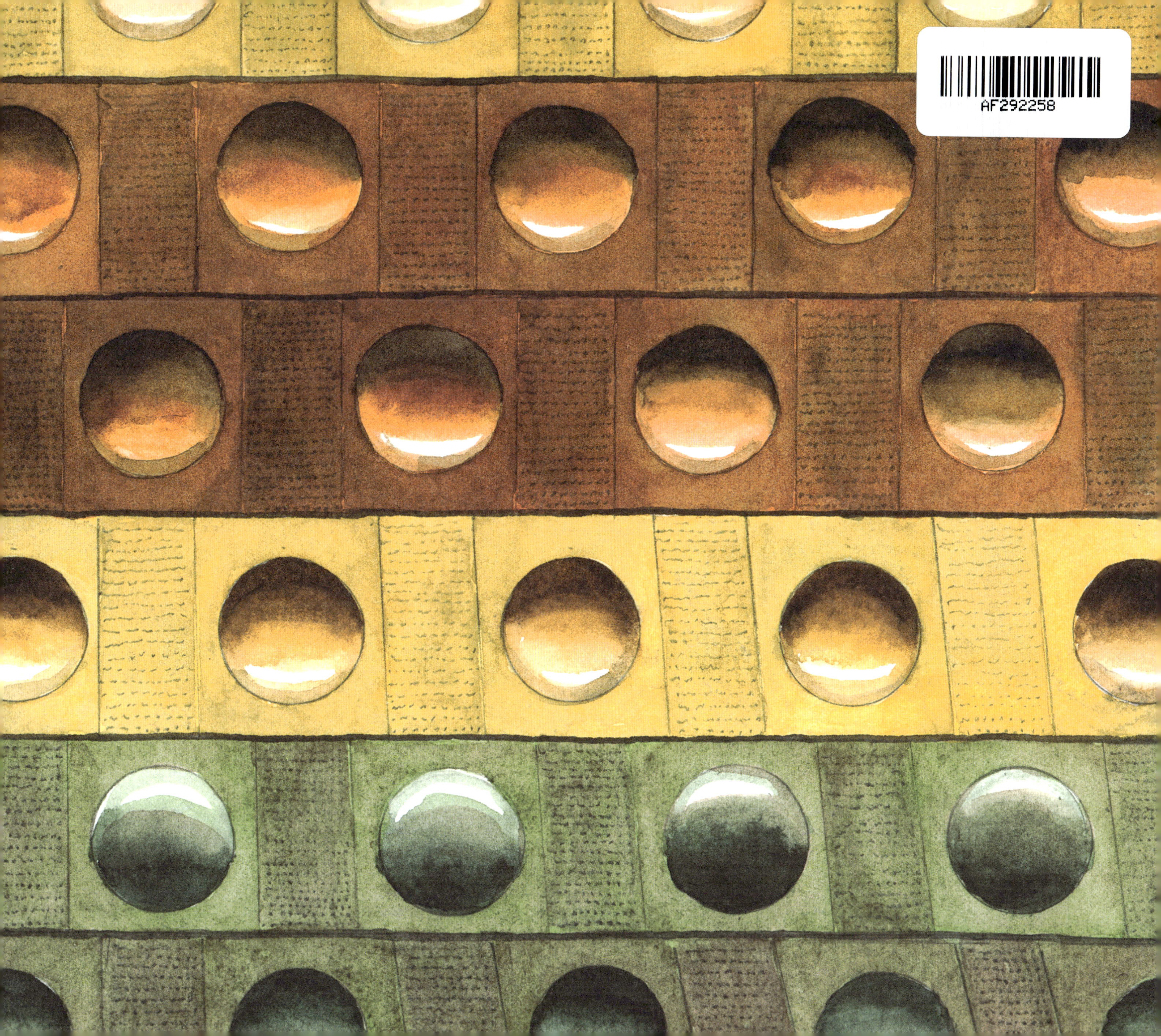

PRAGUE

sketchbook

Special thanks to Thierry Théault
for making this book a reality.
In 2019, while running the Paris office
of Les Éditions du Pacifique, Thierry was
approached by Tom, a Fabrice Moireau
superfan, eager to collaborate on
a watercolor book. With no immediate
plans, Thierry casually tossed out
Prague as a potential city–no pressure,
just a suggestion. Fast forward to 2023,
and despite having zero personal
ties to Prague, Tom (a Canadian living
in Berlin) took that suggestion a little
too seriously. He visited Prague more
than forty times, capturing its beauty
in watercolors–still not quite sure if
a book would come of it. And yet, here
we are now–bringing this book to life!
Alexandre Millet

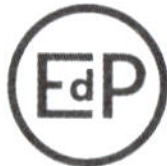

© Les Éditions du Pacifique, 2024
29, rue des Trois Bornes, 75011 Paris
www.leseditionsdupacifique.com

In loving memory of Marie-Claude Millet,
the timeless collection manager
of the sketchbook series.

Project manager: Clara Paumier

Text editing: John Kenny
Captions: Anne-Sylvie Homassel
Captions translation: Sheila McCarron

Design and typesetting: Benoit Dupré

Reprography: Fotimprim

Printed à Saint-Just-la-Pendue
by Imprimerie Chirat, France
on Munken Print White

Legal deposit: October 2024

Front cover:
Neo-Renaissance and Baroque
facades in the Old Town square.

Below:
House of the Three Little Fiddles
(Dům U Tří housliček), Neruda Street.
It housed Pradter and Edlinger,
renowned 18th century violin makers.

Title page:
Almond trees in bloom
in the seminary gardens
(Seminářská zahrada) on Petřín Hill.

Back cover:
Wenceslas Square and
the equestrian statue of the prince,
saint and martyr of the same name.

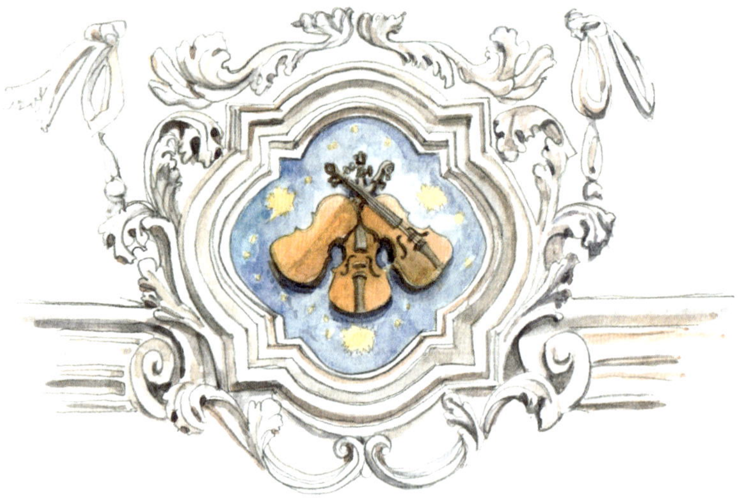

PRAGUE

sketchbook

PAINTINGS TOM MAIRS
TEXT JAROSLAV KALFAR

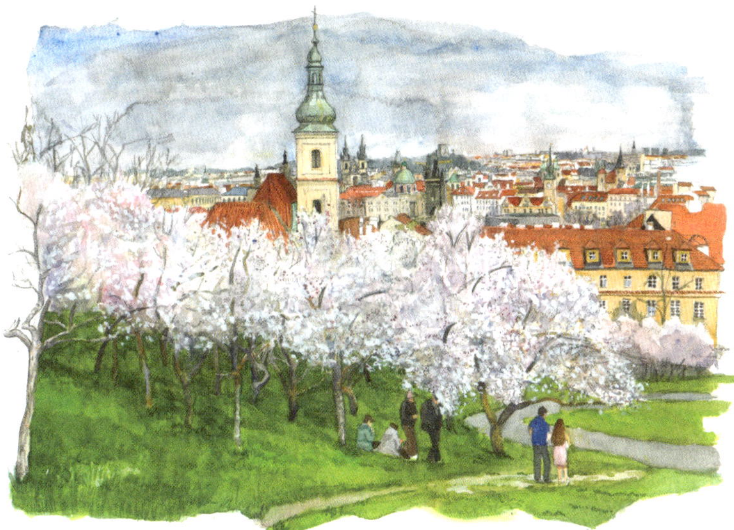

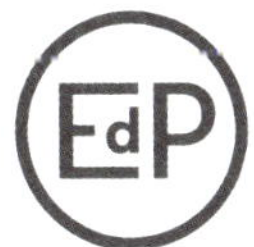

Contents

Prague Won't Let You Go

A life in Old Town

Prague. The city I yearn for and the city I've run from. "Prague won't let you go, the little mother has claws", Franz Kafka once said of our shared birthplace, knowing that to fall in love with a beautiful city guarantees a life of suffering.

I was born in the middle of a tourist attraction—and a revolution. For the first three years of my life, my father, a plumber, my mother, a hotel receptionist, and I lived in one of the most sought-after zip codes in Prague. We occupied a ground-floor apartment on a street called Dušní (translated as "of the soul"), tucked into the city's famous Jewish Quarter. The birthplace of Kafka, the Quarter is home to stunning 15th century synagogues and the iconic Old Jewish Cemetery. Over the centuries, it withstood the whims of European emperors who flattened and rebuilt it several times over, as well as the Nazis, who plundered its artifacts and planned to preserve it as a museum to "an extinct race".

To my family, the Quarter was simply the neighborhood. Beloved Czech movie stars watched passively as their dogs defecated in front of our doorstep. The grocer's clan next door had known our family for generations and allowed us to shop on credit. A phone booth installed too close to our building entrance irritated my father, who attempted with my grandfather to rip it out of the ground and move it down the street (it didn't work out). Amidst these petty concerns of daily life, on this street and in our city, morose and tragic decades were coming to an end. When I was just one year old, my mother took me in my stroller to Wenceslas Square, a twenty-minute walk from our house, to see the final movement of a revolution so gentle historians have dubbed it "Velvet".

Facing mass protests and a lack of support from the collapsing Soviet Union, the Communist Party leadership had resigned in the winter of 1989. Tens of thousands of Czechs filled the long slope of the square and shook their keys to celebrate this momentous occurrence as the policemen who had beaten them with batons just days before stood still and watched. I was too young to remember any of it, and yet, I can conjure distinct images of what I saw that day from my stroller when I close my eyes. I see the statue of Wenceslas the Good, glorious atop his horse, whose virtuous nature and assassination by his brother made him the patron saint of Bohemia. I see the saint's statue adorned with Czech flags and handwritten signs, bidding us to "wish truth upon all". I see people sitting and resting from an excess of revolutionary

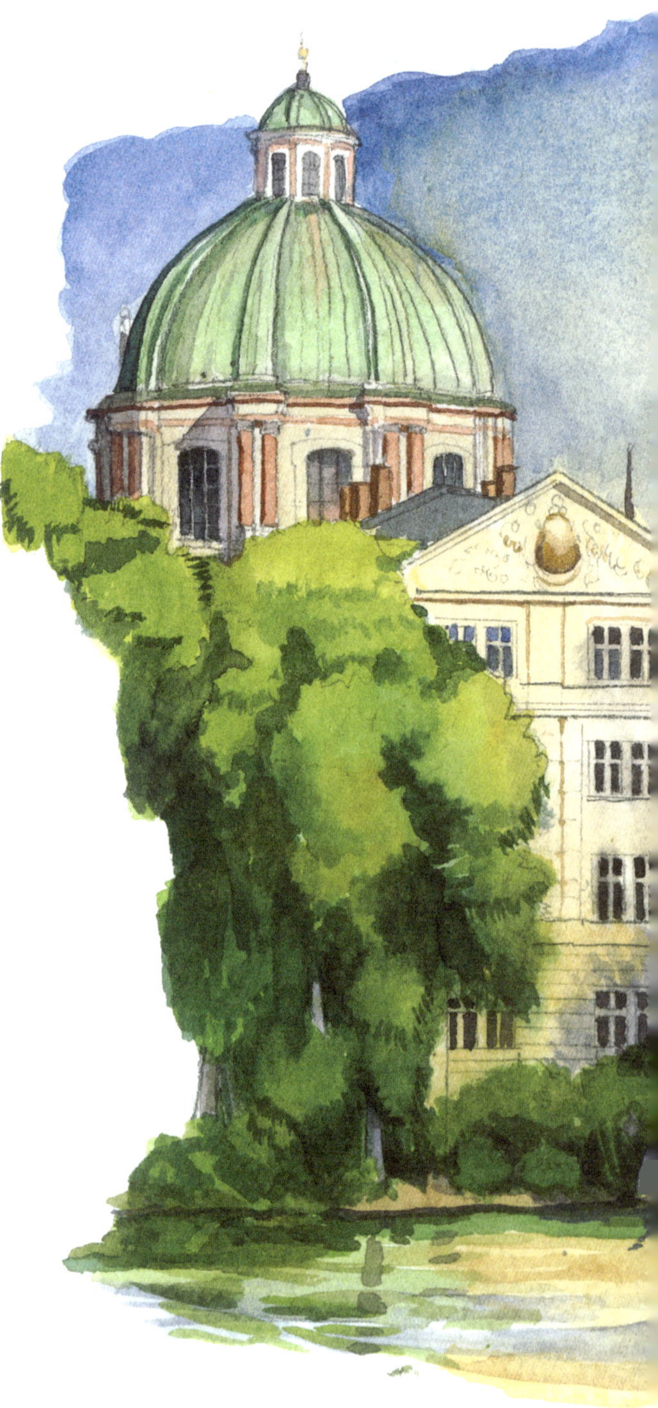

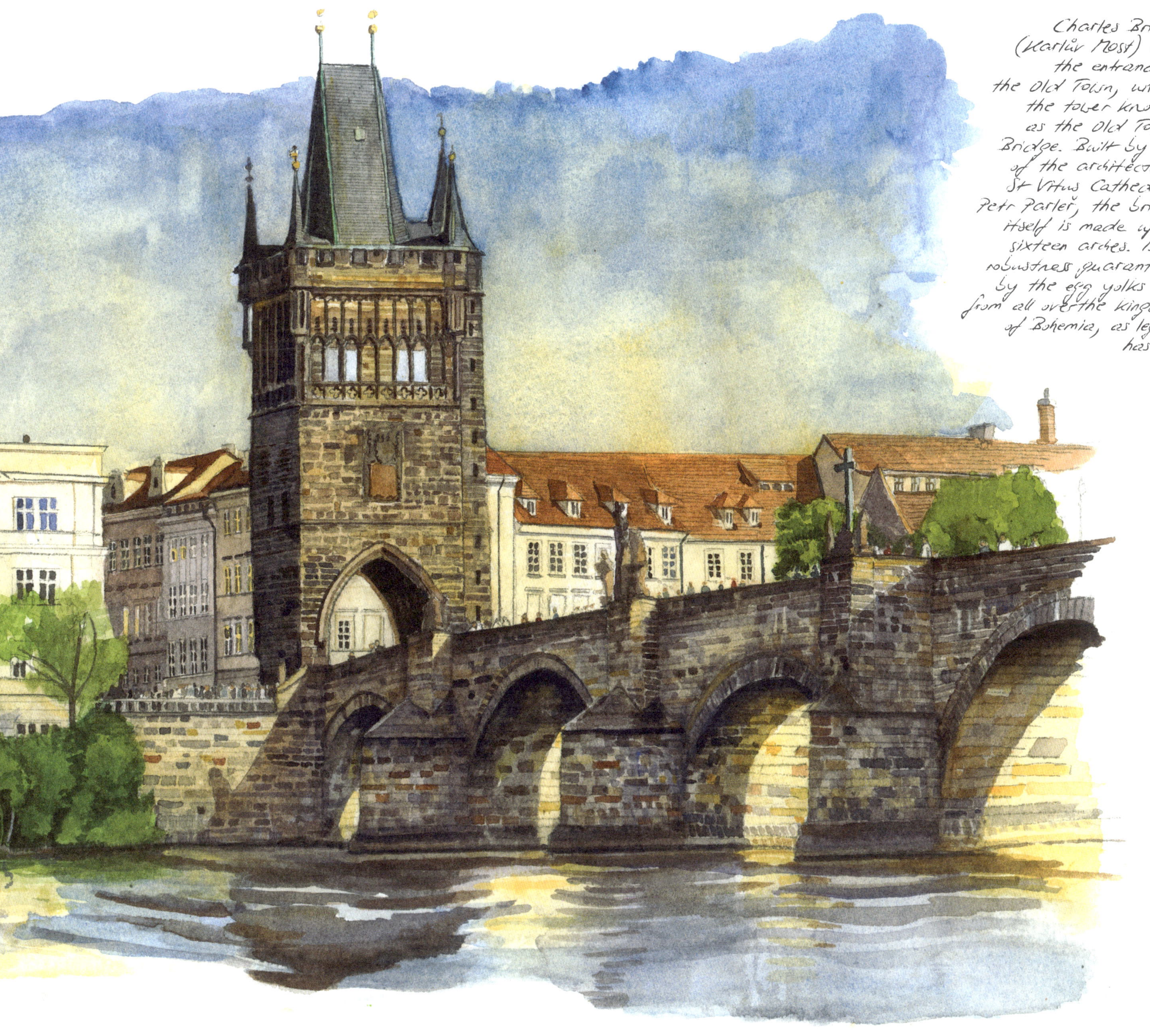

Charles Bridge
(Karlův Most) and
the entrance to
the Old Town, under
the tower known
as the Old Town
Bridge. Built by one
of the architects of
St Vitus Cathedral,
Petr Parléř, the bridge
itself is made up of
sixteen arches. Is its
robustness guaranteed
by the egg yolks sent
from all over the kingdom
of Bohemia, as legend
has it?

fervor on the iconic steps of the National Museum, whose facade still bore the bullet holes from the Soviet machine gun assault of 1968. I see my mother smiling down at me, knowing the nightmare of totalitarian life was over. On any given day, I am not quite sure which of my memories of Prague are true and which are merely a dream, a wish, a night terror.

As is the case with the revolution, I do not remember much about my early years of living in the most famous section of Prague. The Jewish Quarter is situated in Old Town, the city's most popular destination, where the area's monuments draw over eight million visitors every year. Here, at the heart of our economy, the city offers visitors our famous Czech crystal, the best beer in the world, sold for a song, the aggressive scents of spit cake filled with Nutella, and absinthe set afire. After the revolution, it didn't take much time for Prague to become the hedonistic city it is now. With the fall of communism, the borders were swung open to capitalist commerce, and nothing stood in the way of a West-adjacent tourist industry, embracing the joy of debauchery.

But I wasn't meant to watch this transformation of my city with my own eyes. At the age of three, I had my first real birthday party at the newly opened McDonald's—sinking my teeth into and falling in love with the novel sweetness of a cheeseburger bun—and the celebration doubled as my first farewell to Prague. Just as I was becoming aware of my surroundings, able to create a sensory bond with the city of my birth, my parents divorced, and my mother and I moved to a small town in Northern Bohemia. Prague turned into a mere abstraction for me, a Proustian collection of early scents and dreamlike images without context. For the next seven years, I was forced to abandon my town before we could truly get to know each other, and this motif of leaving and returning to the city would come to define my life.

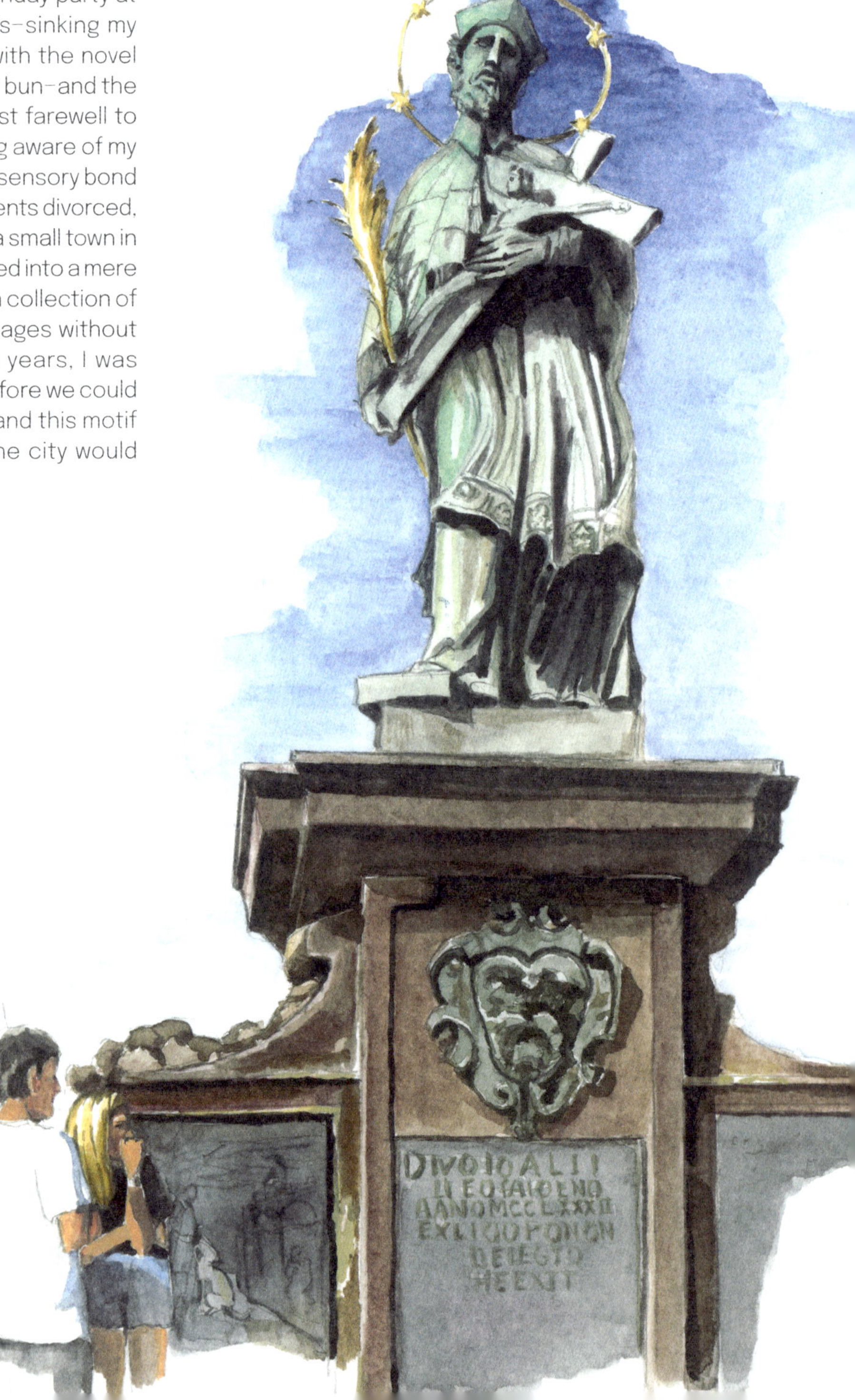

Statue of St. John of Nepomuk on Charles Bridge. He is one of Bohemia's most famous saints. King Wenceslas IV had him tortured and drowned in the Vltava. A crown of five stars appeared in the heavens as his body was being recovered. He is the patron saint of all aquatic activities.

A City of Secrets

At the age of ten, when the first formative phase of my life was over, I returned to Prague to live with my father. But by then, the apartment we lived in on Dušní had been returned to the original owners, from whom it was confiscated by the communists in the 1950s, and my family was driven out of Old Town for good. My new neighborhood, Chodov, was no tourist destination. It was a suburban aberration on the outskirts of Prague, composed of Brutalist concrete structures that were once meant to form a communist utopia. Suddenly, my childhood bore the aesthetic of gray sludge interspersed with rusting playground climbers, discarded syringes freshly emptied of heroin, and shattered Pilsner bottles. This, too, was Prague, but it was not a picture to be found on postcards. Yet, to me and the other children in the neighborhood, the desolate landscape defined the aesthetics of Prague more accurately than its adored Castle or some astronomical clock. It was our immediate reality. It was *us*.

My peers and I scorned the pretty version of Prague—the version that defined the early years of my life—in the way only cynical teens can. That version of our city was meant for the wide-eyed visitors and their clunky cameras, the gaggles of suckers who stood in front of the Orloj looking up like dogs begging for scraps. The tourists flooding our country after the Velvet Revolution wanted immersion in Czech culture, to sit in a basement pub with a liter of beer and a bowl of guláš. My peers and I yearned for Big Macs and Vans sneakers, yearned to stroll the beaches of Los Angeles like our heroes on Baywatch. Throughout these years, I forced myself to forget the little I remembered of my old neighborhood of Dušní: the beauty of the Spanish Synagogue at the end of our street, the memorials to Franz Kafka, that pesky phone booth. I was born in Old Town, but I was a Chodov boy through and through. I had decided that historic Prague, pretty Prague, was for the outsiders, the uninitiated. The uncool.

As my friends and I got older, our hostility toward our historic city drove us to action. We'd organize excursions to Old Town, the former medieval marketplace from which Prague grew, to wreak havoc. In the 9th century, traders had peddled their wares

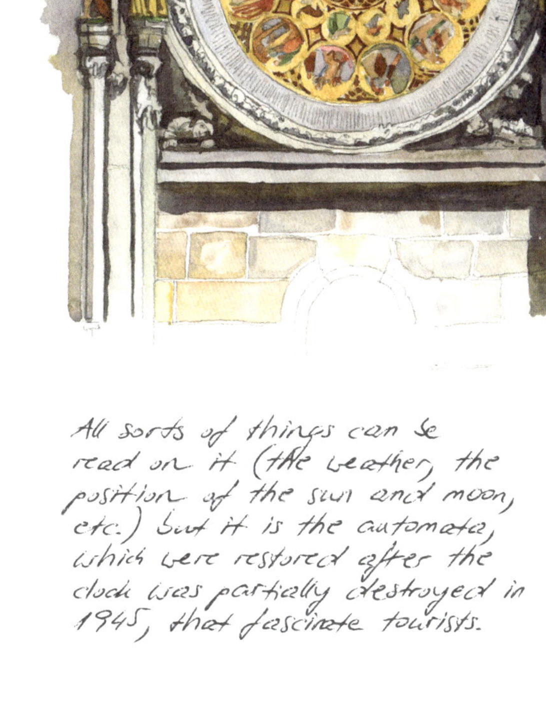

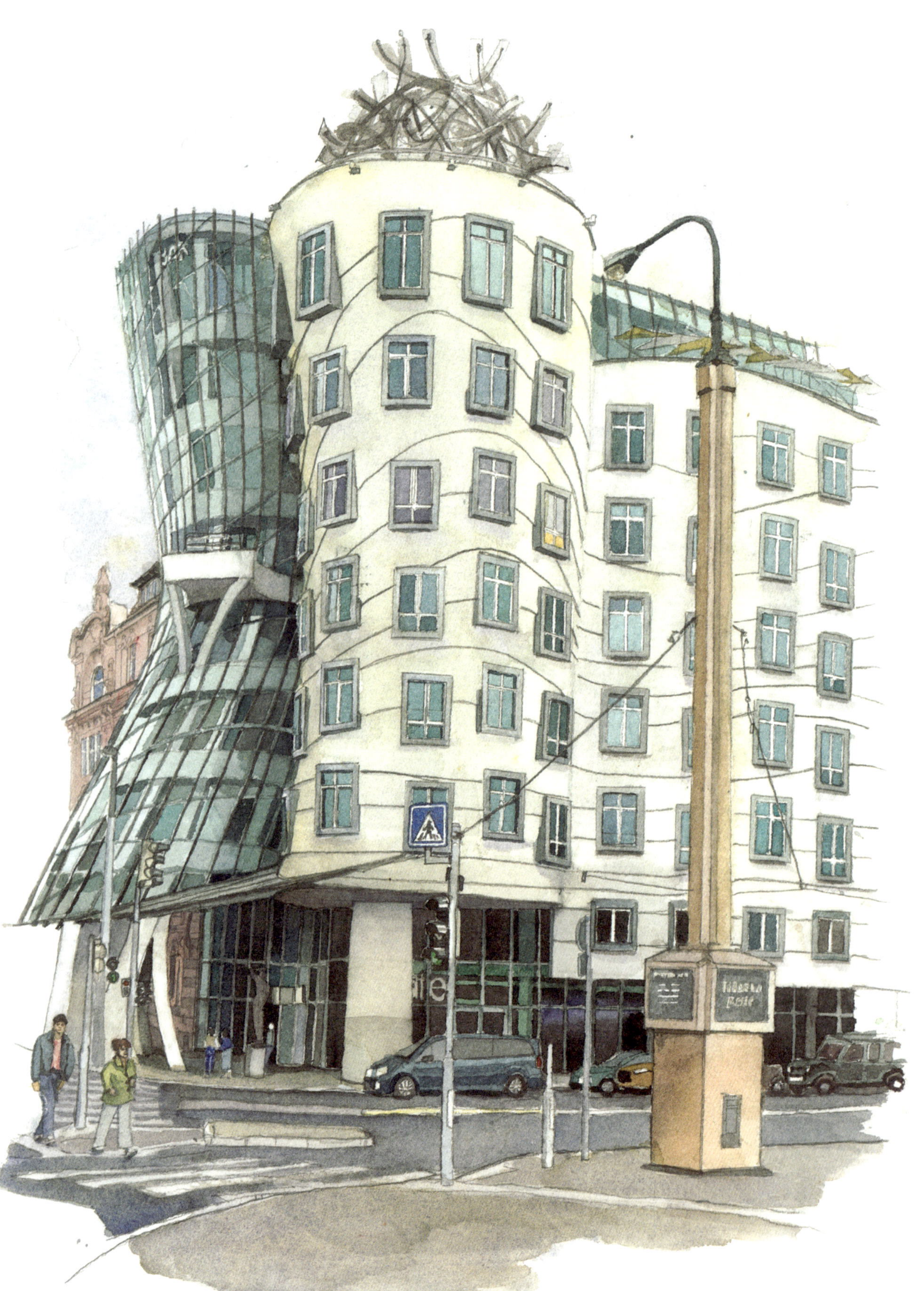

on the abundant shores of the river Vltava, and this early seed of commerce sprouted a group of settlements in its vicinity. Brick by brick, the early Czechs built up the city until Prague became the toast of Europe when it served as the seat of Charles IV (Wenceslas), Holy Roman Emperor, from 1355 until his death in 1378. From there, Prague managed to survive a series of existential threats. During the Hussite Wars (1419 – 1434), citizens drove out the crusaders who'd come to occupy the city on behalf of the Pope. The Thirty Years' War (1618 – 1648) saw the armies of Sweden lay siege to the city, looting the wealthy quarters surrounding Prague Castle and the Little Quarter. But the sack of the city was repelled by the city's militia as the Swedes attempted to cross Charles Bridge. And when the tide of World War II turned and the Czechs rose up to drive the Nazi scourge out of the country, Hitler threatened to annihilate the city as an act of revenge—yet, the only bombs that ever touched Prague's spires were those dropped by the US Air Forces, who attacked the city and destroyed a few landmarks due to a navigational error. The site of the apartment building that was destroyed by bombing is now the Dancing House, a deconstructivist wonder built around the yin of our communist past and the yang of the country's leap toward parliamentary democracy. Unlike the many metropolises of Europe devastated by the war, our city had escaped relatively unscathed.

Dancing House
1994–1997
The Dancing House, also known as Fred and Ginger, is one of the city's most iconic buildings. The building was managed by Canadian Architect Frank Gehry and has many architectural deconstructivist elements that he is famous for.

But American bombs were nothing compared to the angst of the city's teenagers. On our excursions to make Prague ugly, my comrades and I weren't burdened by history. We brought our permanent markers and spray-paint, and we went to work on ruining Prague's famous beauty, making it our own. We signed our names on the Powder Tower, drew obscenities on the wall of the National Museum, and spray-painted slogans on the Jiráskův Bridge pillars: *Tourists, Go Home*. In *Notes from Underground*, Dostoevsky posited that utopia is not possible because a person will always resist the perfect world, for no reason other than to feel alive. Unknowingly, my comrades and I became the enactors of Dostoevsky's dark observation, striking against the fate of having been born in one of the most beloved cities in the world. Sometimes I wonder how many remnants of our petty destruction remain, untouched by a new coat of paint.

Between the Old Town square and the Municipal House, the Powder Tower (Prašná brána) is a vestige of mediaeval Prague's fortifications. It was restored at the end of the 19th century in all its Gothic splendour.

For years we made Prague uglier to make it ours, until an escalation in methods led to a fire when a friend of mine brought along a box of matches. Together, we inserted the plastic wrap from my stolen pack of cigarettes into the doorbell panel of a beautiful Art Deco building in Old Town. My friend lit the match, and I held it to the plastic. The doorbell wires sparked, and a fireball shot out from the panel as my accomplices and I ran for cover. We watched from a distance as the shirtless, sweat-drenched owner of the ceramic shop on the ground floor quenched the flames with buckets of water. Soon, the sirens of fire engines squealed nearby. I ran for my life. My friends and I wanted to disfigure our Prague, but we didn't want to watch it burn.

At the age of fifteen, I would flee my utopia once again and exchange Prague for the beaches of Florida, where my mother had relocated after divorcing my father. In the months before my emigration, something had changed in me. Perhaps the doorbell fire taught me that Prague would defend itself against my assaults, or I had simply matured with age. But suddenly, I no longer craved the city's disfigurement. Instead, I wanted to enjoy the parts that had eluded me all this time, the parts I scoffed at when my school took us on field trips to the National Gallery to see Picasso and Mucha, or the National Theatre to sit through a presentation of *Rusalka*.

After school, I would board the train from my neighborhood, and I would go on secret solo trips to become lost among the city's attractions. There were no smartphones yet, no GPS apps, and my only guide to the city was my own sense of direction, acquired through years as a native child, and the occasional glance at the maps inside the subway trains. That summer I strayed into the melancholic Vojan Gardens, a former monastery garden from the 1200s, where majestic peacocks stroll the narrow paths among blooming spruces and Baroque chapels, and where locals and tourists alike rest on the benches of the panoramic terrace surrounded with pink rose adorned pergolas while admiring the glimmering sundial above their heads. For the first time I entered the Klementinum, made famous by Jorge Luis Borges' magnificent short story 'The Secret Miracle', in which librarians search their books for the word that contains all of God. I could see why Borges found this to be a place so close to divinity. Hosted inside the building where Einstein gave lectures on molecular physics and Mozart played the organ in the Mirror Chapel, the Baroque National Library caused me to strain my neck as I looked up at the ceiling frescoes portraying stunningly elaborate scenes that encapsulated the timeless pursuit of scientific knowledge. Handcrafted book-shelves extended as far as my eye could see, bearing the weight of over six million books and documents dating as far back as the 1st century, intermixed with antique Jesuit globes and clocks adorned with gold.

I told no one about these trips into historic Prague. My friends thought I was spending the afternoons at home playing video games. On these journeys, I felt both shame for suddenly loving my city in the way the tourists did–creaking my neck to gaze at its spires–and exhilaration, discovering for the first time what it meant to admire my place of birth.

Quickly I became addicted to the postcard Prague, and I began to visit Old Town on weekends, too, instead of going to pubs with friends. With my allowance, I purchased tickets to cathedrals and museums and visited tourist-trap cafes where the waiters spoke to me in English. For the first time I strolled the famed Charles Bridge not because I was trying to get somewhere, but simply for its own sake and to get lost among the enthusiastic crowds looking up at the Prague Castle looming over the West side of Vltava's riverbank. Lovers from Italy and Japan and Egypt took photos together with Kodak disposable cameras next to brooding statues of saints and the lamenting Christ. These were the same statues I had once

defaced with a permanent marker, signing my initials in the late hours of the night. At the end of Charles Bridge I reached the notorious painter of caricatures, who always reeked of rum and slurred at his patrons in Czech (addressing them in the informal "ty" instead of the expected "vy", a rude technique utilized by Czechs looking to disrespect foreigners) while he decorated his paintings with crude additions: genital-shaped chins, green clouds of gas signaling his customers' bad breath. The customers loved it. That day, I wanted to become one of them, but there wasn't enough cash in my wallet to afford this memento.

One week before my flight to Florida–where I was meant to spend the summer, then return to Prague, a homecoming that wouldn't come to pass because I decided to stay in America with my mother–I walked up Nerudova Street, which runs parallel to the Prague Castle. This short but famous vein of the city has become one of the main attrac-tions of Malá Strana, or the Little Quarter, the neighborhood living in the castle's shadow. Little Quarter was another part of the city that had eluded me, because of my own childish disinterest and my family's neglect in exposing me to Prague's charms. As natives, we took it all for granted, as Prague was not a museum attraction but a place where we did our best to afford bread and rent.

Nerudova Street was of particular interest because of a book every Czech schoolchild reads, one I hated when I encountered it in school and have since come to embrace as one of my country's great literary treasures. The lane is named after Jan Neruda, one of Prague's most beloved writers, who lived inside a Little Quarter landmark building named Of the Two Suns. The book I used

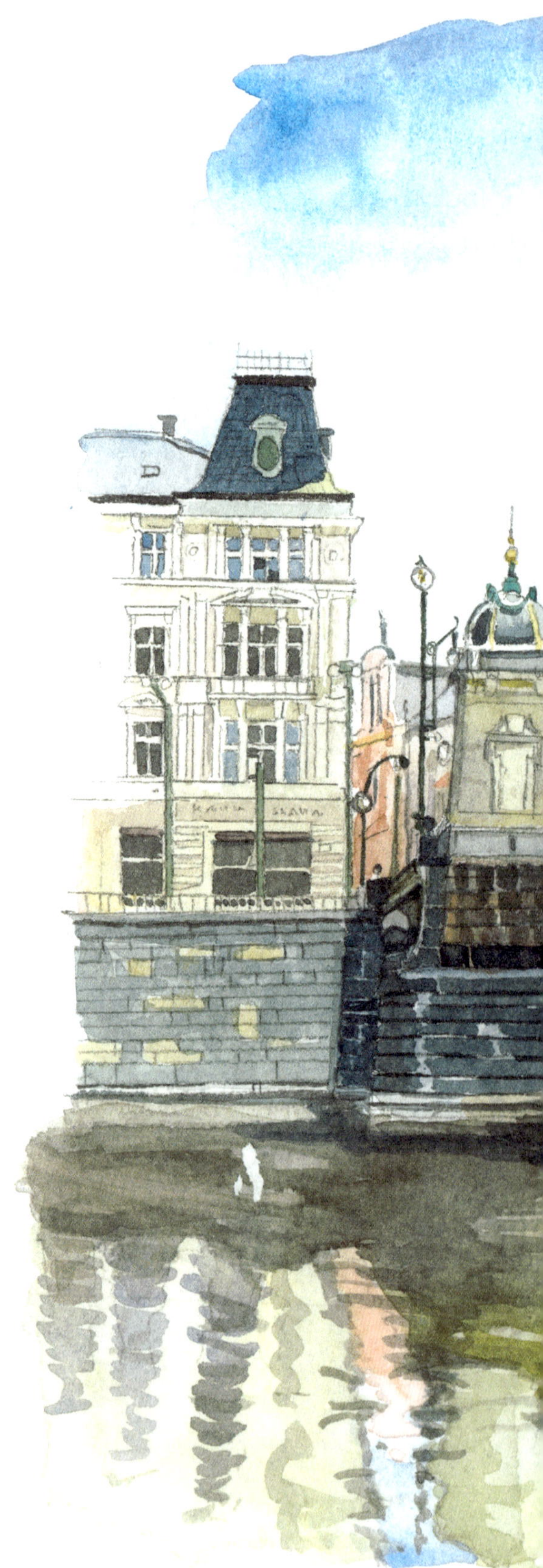

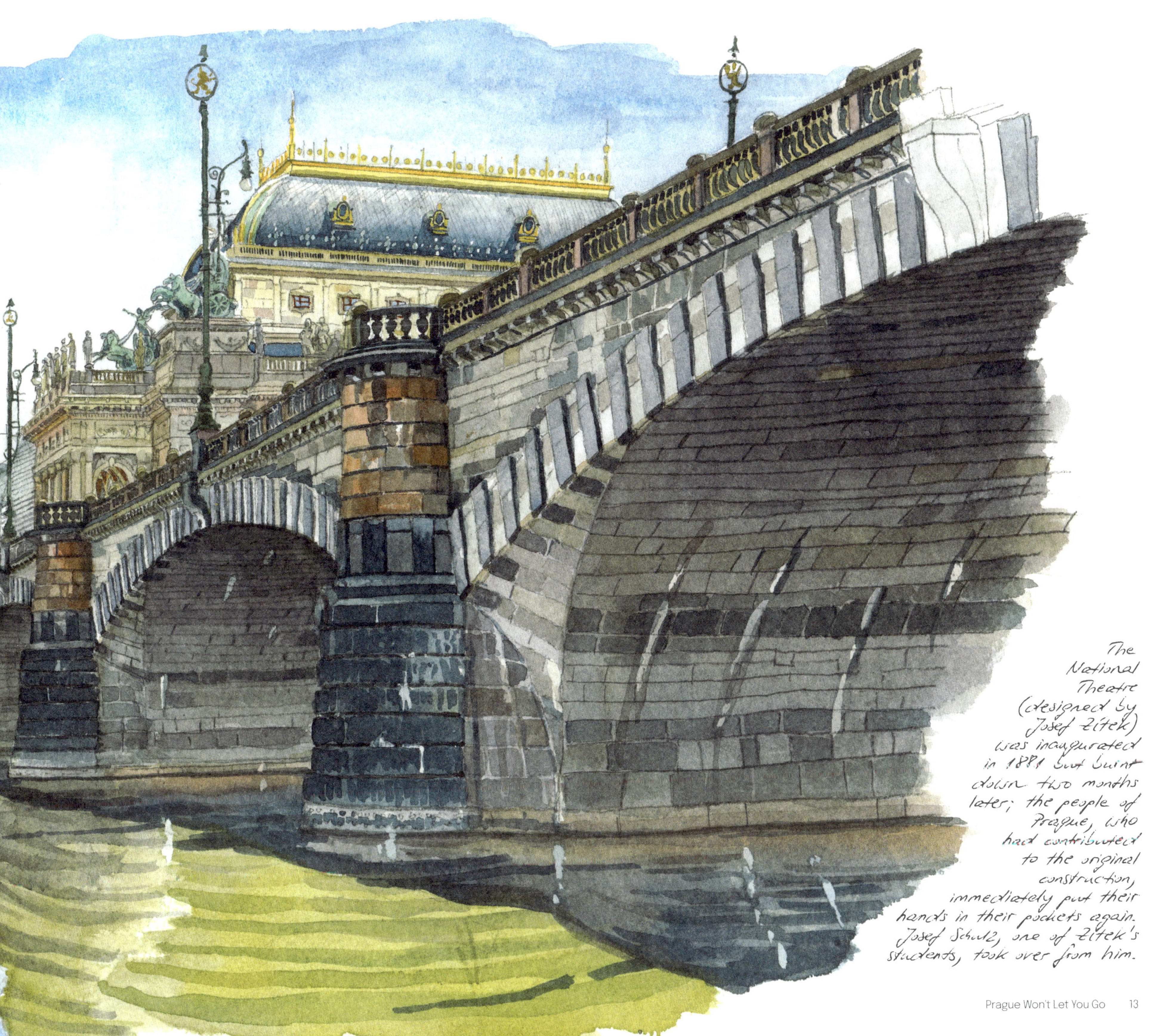

The
National
Theatre
(designed by
Josef Zítek)
was inaugurated
in 1881 but burnt
down two months
later; the people of
Prague, who
had contributed
to the original
construction,
immediately put their
hands in their pockets again.
Josef Schulz, one of Zítek's
students, took over from him.

to resent was Neruda's celebrated short story collection, *Tales from the Little Quarter*, wherein the author's upbringing in the Little Quarter informs tales of everyday citizens of the neighborhood, both bourgeois and working class, coexisting in a swirl of human joy, work, death, love, and pettiness. In one of these tales, a law student who resembles the author is constantly distracted from his studies by engaging with the neighbors in his building, listening to their stories, discovering the endless universe of his community, until his fascination with those around him threatens his future career. In other stories, a band of young boys plot to overthrow the Austro-Hungarian Empire, a funeral procession is divided between the haves (who travel to the cemetery via carriage) and have-nots (who must plod to the funeral on their own two feet), and a local woman attends funerals of people she didn't know to spread gossip about them.

Neruda strove to capture the richness of the people living in our city and his neighborhood, creating a kaleidoscopic view of Prague before wars and totalitarianism swallowed it up, all while satirizing the pettiness of bourgeois mores. As I strolled the streets of his youth and sat inside the Of the Two Suns Inn, which honors Neruda with a plaque, I couldn't escape the desire to see myself as one of Neruda's characters, a citizen living in Prague during an age the writer couldn't possibly fathom, preoccupied as I was with my own petty concerns and aspirations, which were tied intimately to the city. Among those concerns were my daily trips around town, which I'd hidden from my friends, those trips serving as an escape from the perilous living conditions with my tyrannical father, and my wish to become a writer, along with the troubling thought that within the small literary market of the Czech Republic, writing would most likely always be a hobby, not a career. I thought about my mother living across the ocean in Florida, knowing that I would soon see her, and that with her having acquired a green card in America, an

entirely different future had opened up for me, far from the city I was beginning to love. I believe I knew then for the first time—as I sat inside Of the Two Suns Inn on Nerudova Street, contemplating Neruda's characters and imagining him strolling through the lane and weaving a vast tale behind every face he encountered—that I wasn't going to call Prague home for much longer.

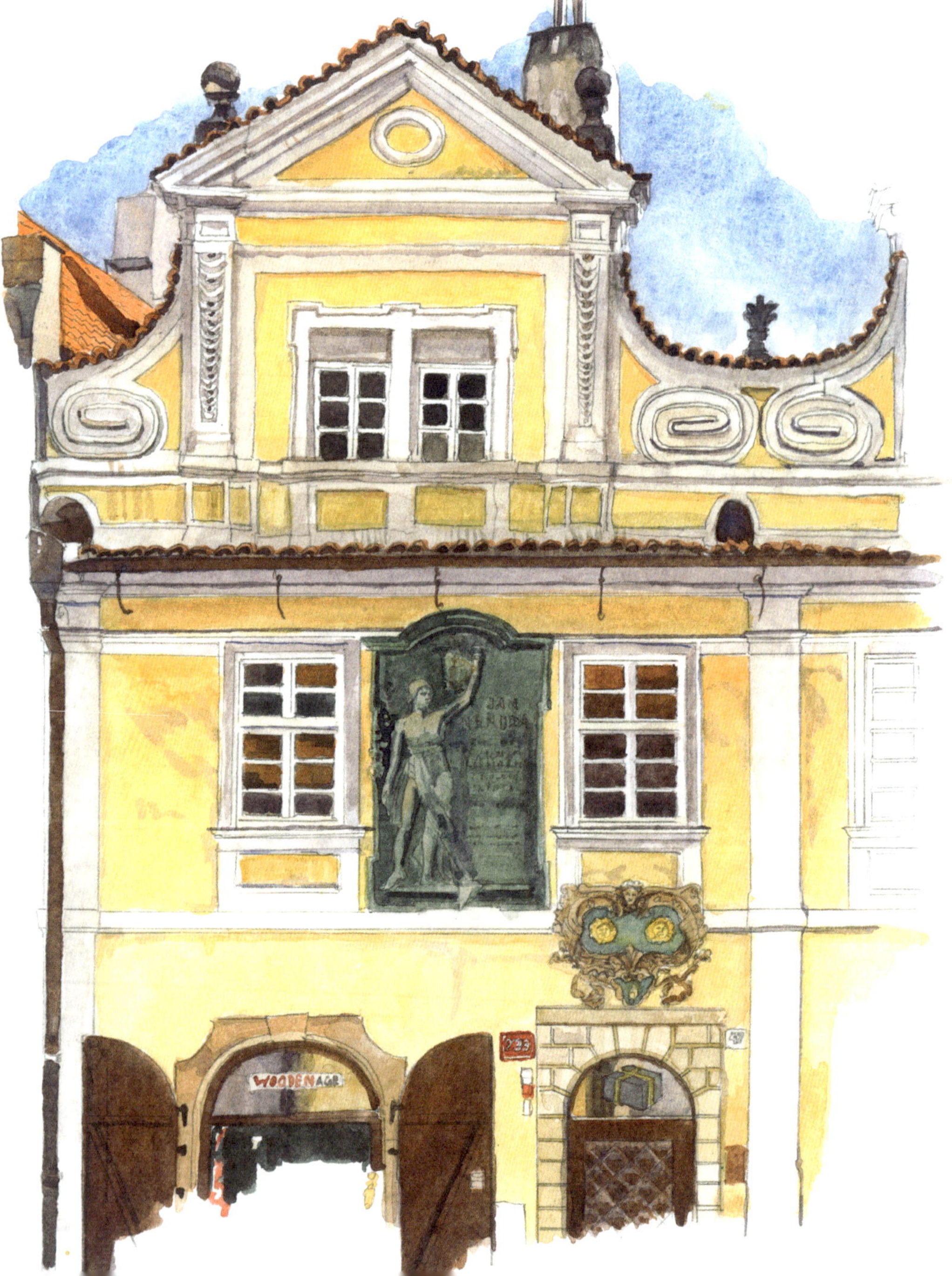

The House of the Two Suns (Dům u dvou Slunců), Neruda Street: the street was named after Czech writer Jan Neruda, who lived here, as the bronze plaque above the two suns reminds us.

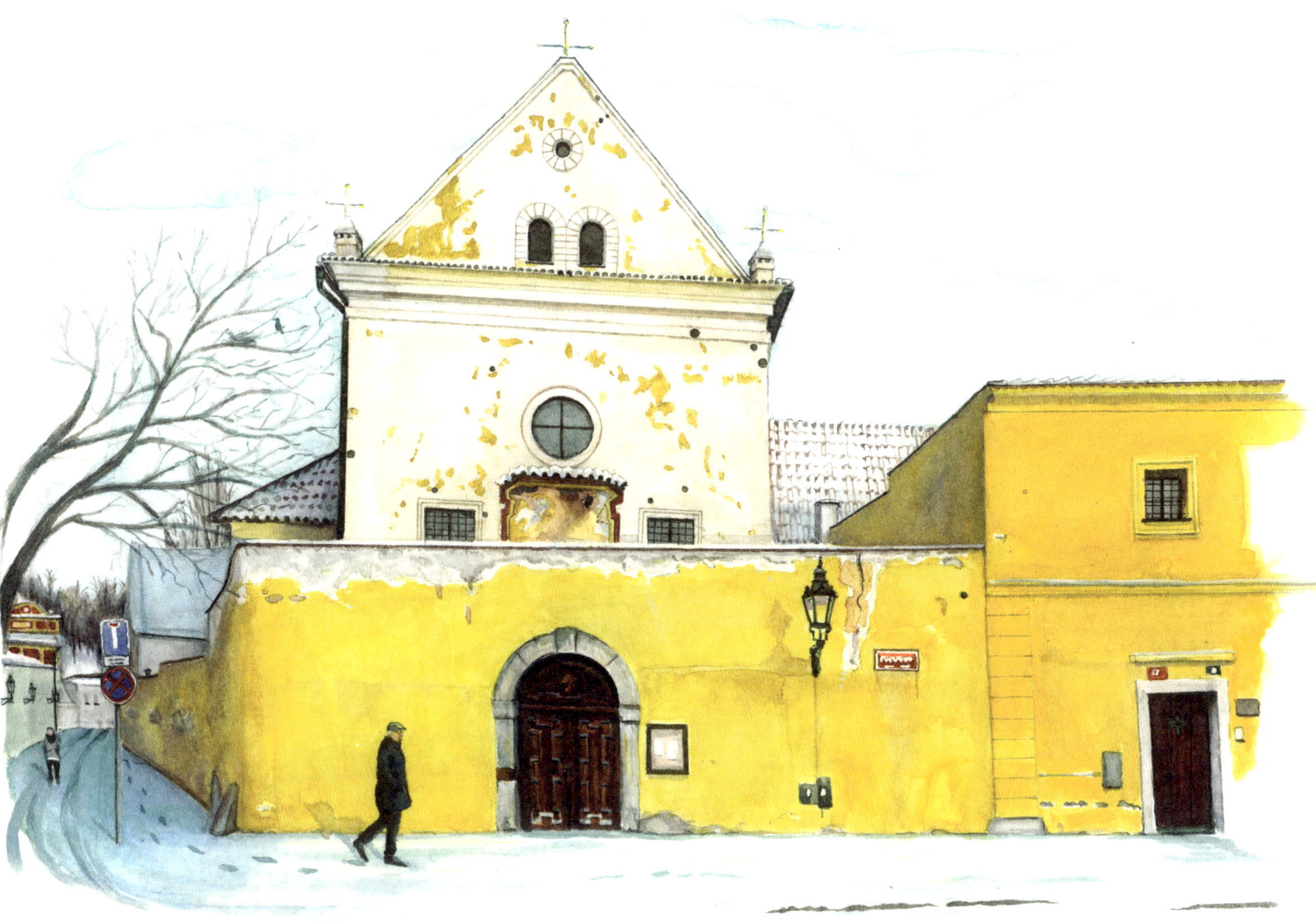

Visitors, Welcome

The summer following my farewell to Prague, I found myself in Florida, having landed on July 4th to the kitsch fireworks display of Independence Day. The state's aggressive sunshine scorched the colors out of grass, palm leaves, and building facades, turning the landscape pale and monotone. I had to keep my eyes half-closed because I feared the sun would burn through my retinas. Florida's flat plots of strip malls were the first thing to make me feel something like desolation of the soul. There was little history here, no cathedrals or monuments reminding me of the gravity of all that came before me the closest the place seemed to get to history was in the form of Confederate flags fluttering from rusted pickup trucks. The people smiled suspiciously often, asked me "How are you?", and walked away before I could answer. I couldn't board a train to get anywhere in the new city: the buses roaming the land came only once every hour and smelled of vomit. I had made a mistake. This place was nothing like me, nothing like my culture. My longing for Prague, for home, asserted itself, and was immediately unbearable.

Yet, Florida was to become the unsatisfying imitation of home. After my emigration, I became stuck in a cycle of working minimum-wage jobs to stay afloat in a country where life is only good with money, and playing the game of catch and release with the broken US immigration system, which stretched out my application for a green card over a decade. Barred from doing so both by poverty–as a newly-minted member of America's working class, I couldn't afford to miss a shift–and by limitations impressed upon me by the immigration process, I was unable to return to my city of birth for eight years. Not in waking life, anyway. In my dreams I strolled Prague just as I had when I was young, though its monuments became increasingly blurred, and I couldn't quite tell if the memories I experienced were forgeries conjured by nostalgia, the mind's deepfakes, where I had an intimate relationship with every inch of my city when, in reality, my childhood had been confined to those early years in Kafka's Quarter and the gray desolation of Chodov.

After eight years of being trapped in Florida, I finally received my green card and saved up enough money for a plane ticket to Prague. I returned to my birth city and learned a cruel lesson of time. Much like ex-lovers, cities do not wait for us. When we depart, they live and shape-shift, whereas our idea of them becomes frozen, a memory we worship and embellish.

I'll never forget that first day of my return. The cab driver attempted to speak to me in English, shocked that I was a native, disappointed he couldn't rip me off in the way he could cheat German or American visitors. Prague looked nothing like I'd remembered. Certainly, there was more graffiti, created by the new generation of children who wanted to make their beautiful city ugly to make it theirs. The city showed more signs of decay, in the form of the neon-lit fast-fashion shops violently shoved inside Neo-renaissance palaces, shuttered methamphetamine nests ruining the otherwise picturesque quarters. Streets I had seen in my dreams turned out not to exist, the facades of Gothic monuments looked nothing like the pictures in my mind. The buildings were taller and more difficult to fathom, and I gaped at the smallest adornments they carried–the Latin phrases carved into stones and ceiling frescoes displaying divinity–wondering how my ancestors were able to build these wonders that last through centuries. I've always been suspicious of the pathos of patriotism, yet suddenly, I was moved by the statue of Jan Hus gazing far into the distance, as if contemplating the nation's future potential and woes with an expression that lands somewhere between hope and tragedy. Having come back to the motherland, I looked upon everything with the fresh, innocent eyes of a tourist, yet also with the yearning of a long-lost son returning home. I didn't yet know that reconciling these two sentiments toward Prague would become the greatest project of my life.

In 2016, my debut novel about a Czech astronaut flying into space, far away from his beloved Prague, came into the world and changed everything for me. The protagonist spends much of his time reexamining the flawed memory fragments of his city as he withers away on a spaceship. Streets shape shift and change their names, the city's appearance morphs to accommodate nostalgia. The launch of the novel's Czech edition took place inside another of Prague's wonders, the Gulliver Airship. Built atop the roofs of the DOX gallery in Holešovice, a hub for Prague's robust art scene, the Gulliver is a Zeppelin replica made entirely of wood and steel, a space that hosts many of the city's book release parties and gallery openings.

Introducing the novel to the Czech reading public ushered a new era in my relationship with the city. *Spaceman of Bohemia* was born from my longing for my culture, the isolation of an immigrant trapped in a country and language so far from his own. The Gulliver Airship launch, I felt, was an opportunity for something new. I would no longer dwell on Prague as something that I'd lost. I was to devote myself to rebuilding my relationship with the city and my Czech identity, create a future to make up for my absence in the past. It was the book's success that allowed me to begin returning to Prague every year, to spend months at a time back in the motherland, and to reforge my relationship with it. I am plagued by a pathological need to ensure I never forget the real Prague again. When I visit my city now, I book hotels in Old Town and linger in the neighborhood just like a tourist. I watch the bands of Brits chanting football war cries, the stag partiers and absinthe enthusiasts flooding to Old Town like mosquitoes to a

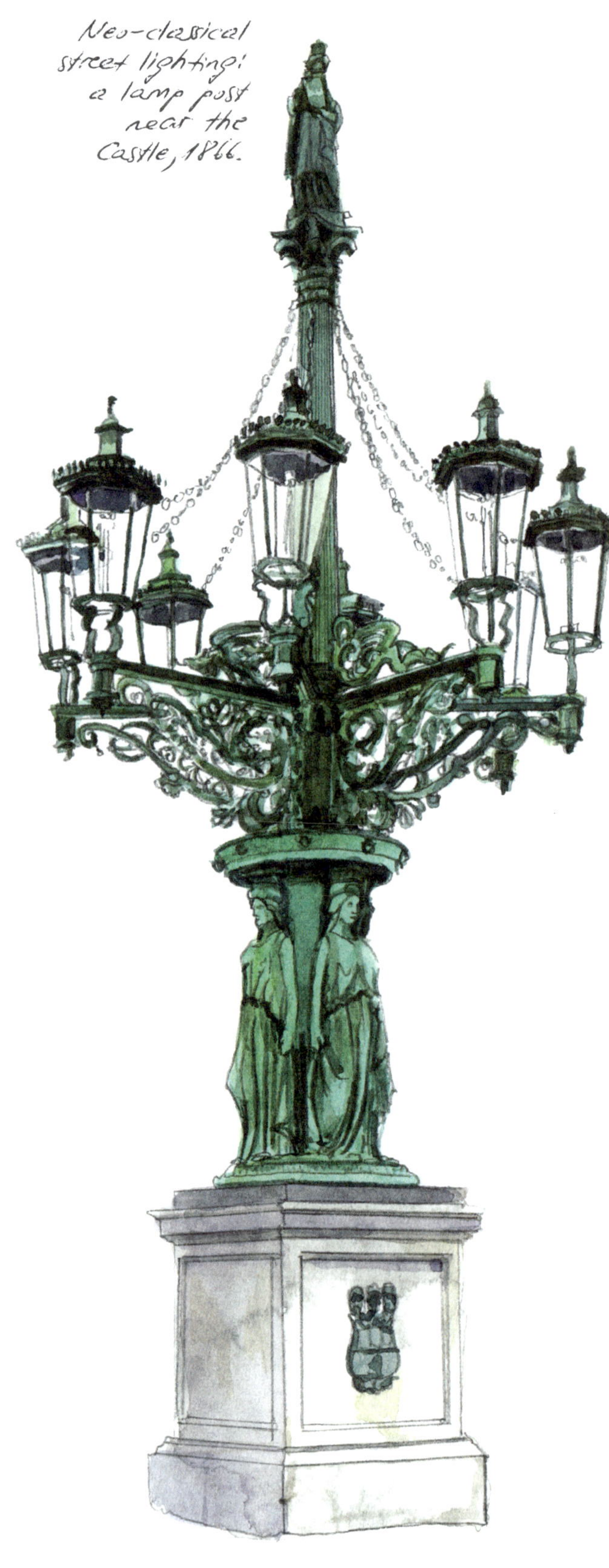

vein, and my former hostility toward tourists has morphed into empathy. Prague is a place that brings joy to people. They seek it out, they strive to spend their precious summers among its living history, they devote their yearly travel budgets to stroll the memorial to the Velvet Revolution by day and lose themselves in the cheap vodka of five-story nightclubs at night. What is more human than this? To seek out the seriousness and hedonism of the world's famous cities in equal measure. Every band of disrespectful teens spitting on the monuments is balanced by a guided group gazing up in awe at the Gothic wonder of the Saint Vitus Cathedral, a family carefully guiding their children by the hand through the crowds, the lovers flocking to Charles Bridge for selfies. Despite its ugly side–one that any city's occupants have the right to rail against–tourism infuses a city with life and new appreciation, the kind of adoration Prague deserves.

In the interconnected world of the 21st century, a new kind of person emerges: a chimera combining the tourist and the local, the native who has left and yet strives to return all the time, seeking the warmth of home without commitment. Loving this beautiful city means I've become a tourist in my place of birth. I know I am this chimera, as I observe the tension between tourists and locals and feel my allegiances ebb and flow. Revisiting Prague is a religious experience, one I've become dependent on–during the occasional year I must skip the visit, I feel heartbroken and frustrated, unfulfilled. When I am finally back on my city's soil, I take each step carefully, the sensation of smooth cobblestone under my feet a resonance more pleasant to me than grass in spring or sand on a beach. I join the suffocating crowd of Orloj onlookers, another chump waiting for the clock to ring on the hour. Along with them I raise my smartphone to take photos of the astronomical clock I grew up ignoring. I enter souvenir shops in stray alleyways, where painters reproduce the many attractive parts of my city on canvass, and I pay the tourist prices to bring these paintings back to Brooklyn.

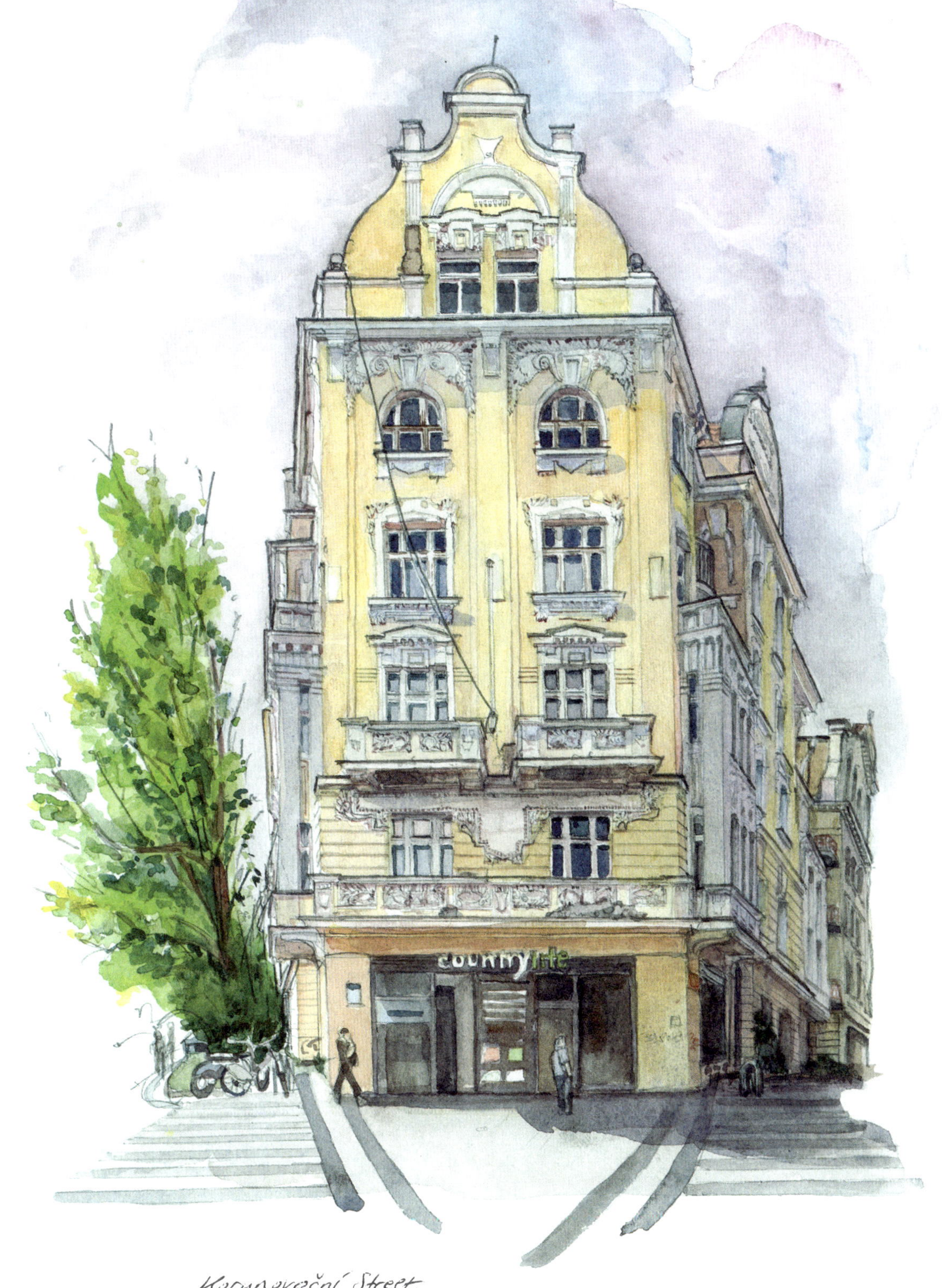

Korunovační Street.
Prague City Council shortened it in March 2022, renaming the section that houses the Russian embassy 'Heroes of Ukraine Street'.

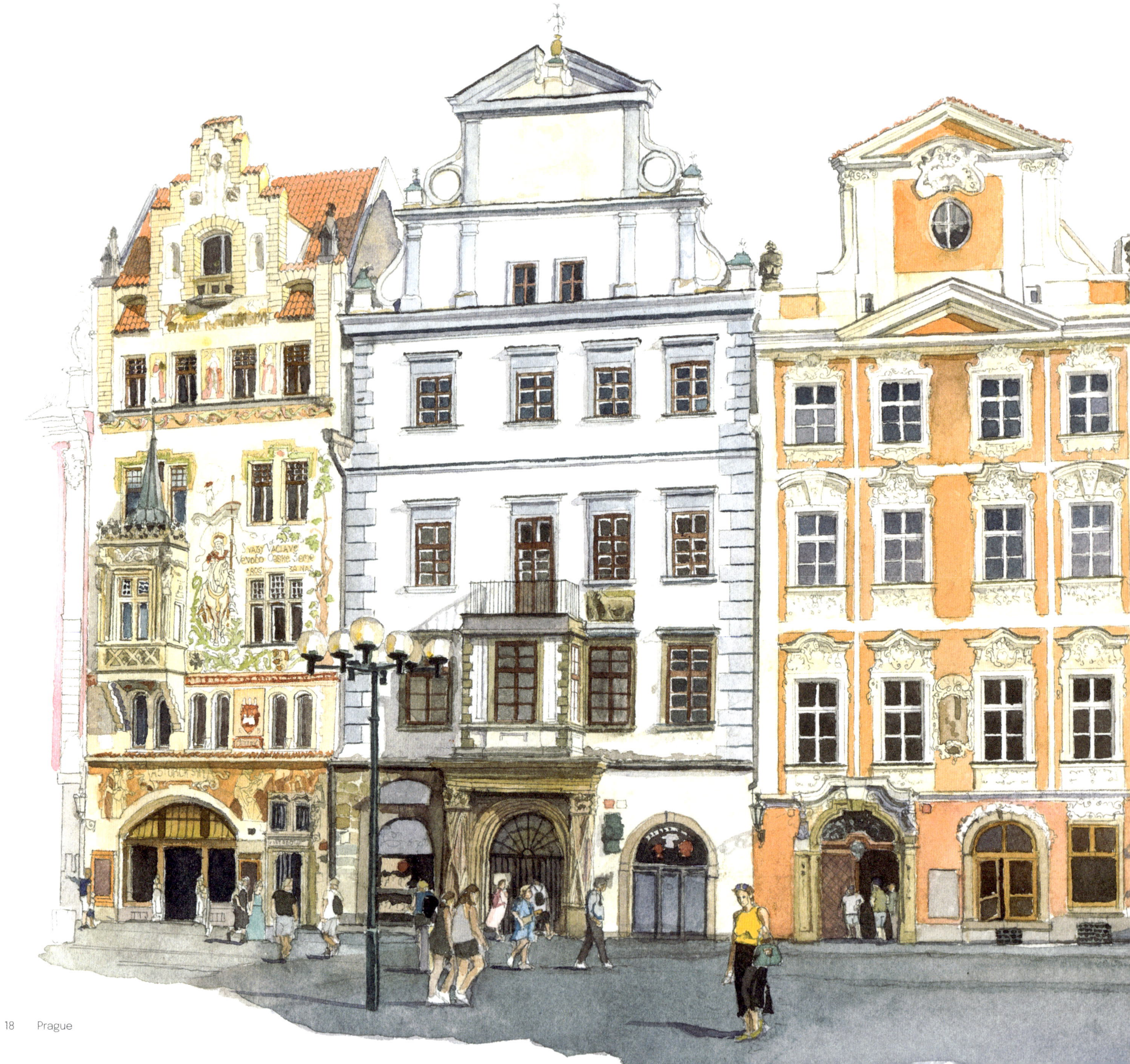

SVATY VACLAVE
VEVODO CESKE ZEME
PROS — ZA NAS

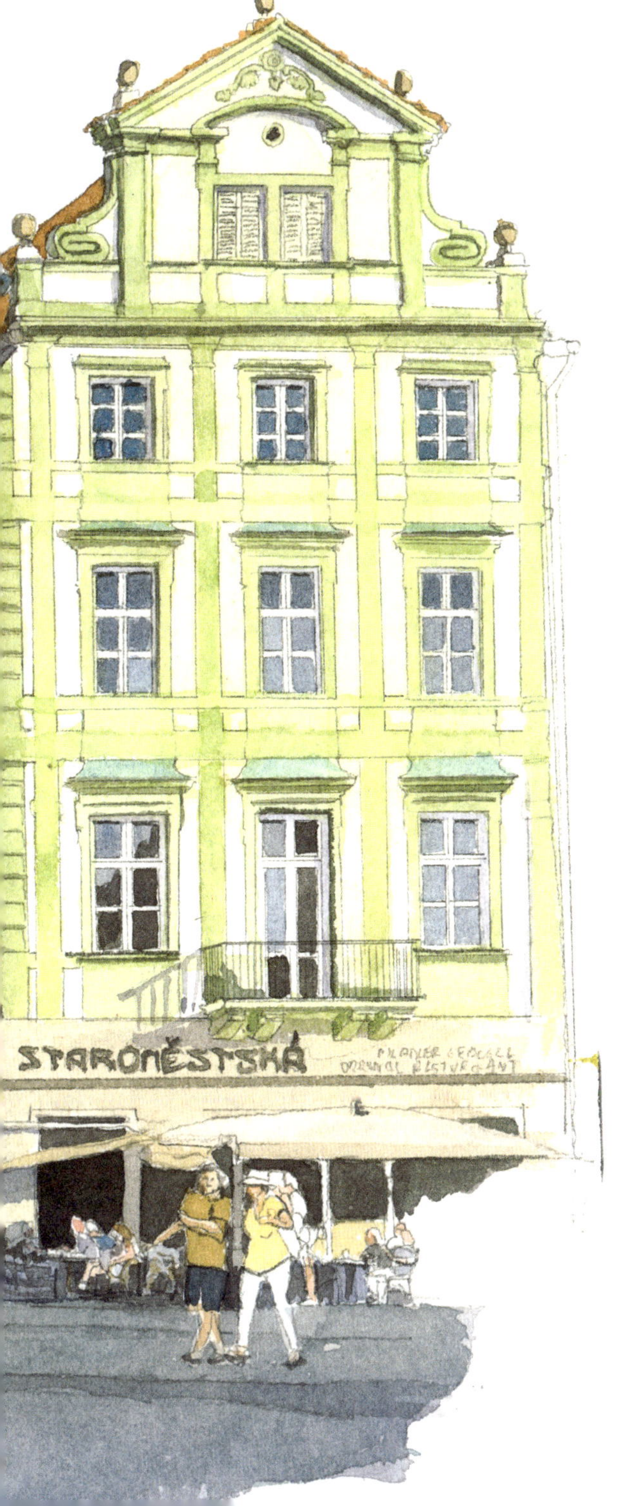

Neo-Renaissance and Baroque façades in the Old Town square. From left to right: the Storch house and its fresco by the great Czech illustrator Mikoláš Aleš; the House of the Stone Lamb; the House of the Stone Table, where Mrs Fantova hosted her literary salon; and the Lazarus house.

Such is the path of the tourist living in me, but as a chimera I am able to switch between identities. Often, I abandon the path of the visitors and retrace the trails of my childhood, return to the places that mean little to a tourist and everything to a prodigal son. Across from the iconic Tesco shopping mall on Národní Třída, I dodge the ringing red trams (as a local, I know to hurry; my pedestrian immunity doesn't apply, and the trams would gleefully run me over) to pop into the computer game shop where I used to go on weekends to spend my allowance on games I couldn't yet play because we didn't have a PC. Afterwards I sit on the ground floor of the Tesco shopping mall, officially named Máj after my birth month, and eat a greasy slice of Little Caesar's pizza, so much better in Europe than in America thanks to the strict food quality laws that many Europeans curse as a regulatory burden. As a Crohn's sufferer, much of American food is taboo for me, and visits to restaurants are perilous. But in my country of birth, I can eat anything and everything I like–even the forbidden dairy–without the smallest ache. This local's body remains attuned after all these years to the local food.

Between the tourist must-sees generally avoided by the local population–Prague Castle, Charles Bridge, Old Town Square–and the small spots that hold meaning only for locals are the middle-of-the-road destinations where locals and tourists mix the most, places too low on the tourist guides to inspire massive crowds. These casual attractions offer some serenity away from the city's busiest traffic veins connecting the Eastern shore of Old Town and the Western shore, which hosts Prague Castle and the charms of Neruda's Little Quarter. Just north across the river

from Old Town, on a plateau above Vltava's steep embankments rests one such place of respite, the breathtaking Letná Park. Here, too, the Velvet Revolution touched when 750,000 Czechs convened inside the park to overthrow the government in 1989. Once upon a time, the park was even the home to a statue of Joseph Stalin. Now, the site of the tyrant's memorial is occupied by the 23-meter-tall Time Machine, its functioning metronome swinging back and forth. *In time, all things pass*, declares the plaque at the metronome's base, where Prague's skateboarders gather to record their athletic feats for their TikTok accounts. Lovers come to the edges of the park to nestle on benches and look over Prague's glory. Behind them, runners and bikers practice their sport. Despite the park's bustle, it has been for me the site of many quiet, serene walks, where I feel completely alone with my city, planning in my head the events of my next novel about Prague.

Even further North, near the city's edge, rests the massive complex of Trója, a place just as worthy of stepping off the beaten path. It is home to the city's Botanical Gardens, 25 hectares of carefully curated and preserved natural habitats that include the Peony Meadow, a stunning collection of the country's peony species. The Trója Chateau, modeled after the lavish suburban villas of Rome, is a decadent display of frescoes and galleries portraying scenes from ancient myths and Biblical legends. But the most beloved part of Trója must be the Prague Zoo. This, too, is a place for mandatory visits every time I return home. The startlingly fast aerial chairlift within the complex carries visitors between the low points and high points of the zoo grounds, and children squeal just as I used to while they are carried upwards on small plastic chairs, fastened with nothing but a thin swinging chain and the power of gravity. After the chairlift journey, I sit on the same bench where my grandfather and I used to rest and eat Keks butter cookies for strength before heading for the Valley of the Elephants. As a reader and writer of speculative fiction, I never fail to visit the giant salamander exhibit, where those uncanny animals rest lazily in their water tanks, their beady eyes and blubbery faces pressed against the glass. The exhibit is the largest of its kind in Europe, a tribute to one of the country's greatest novelistic achievements, Karel Čapek's science fiction classic *War with the Newts*.

Prague does not lack nature to explore–setting aside its many parks, built out over the centuries with the plentiful coin of monarchs, the city offers massive natural reserves where visitors can get irreversibly lost. The best of them is Divoká Šárka, the rugged valley where the early Slavs built the first fortified settlement of Prague in the 8th and 9th centuries. There are few things as satisfying in life as a bustling metropolis that offers enormous areas of real nature for locals and visitors alike to escape to, a luxury I sorely miss within the man-made, garbage-littered parks of New York City. It is a distinct pleasure to take the short tram ride from Old Town and ascend the abundant Šárka plateau, stroll among the meadows and dwell beneath waterfalls, take in the breathtaking high-point views of Prague's entirety while sitting outside one of the park's pubs, and overhear the dozens of languages around me–mothers and fathers drinking Pilsner while their tiniest hikers enjoy Kofola. In places like these, the difference between tourist and local is erased, as all of us sit clad in our hiking sweatpants and massage our sore feet and calves, feeling that together we have uncovered one of Prague's many profound secrets.

Of course, as in many of Europe's finest cities, pubs are at the center of Prague's communal life. While a charming establishment can be found anywhere, including within the vast valleys of natural reserves, one must return to the bustling city center to find the pubs that carry, soaked into their walls, the perilous history of my nation. Among them are several famous establishments where one is sure to find a seat at any time of day. U Zlatého Tygra is the classic small pub where the first post-communist president, Václav Havel, hosted Bill Clinton for a night of beer drinking. It is also a place once favored by one of the most famous of Czech novelists, Bohumil Hrabal. Perhaps the most well-known Czech beer hall, U Fleků, was founded 500 years ago, and offers eight themed medieval feasting halls. The pub U Pinkasů has hosted the most prominent members of the Czech intelligentsia over the past three hundred

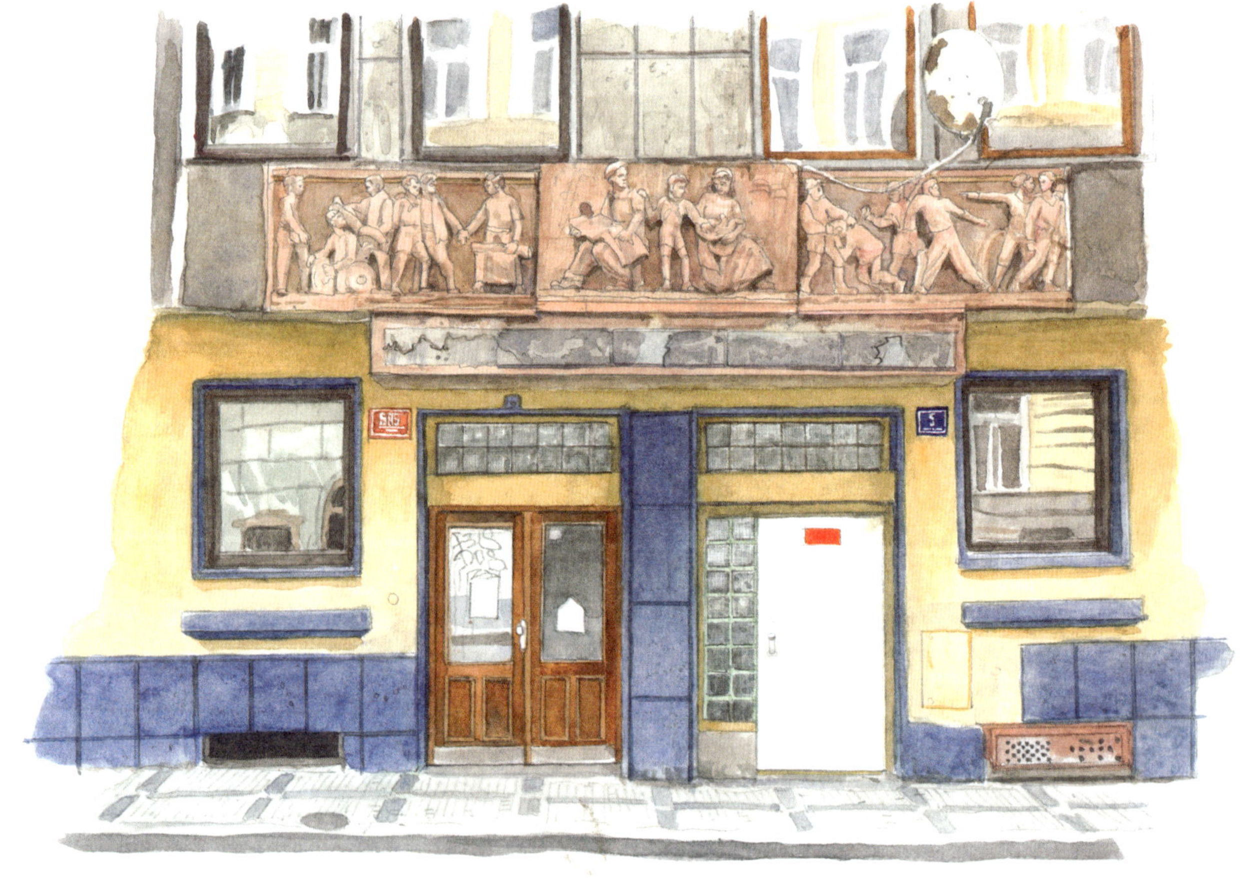

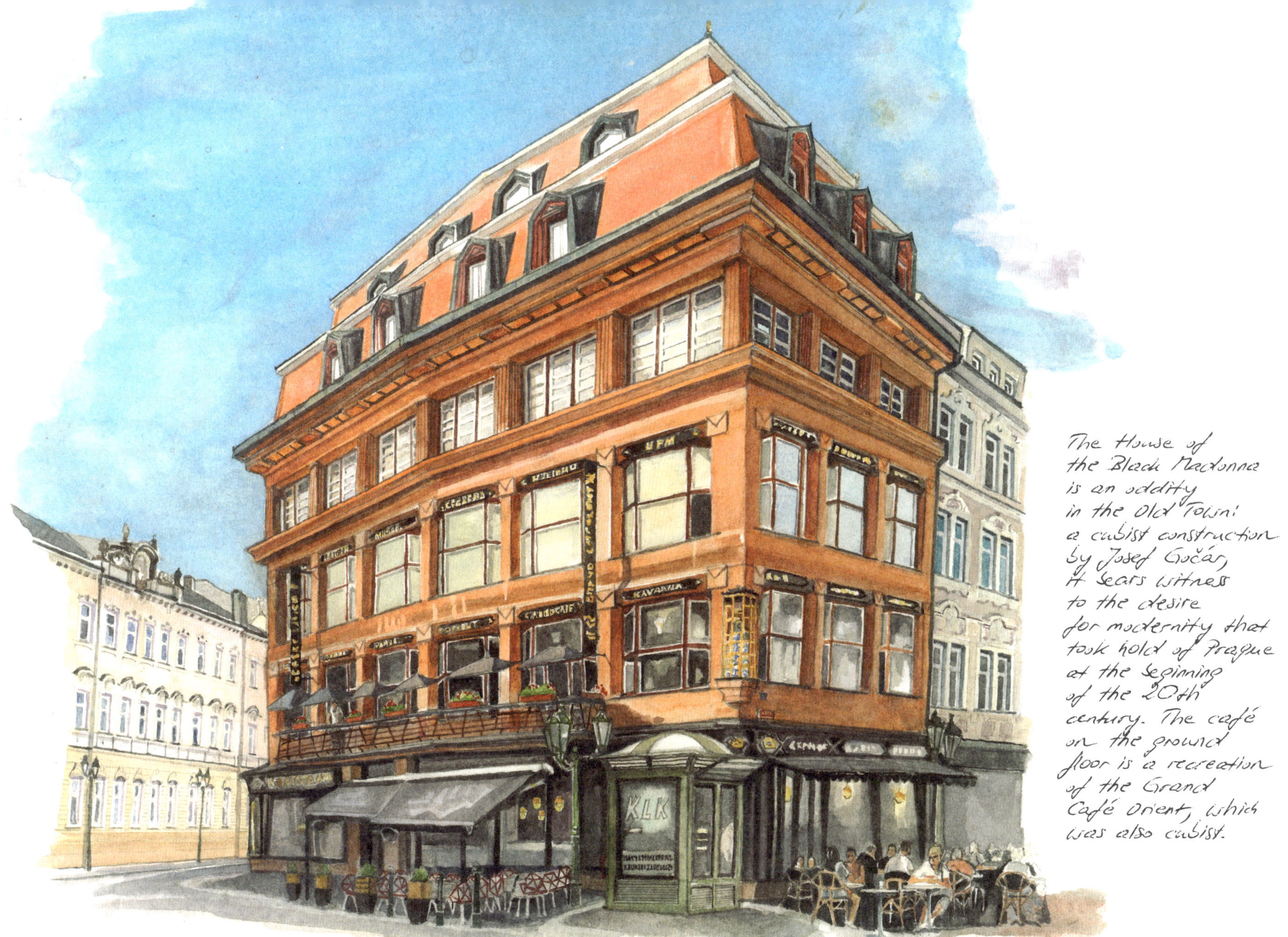

years, including T.G. Masaryk, the nation's very first president, who secured the rights of Czechs to split away from the Austro-Hungarian Empire and form an independent nation. Cafe Slavia may not be strictly a pub (but, as anywhere in the country, a thirsty visitor will find a life-sustaining glass of beer), but it may be the nation's most famous cafe, where Rainer Maria Rilke was a regular and where dissidents like Václav Havel and Jaroslav Seifert–recipient of the Nobel Prize in Literature–met during the normalization period to discuss their resistance against the regime and ponder the country's future. Over the years, I've become fond of frequenting the many pubs where dissidents hunched over and discussed their strategies for rebellion or simply drank away the terror of life under totalitarian surveillance. There is something extraordinary about the pub being a safe place to gather when the secret police had its informants everywhere, looking to collect the smallest bit of information against the dissident movement. The places where dissidents felt safe to be themselves ought to be memorialized as the cocoons where the seeds of the Velvet Revolution were sown.

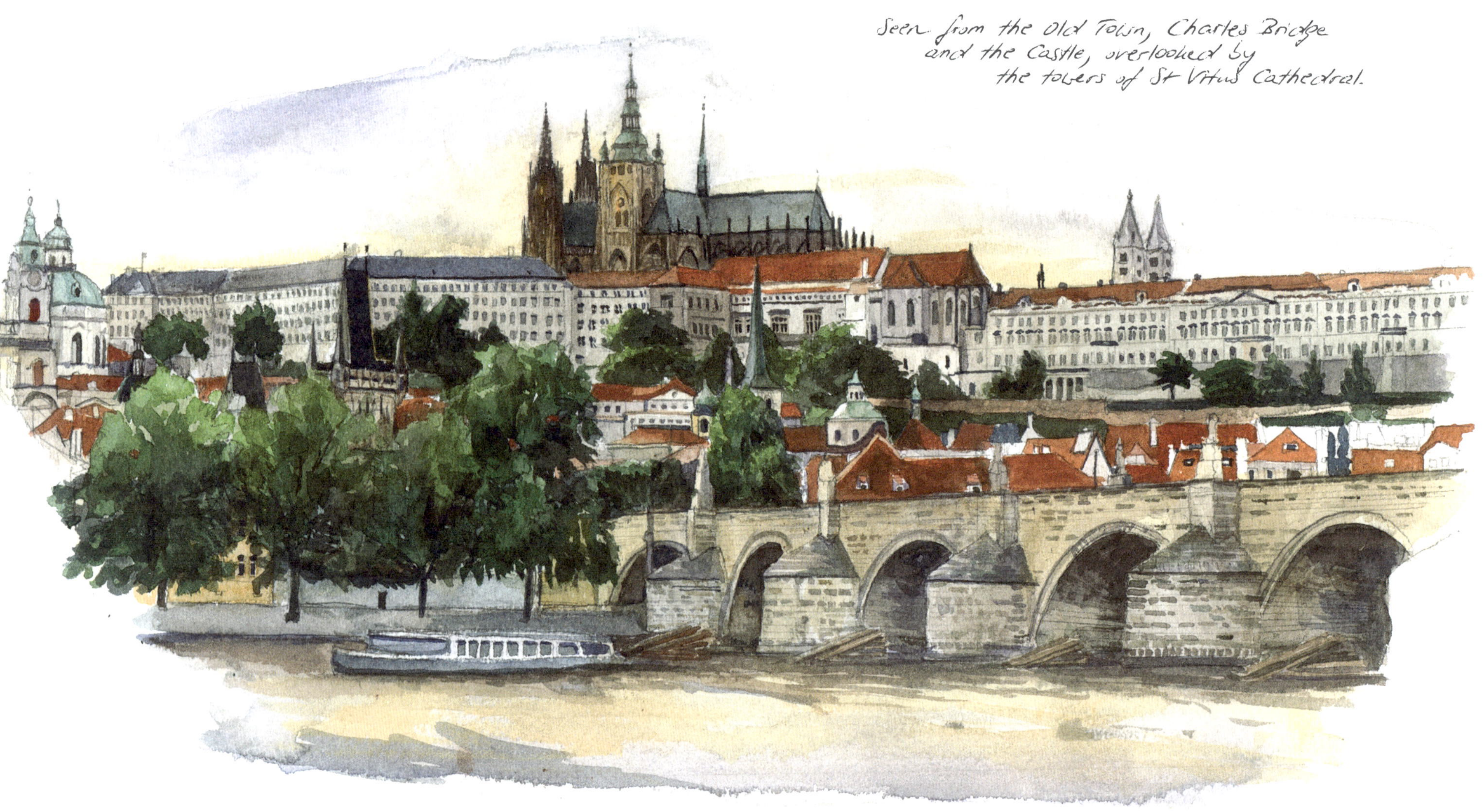

Prague is for Lovers

On my travels to Prague, I often think about the spray-painted slogan *Tourists, Go Home*, which my friends and I weaponized when we were children, a slogan I have seen echoed across cities of the world as recently as during the summer in which I write this essay. It is a puzzling sentiment, of course, one that is undoubtedly steeped in the same hypocrisy my young comrades and I were guilty of. The implication of "tourists going home" is one of *all* tourists going home. The suggestion that no one ought to travel any longer to visit any place is a foolishly isolationist and economically troubling sentiment that doesn't dip a single toe into the reality of how the world has functioned since our species emerged. In short, we visit each other. We travel to admire each other's cities and countries and languages and cultures. The world is made better by the admiration we have for places far away from the dirt on which we were born. My friends and I would confidently spray-paint *Tourists, Go Home* onto Prague's walls mere weeks before we dispersed for our own summer holidays, traveling with our parents to become tourists in Spain, France, or Egypt. We are all tourists somewhere. Living between countries and identities, I feel like a tourist almost everywhere, especially in my home cities of New York and Prague.

While I wasn't able to share the earnest discovery of Prague with my childhood friends as we grew up, nor with my family, the years of my reconnection with the city have offered the pleasure of introducing my birthplace to my American friends. Their enthusiasm is that of visitors seeing the city for the first time, which allows me to play both the role of the local who can introduce them to Prague's wonders and that of a visitor who shares in their awe without a hint of cynicism. During their early days in the city, my New Yorker friends were too polite and plagued by tourist's guilt to look the people of Prague in the eye, let alone try to interact with the Czech greetings and pleasantries I had taught them. A week later, having experienced the host culture expressed by most of Prague's citizens, who are proud to present the city to visitors, my friends were asking every hot dog vendor about their day in the chattiest Czech. They laughed and insisted, "to je okay" as the young woman setting our serving of absinthe aflame lost control of the burning liquid and dropped it straight into my friend's hair.

Inside underground student bars, my American friends and I could barely see each other through the thick haze of cigarette smoke that filled establishments before the smoking ban in the city went into effect. We purchased our own packs of vogues from the bar's vending machine and joined the revelers as I watched one of my friends mount a table and attempt to play the lute hanging on the bar's wall. With me they climbed the steep stairs leading up to the gates of Prague Castle and ascended the Saint Vitus Cathedral's southern tower via the 100-meter-tall winding staircase. The cathedral allows visitors to admire the city from one of its finest vantage points, a 360-degree view of Eden. Its southern tower may hold prophetic qualities: in 2002, the literal heart of the 500-year-old bell that lives within the tower, Zikmund, burst open during the celebratory ringing acknowledging the name-day of Saint Zikmund himself. According to legends, the bursting of the bell's heart is a grave omen, and later that year, the Czech Republic was struck by the most catastrophic floods in a hundred years.

Prague, of course, is rich in towers. My American friends' AirBNB was located in the troubled neighborhood of Žižkov, and from their window, they could see the unsettlingly absurdist installation of giant metal toddlers climbing up the city's famous Žižkov Television Tower. This bizarre art project is another fitting tribute to Prague's many faces, and its legacy of producing one of the most accomplished absurdists of all time, Franz Kafka. Much like my neighborhood of Chodov, Žižkov is a quarter historically plagued by drug abuse and the whims of troubled youth; yet its proximity to Prague's center and its own landmarks, such as the television tower, the eerie Olšanské

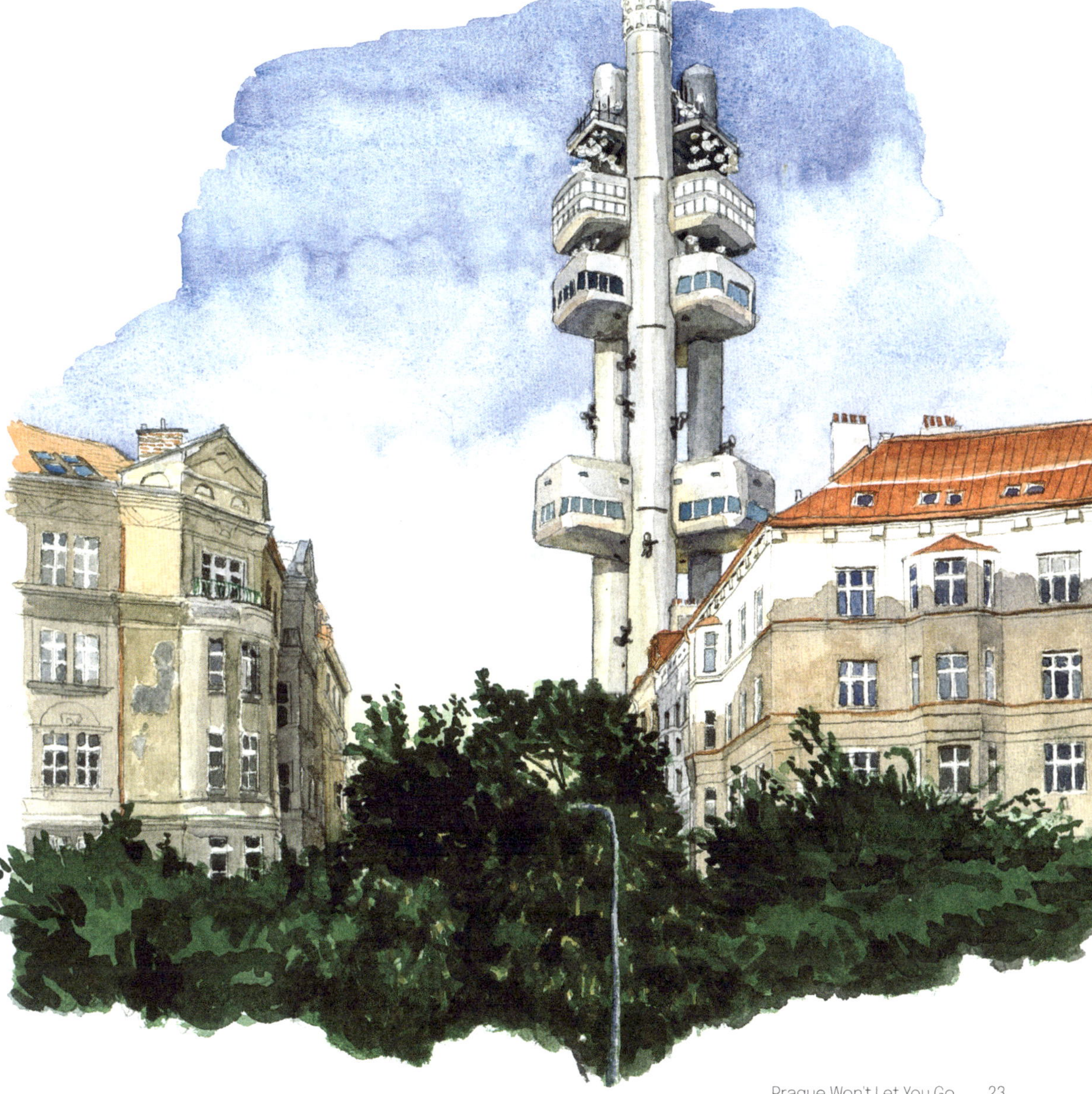

Hřbitovy–the largest cemetery in Prague–and the statue of the Hussite hero Jan Žižka, make it a sought-after destination for tourists looking for secrets beyond Prague's well-known spots. Even the underdog quarters of the city have an undeniable charm bound to win over its visitors.

As much as I've enjoyed Prague with friends, only recently have I been able to conquer the last facet of the city, which eluded me for decades: Prague's romance. Throughout many partnerships, I have refused to bring my inamoratas to Prague, feeling that my connection to the city was so sacred that I hesitated to share it on an intimate level. But during recent summers, I have finally gotten to experience what it's like to take couple's photos with a Kodak disposable camera next to the morose saints of Charles Bridge. Together, my partner and I have ascended the Park of Lovers, or Petřín, the hill looming over

Vltava made famous by Kafka's 'Description of a Struggle' and Kundera's *Unbearable Lightness of Being*. Here, families and lovers alike climb the steep trails, passing the leftovers of medieval fortifications at the Hunger Wall, the hill's magnificent Rose Garden, or the Mirror Maze, where children chortle at the contortions of their faces, before reaching the ultimate prize: the Petřín Lookout Tower. Dubbed as the Eiffel Tower of Prague, here local and foreign lovers wait in line for the stairs and elevator taking them to the top, where perhaps the best panoramic view of the city is on offer, a view extending far beyond the city limits and into the highlands of Northern Bohemia. There is something truly romantic about this place–perhaps it is the scent traveling from the nearby rose garden and orchards, or the fact that so much of the country is on display. The hundred spires of Prague surrounded by the green hills, forests, and rivers of untouched nature create a perfect balance between fast-paced urban thrills and the enduring serenity of the Bohemian countryside.

In a way, sharing the city of my birth with my partner and soon-to-be-wife is the culmination of the past two decades, a journey that began when my teenaged self had embraced the beauty and attractions of Prague on my own without telling anyone, ashamed of my newfound appreciation for its charms. For a long time, my efforts to reconnect with Prague required a degree of solitude and privacy. The vulnerability of my visits, sparked by my feeling as a foreigner in my own motherland, my false memories of Prague, and my wish to understand where the city belonged in my life now that I'd emigrated, could only be processed on my own, without the pressure of showing Prague to other people and acting as a guide or a nostalgist recalling tender memories of childhood. Now that I know who I am in relation to Prague–half native son, half tourist, embracing the familiar while retaining the joy and hedonism of a brand-new visitor– I have been freed to move on to the next stage of my relationship with the city. I can guide

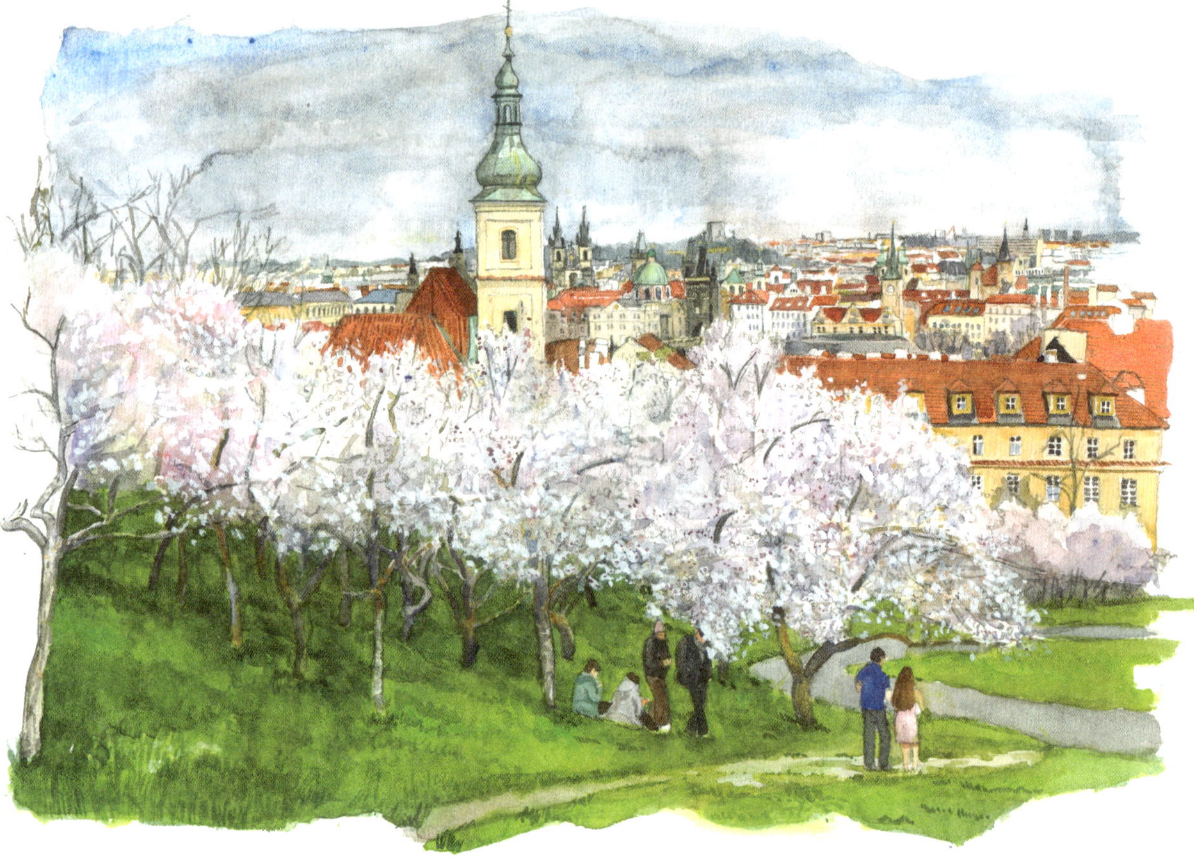

Almond trees in bloom in the seminary gardens (Seminářská zahrada) on Petřín Hill.

Josefov, Prague's Jewish quarter, no longer looks anything like the old quarter haunted by the fictional Golem, with its narrow streets and Gothic houses. They were replaced, thanks to a quasi-Haussmannian renovation at the beginning of the 20th century, by luxury buildings with neo-classical and later Art Nouveau and Cubist facades.

my partner through its streets, eat candlelit dinners inside bell towers, bid the drunken caricaturists of Charles Bridge to capture our likeness, take a great guláš tour to find which establishment serves up the best version of the dish (my partner and I agree: the dingiest basement pub will always serve a better guláš than the clean, English-speaking tourist trap), loiter among the magnificent crystal and art shops in forgotten alleyways to bring pieces of Prague back to New York.

Kitsch or not, tourist or not, falling in love with a beautiful city isn't unlike falling in love with a person. It requires a certain degree of indignity and madness. One must accept he is subject to tropes and clichés. Too much self-seriousness isn't welcome in love. And so, I no longer stroll through Prague as the angry teen who wants to spit on its admirers, or the insecure young emigrant who isn't sure whether the city has any space left for him. I walk through Prague overtaken with shameless adoration, starved for every piece of strange or straightforward joy it has to offer. This is the kind of treatment my city deserves. The tension between my city and me will never dissipate, but I have embraced it. I think of the future, not the past. I think of the half-Czech children that my wife and I will someday introduce to those famous spires. Prague will be so different for my children. I want them to feel safe and sound in their awe, and I want to show them every tourist attraction as soon as they are able to open their eyes. I want them to sense their father's love for the greatest city in the world, and I want them to feel it belongs to them, too, that it will always be there for them, and they needn't do anything at all to make it their own. Prague is a part of their legacy, as it is mine. How lucky to come from such a place. How lucky that Prague will live on in me, and in them, until the end of our days.

How lucky that I will be able to take my children to Dušní, the street of souls, and point to the ground-floor apartment where their family lived through the communist years and the Velvet Revolution. The building has long since been renovated, and the space where our apartment used to be is now a Hawaiian restaurant. The pesky phone booth my father once tried to move was ripped out of the ground decades ago, making space for expanded parking. Czech celebrities have moved on to other, more peaceful neighborhoods, where they still, no doubt, allow their dogs to defecate in front of the neighbors' doors. Some things stay and some things go. But Dušní is still part of Kafka's Quarter. During my wanderings, I never fail to pay my tribute by visiting the statue in Dušní, portraying Kafka as riding an eerily empty suit, commemorating our street as one of the several in which Kafka spent a part of his life. Nor will I ever fail to visit Franz Kafka Square just a block away, where a plaque commemorates the building where the writer was born. Franz never made it far from that address, the same quarter in which he came into existence. He made it the farthest after his death, when he was buried in the Žižkov Cemetery, rather than the Old Jewish Cemetery that graces the quarter from which we both came.

Due to an alphabetical stroke of luck, in bookstores, my novels are almost always right next to those of Kafka, yet our relationship with our city could not be more different. Despite his efforts at building a bigger life, Kafka couldn't escape the small quarter in which he was born until his death. The ambitious life he dreamed of happened only after he passed away, when his books found their audiences and transformed literature as we know it. Unlike its famous son, I left Prague as soon as I could and began the ambitious life I wanted far away from my city of birth. Now I strive to return. I yearn to feel at home and to become smothered, to feel that same choke-hold Kafka felt our city had on him when he wrote about it. I will never halt my efforts to find a new level of closeness within Prague. Always I plot to make my life and hers more intertwined. I want Prague to sink her claws into me and never let me go.

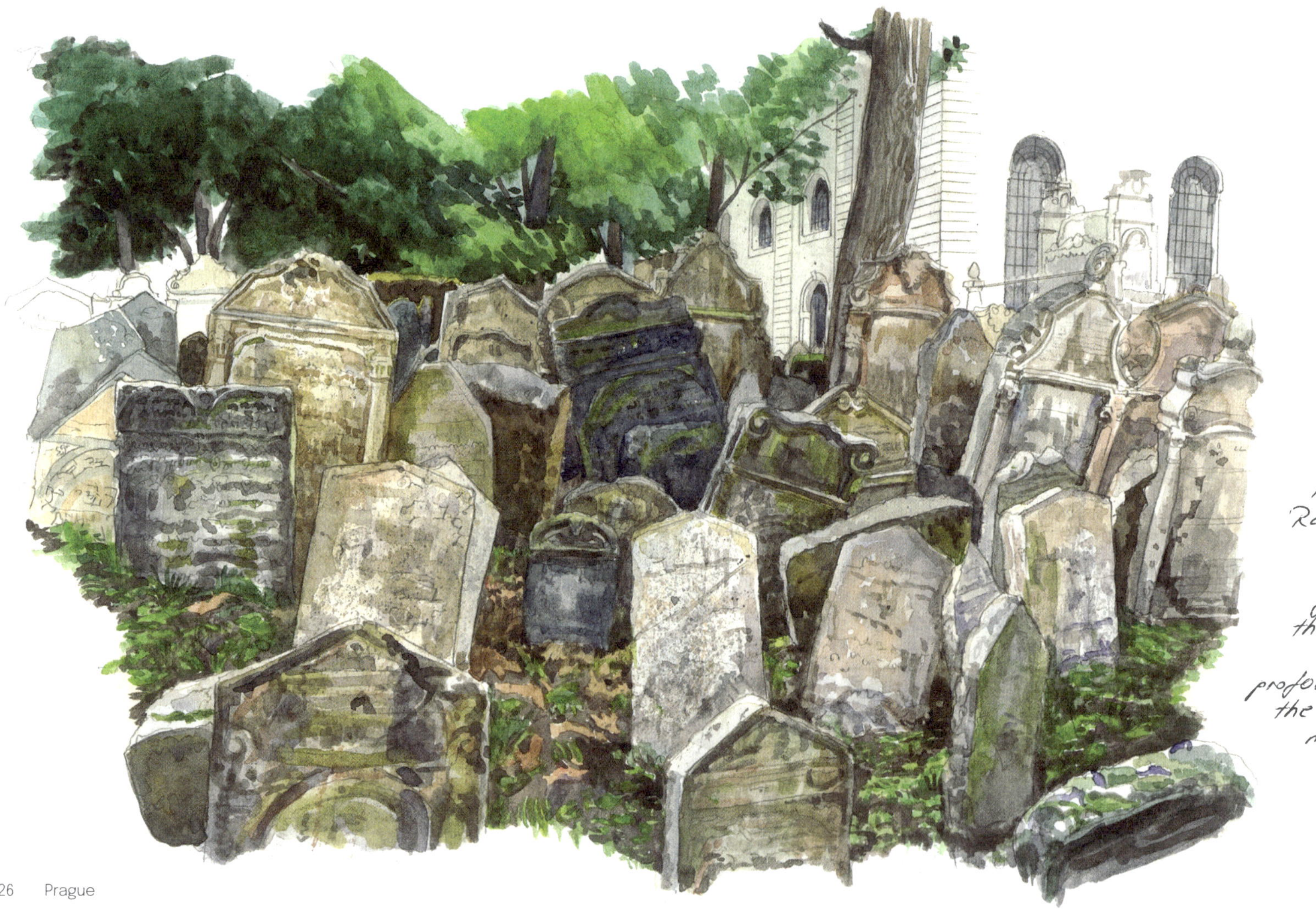

Prague's Old Jewish Cemetery, the still-vibrant heart of the Jewish quarter, is the burial place of Rabbi Maisel, the great philanthropist and leader of Prague's Jewish community in the 17th century, and Rabbi Löw, the profound thinker to whom the legend of the golem is mistakenly attributed.

A City Immortal

Every year, on the last day of my Prague visit, I stand at the edge of Old Town Square, facing the Týn Church, and listen to the chatter from the massage parlor where tired elderly Americans pay for foot rubs. As I leer at the monuments I hated as a child, I struggle to leave them behind. No matter how thick the tourist droves, no matter how insufferable the salesmen peddling city tours and the teens riding motorized scooters are, in that moment, I am alone with my city, bidding another goodbye. It never gets easier. I must stay for a second longer, and the seconds multiply by the thousands. I look upon the faces of people passing me and see they have no features; they turn into mannequins, everything turns lifeless except for Prague's bleeding watercolor, its aesthetic, its sorcery speaking to me, a native child who is once again betraying his city by leaving it behind, boarding a flight back to New York, his adopted homeland.

As in many things, Franz Kafka was right. Falling in love with a beautiful city guarantees a life of suffering. My greatest fear in life, the reason for sleepless nights, is that I will never see Prague again. That this will be my last time among its spires, that it will vanish from the earth, turn again into a mere memory, flawed, inaccurate, colored by nostalgia. I fear my city may survive only in those paintings I've acquired over the years, artists' interpretations that allow me to keep the city alive on my walls when I am long and far away. Has Prague taken me back? Does it love me again? Do I feel like I am part of it, or am I still an outsider looking in? My answers to these questions change daily as I continue to hoard new memories and mementos and hope that the real shine of the city that inspires them will last long after I've said my final goodbye to the only place I yearn for.

And yet, after every brutal farewell comes another summer. The cobblestones rattle the tires of my cab from the airport, and I can tell I have reached the outskirts of Old Town, my birthplace, from the scents seeping through my cracked window. The cab driver stands corrected, speaking at first in English, only to find that he is addressing a Czech son returned home. Such small misun-derstandings can no longer sour my mood. Every year, I find Prague just where I left it, and I know I can count on one thing: that I can adore the most beautiful city on Earth for just a moment longer.

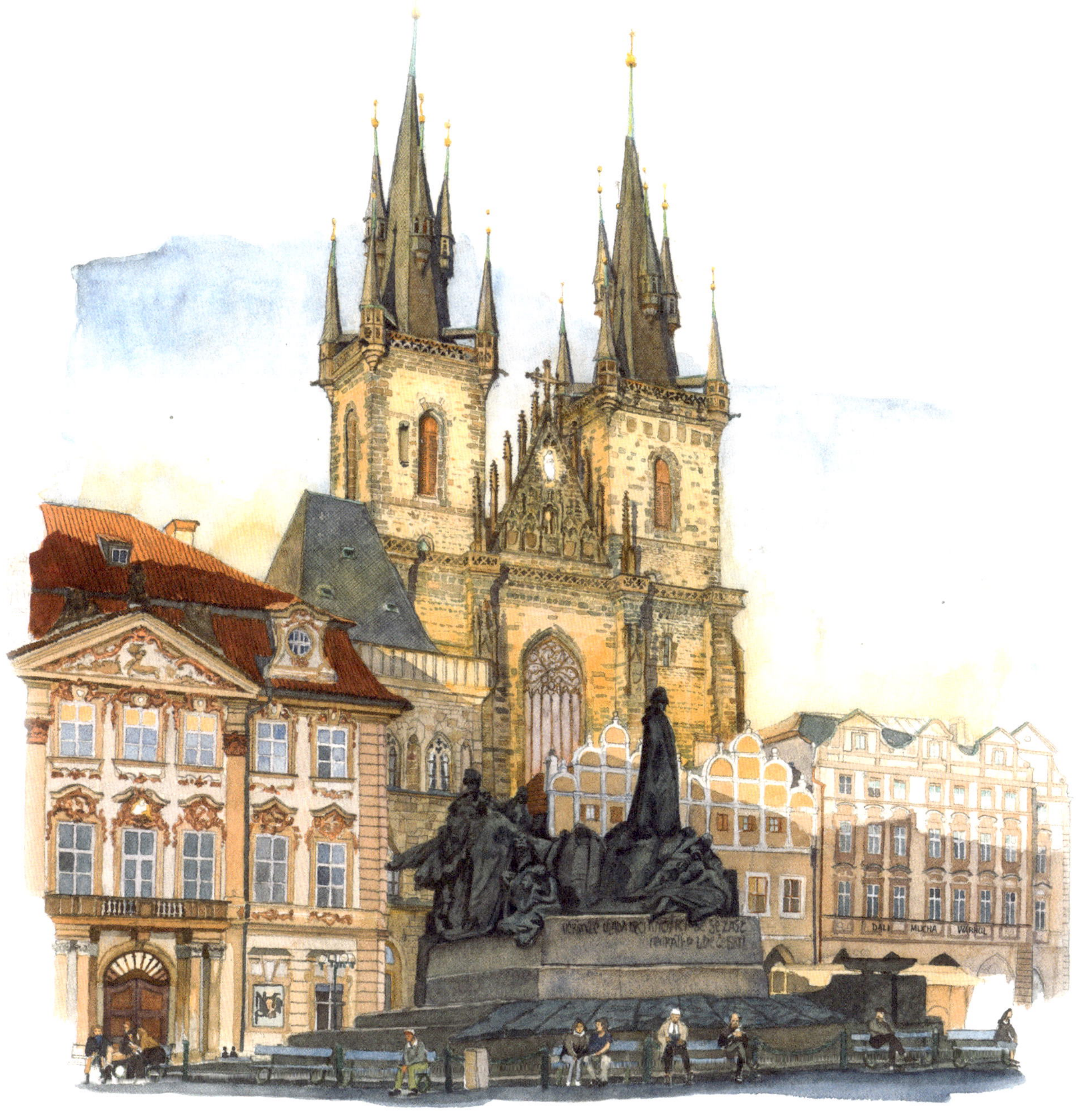

The monument to Jan Hus, a symbol of Bohemian resistance, was erected on the Old Town square in 1915, three years before Czechoslovakia gained its independence. In the background, Our Lady before Týn.

Old Town

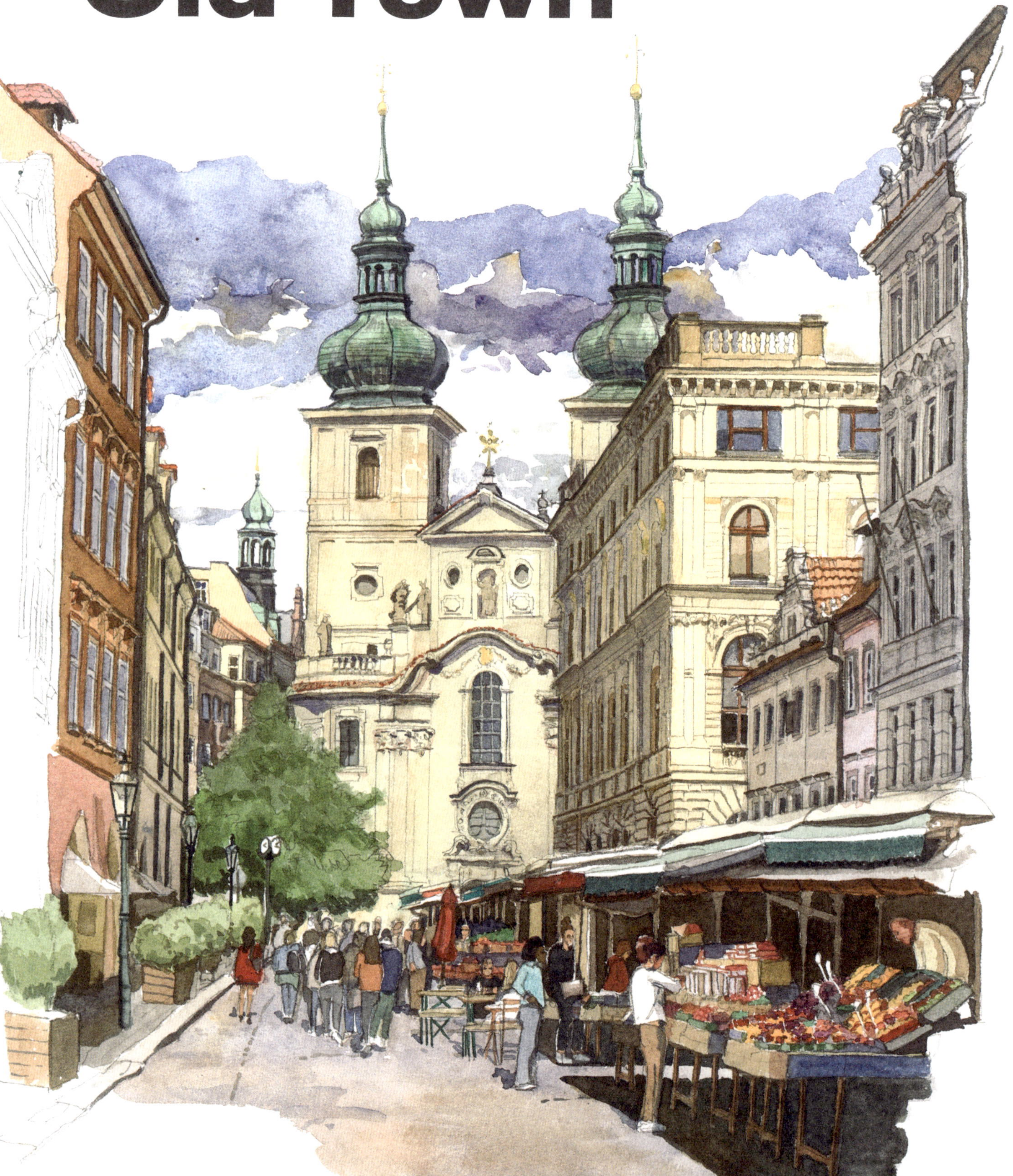

The Gothic Church of St. Gall, whose façade was rebuilt in Baroque style by the architect Pavel Ignac Bayer in 1738, and the Havel fruit and vegetable market, the only one in the Old Town.

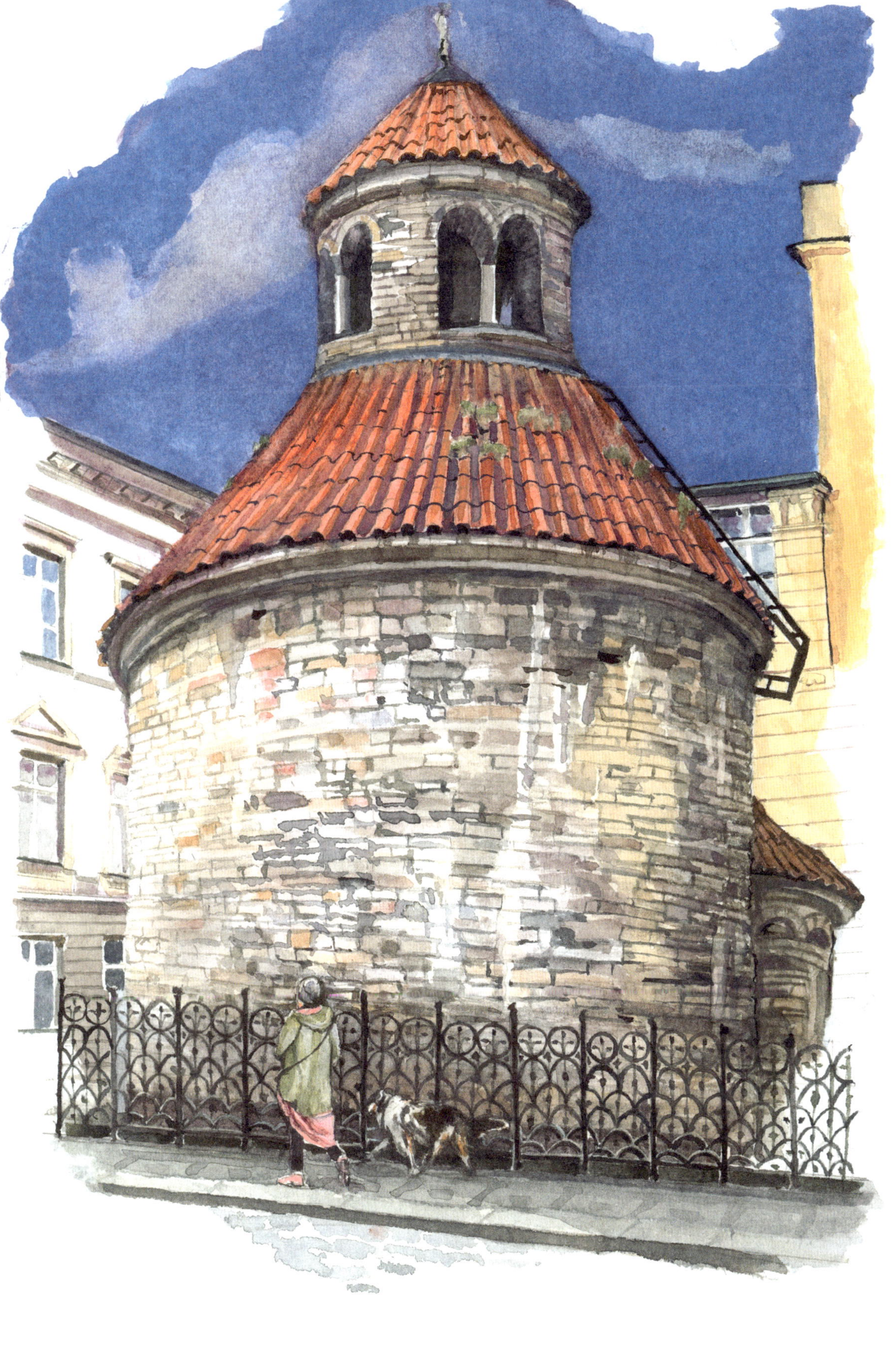

Prague is also a Romanesque
city, as evidenced by its three
rotundas: here, the Holy Cross,
on Karolina Světlá Street,
near the National Theatre.
The St. Martin Rotunda is in
Vyšehrad, and the St. Longin
Rotunda near Štěpánská

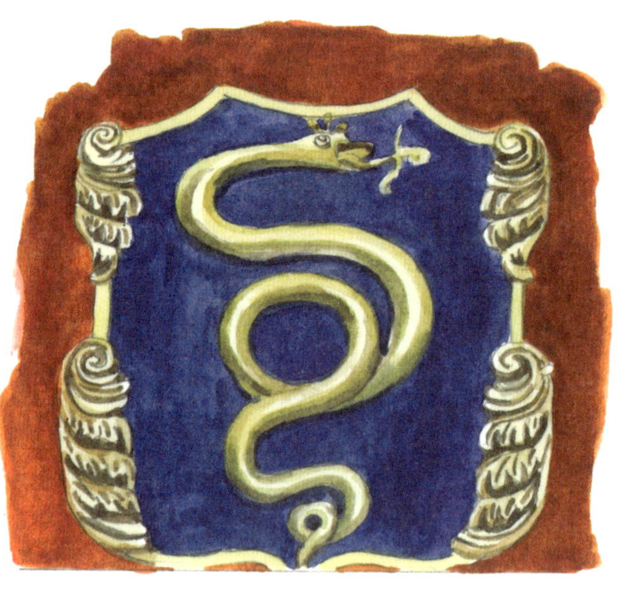

*"By the Golden Snake" –
first coffee house in prague*

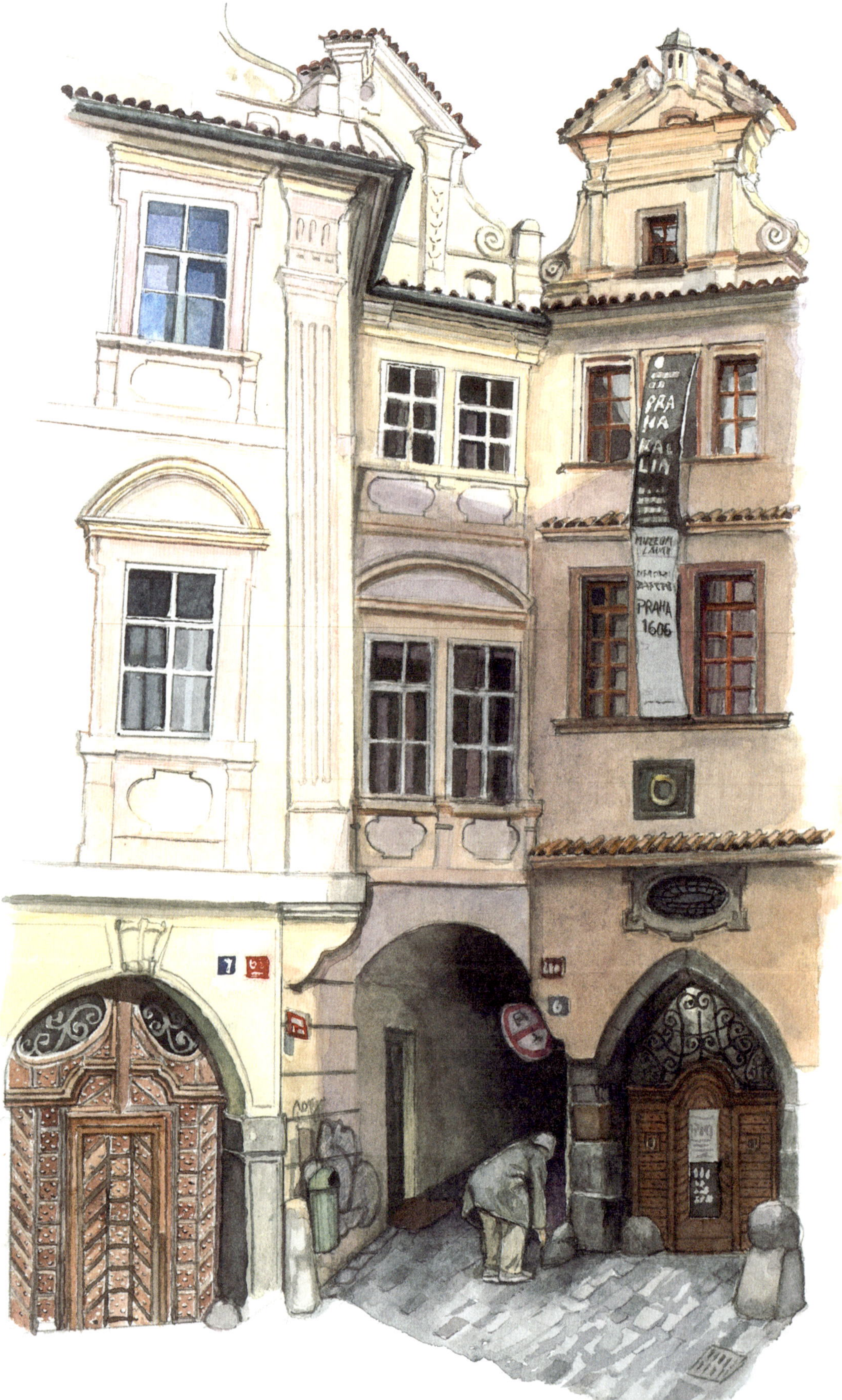

*Baroque houses
on Tynská Street, behind
the Old Town Square.*

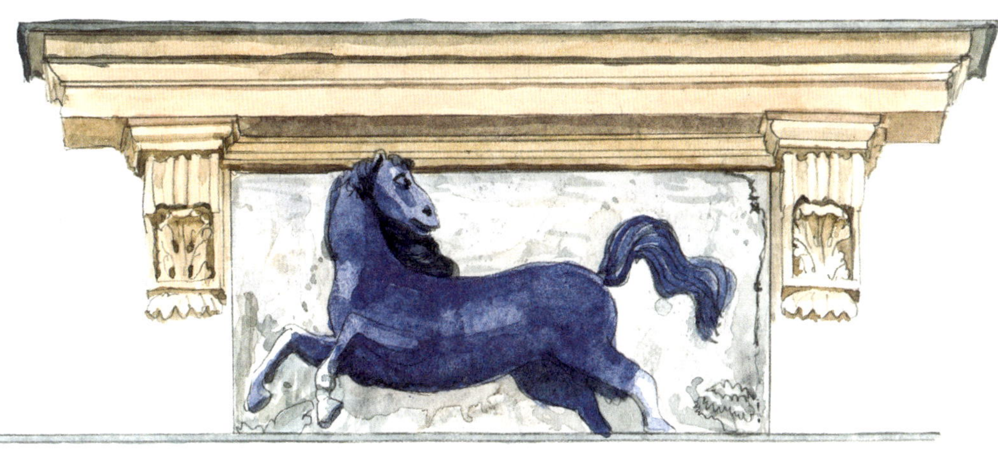

On the Little Square
(Malé náměstí), a stone's throw from
the Old Town square, is a galloping
blue horse, a picturesque example
of Prague's Baroque ornamentation.

Prague's former town hall (Staroměstská
radnice), whose walls house the
astronomical clock on the old square, is
a fascinating construction set. From a
simple town house, converted into the
town hall in 1338, the elected officials,
architects and circumstances have created
a composite Romanesque, Gothic,
Renaissance and neo-Gothic monument.

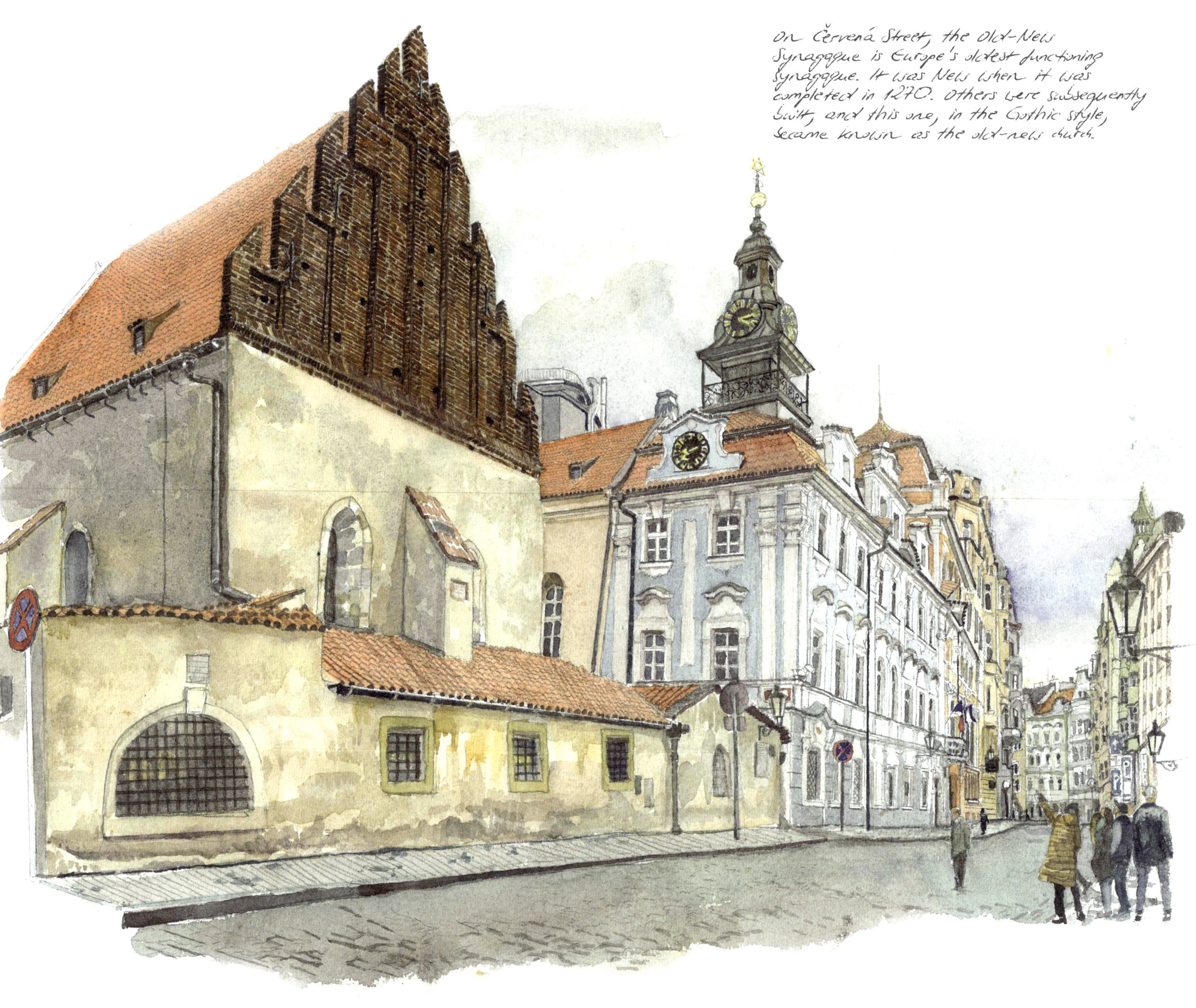

On Červená Street, the Old-New
Synagogue is Europe's oldest functioning
synagogue. It was New when it was
completed in 1270. Others were subsequently
built, and this one, in the Gothic style,
became known as the old-new church.

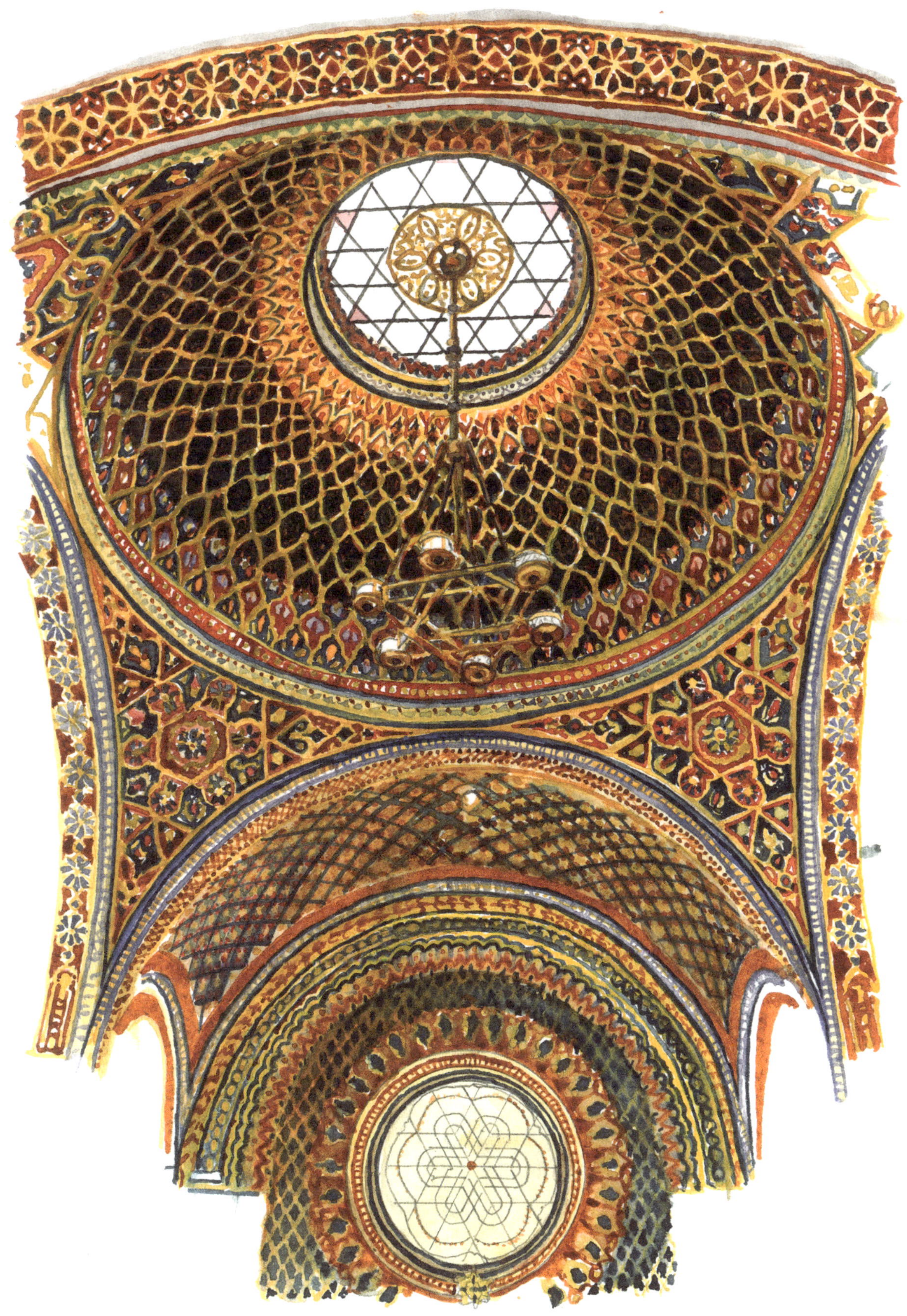

In Dušní Street, the Spanish synagogue replaced the old synagogue, Prague's oldest, in 1868. It is called the Spanish synagogue because its style is reminiscent of the Alhambra, and its beautiful Moorish interior is the work of architects Antonín Baum and Bedrich Münzberger.

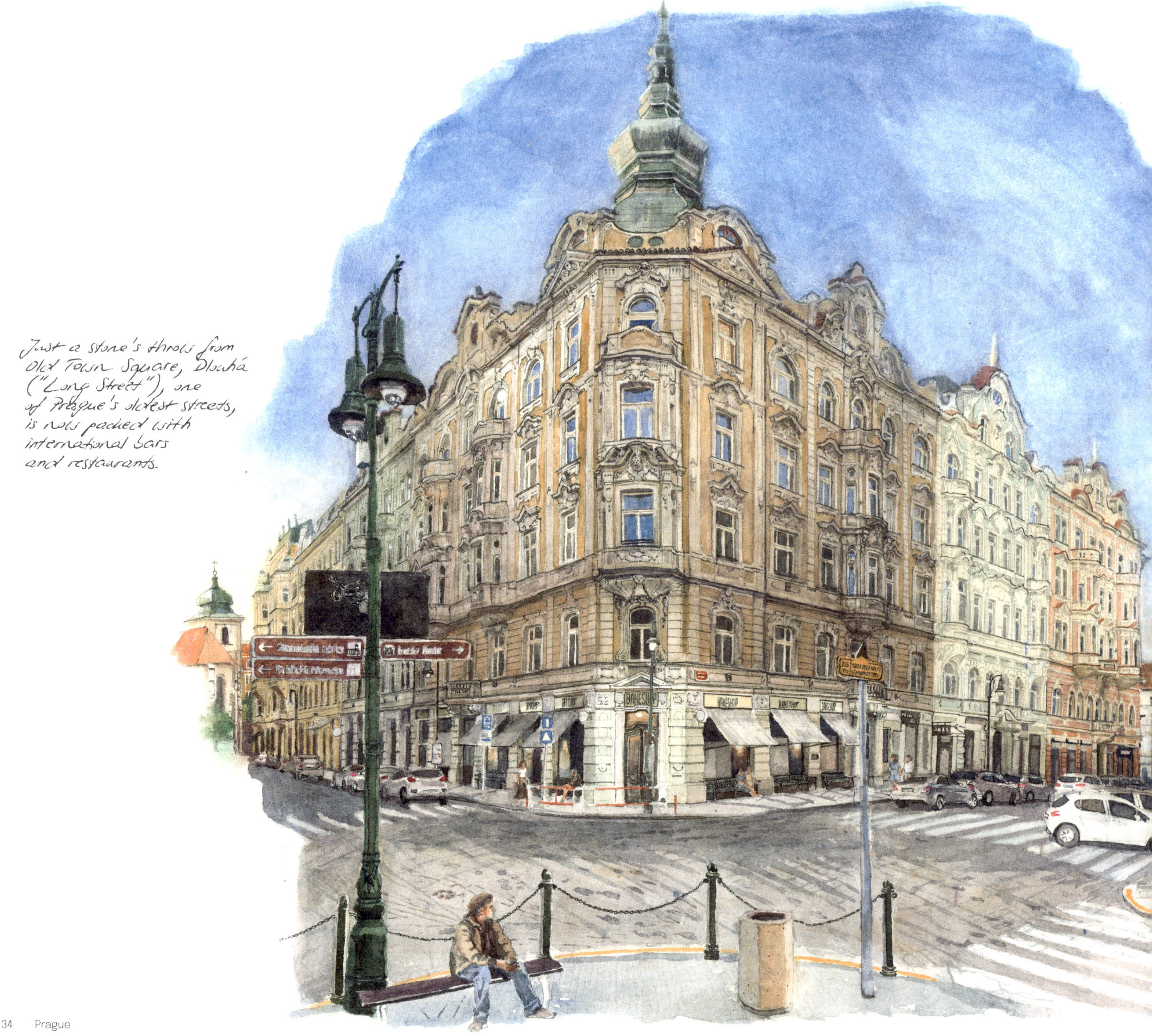

Just a stone's throw from Old Town Square, Dlouhá ("Long Street"), one of Prague's oldest streets, is now packed with international bars and restaurants.

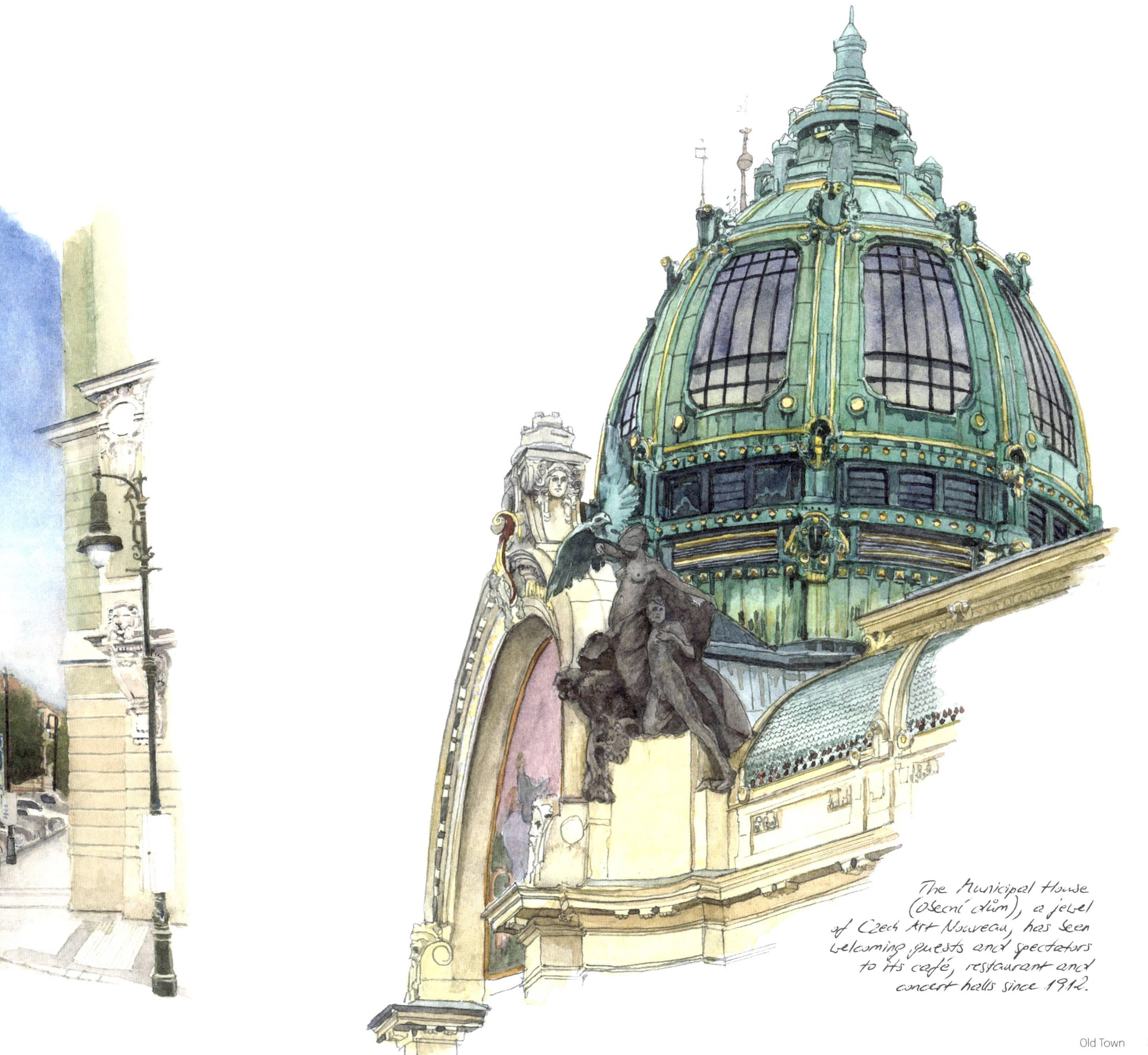

The Municipal House (Obecní dům), a jewel of Czech Art Nouveau, has been welcoming guests and spectators to its café, restaurant and concert halls since 1912.

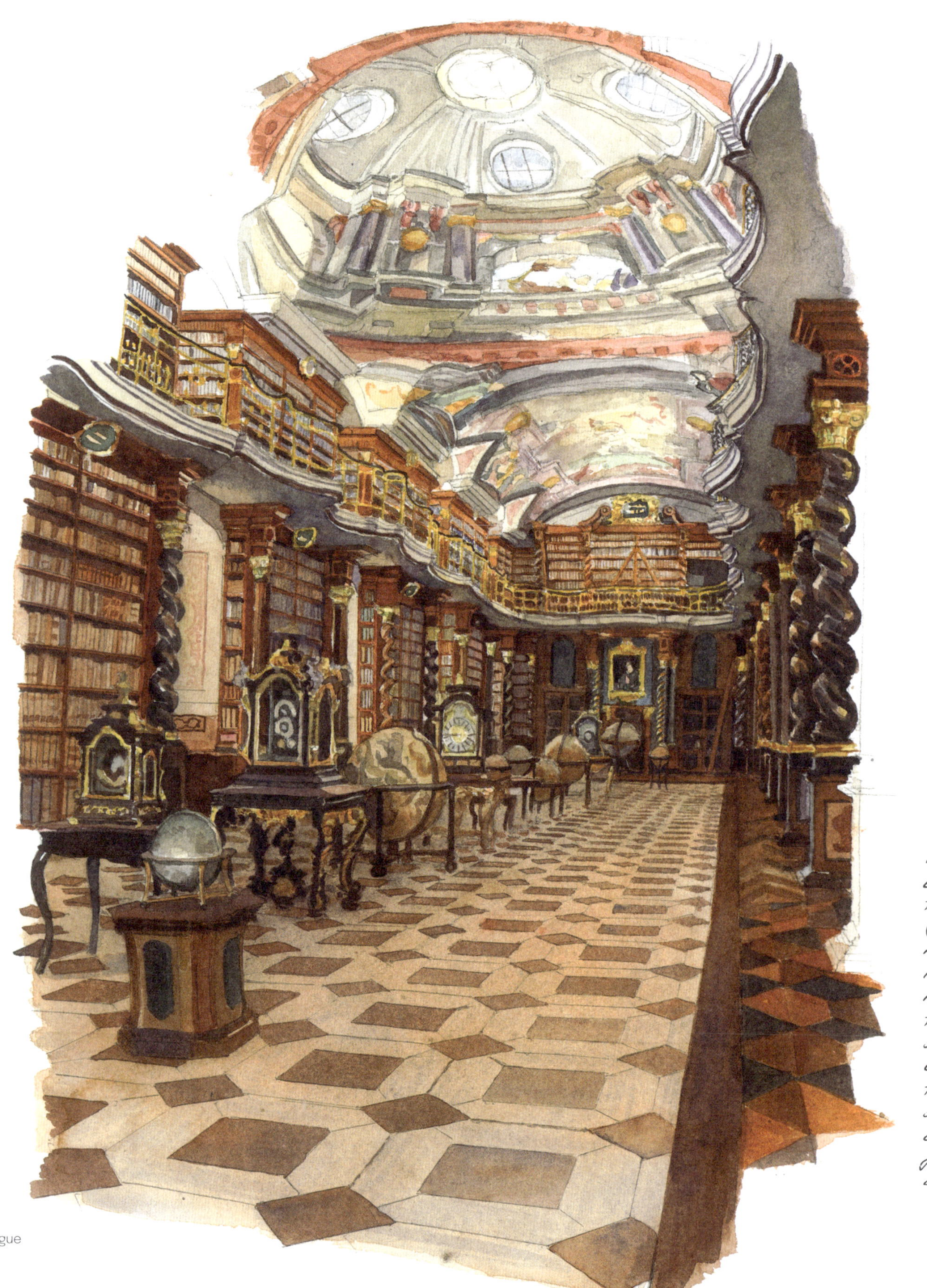

The Czech National
Library, located in
the Clementinum buildings
(Klementinum, Mariánské
náměstí 190/5).
In addition to the six
million books housed here,
there is also a collection
of globes and fourteen
extraordinary sundials,
testifying to the passion
of the Jesuits, who
created the Clementinum,
for geography
and astronomy.

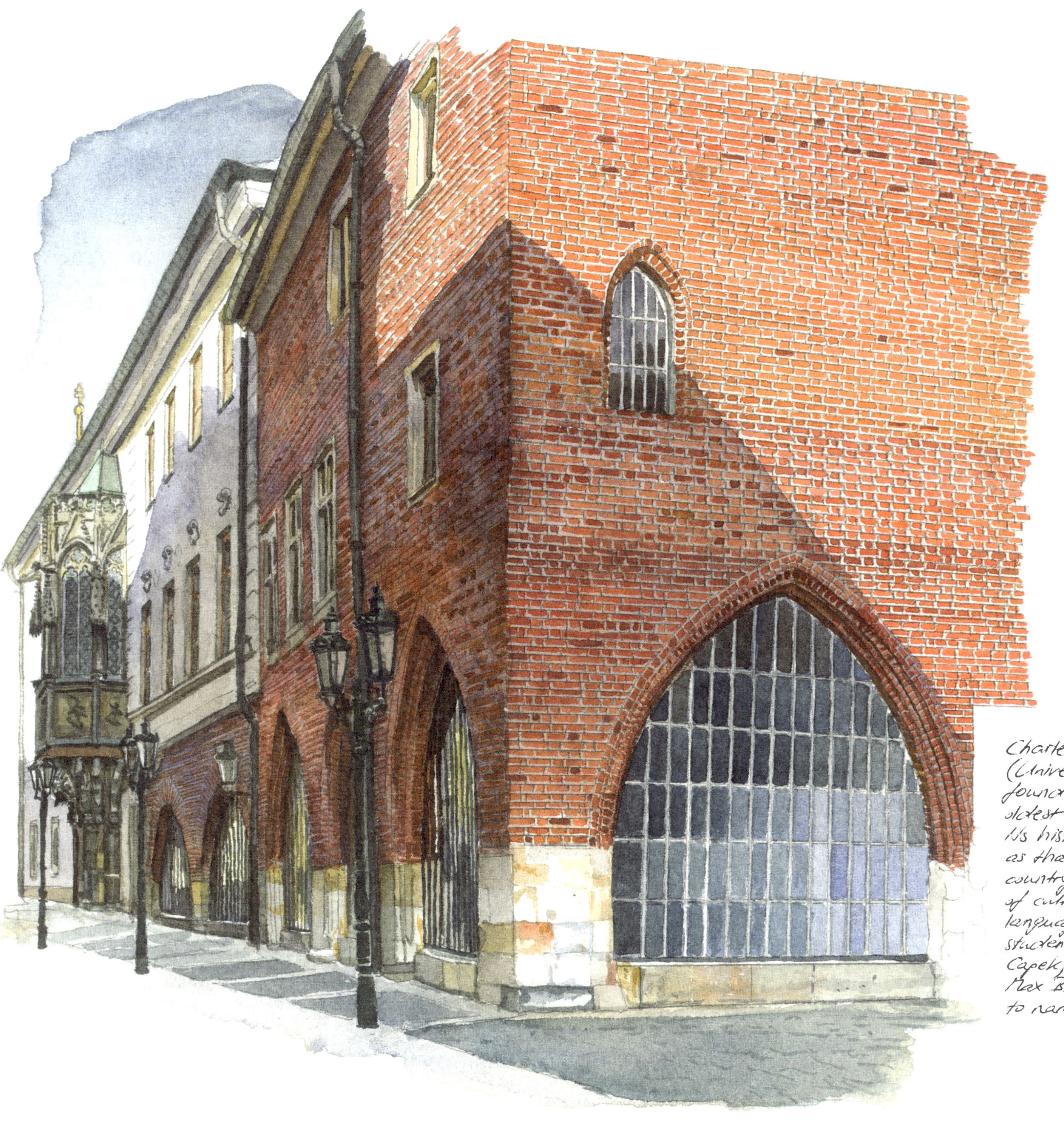

Charles University (Univerzita Karlova), founded in 1348, is the oldest in Central Europe. Its history is as tormented as that of its town and country, a battleground of cultures, religions, languages and politics. Its students included Karel Čapek, Bohumil Hrabal, Max Brod, Franz Kafka to name just a few.

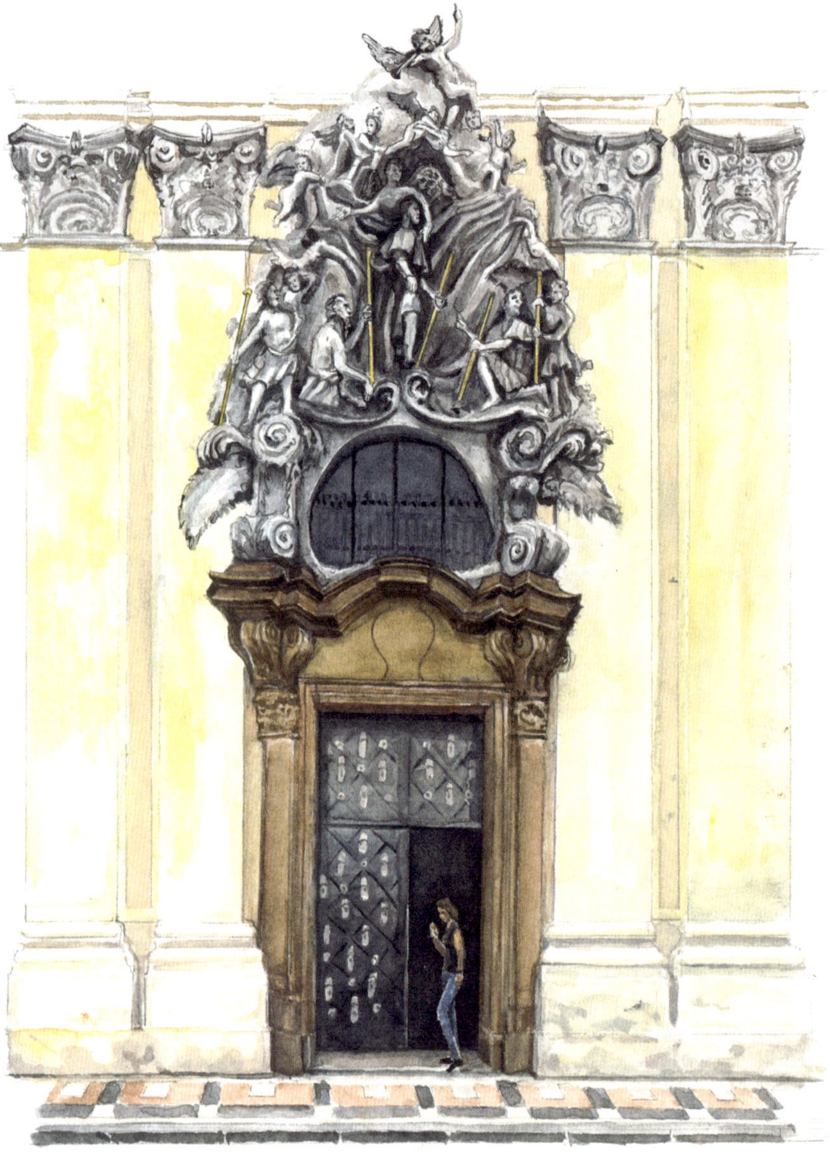

Church of St James the Greater, Malá Štupartská This Baroque church with its remarkable portal replaced a Gothic building that was destroyed by arson in 1689 (or "French fire"), Louis XIV's revenge targeting the Habsburg capitals.

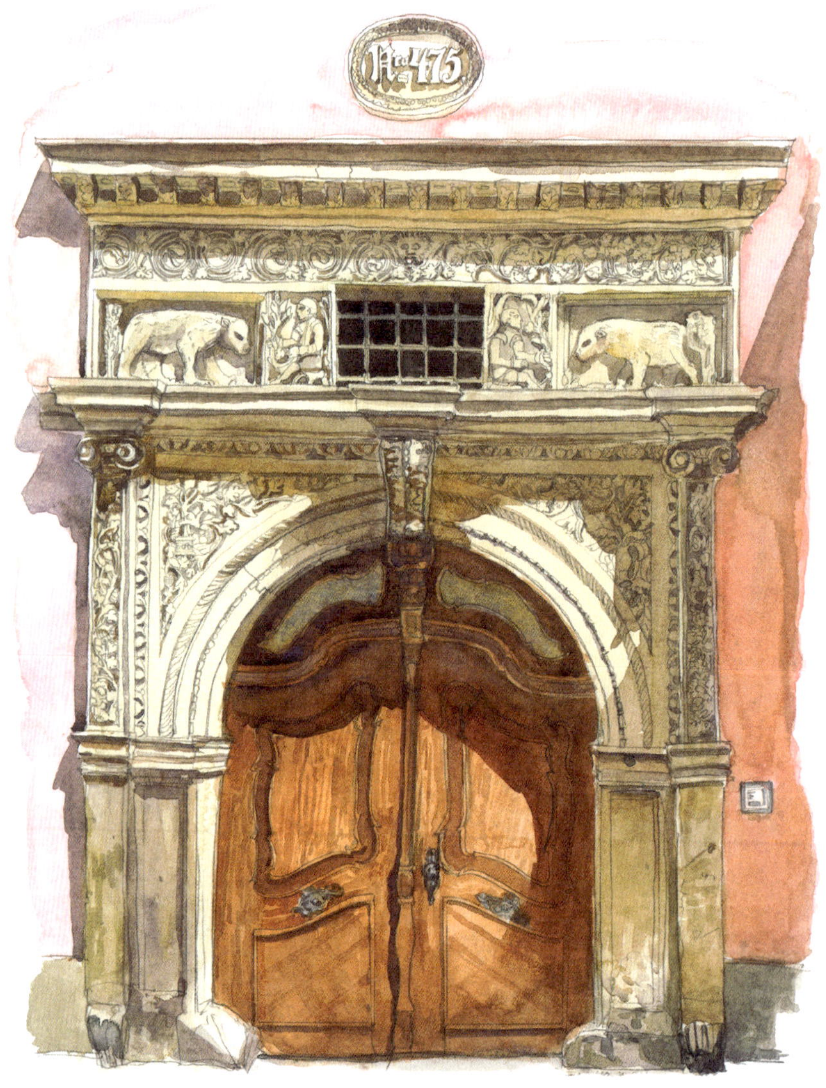

A Renaissance entrance in the old town: the house with the golden bears was the birthplace, a few centuries later, of writer and globetrotter Egon Erwin Kisch (1885–1948).

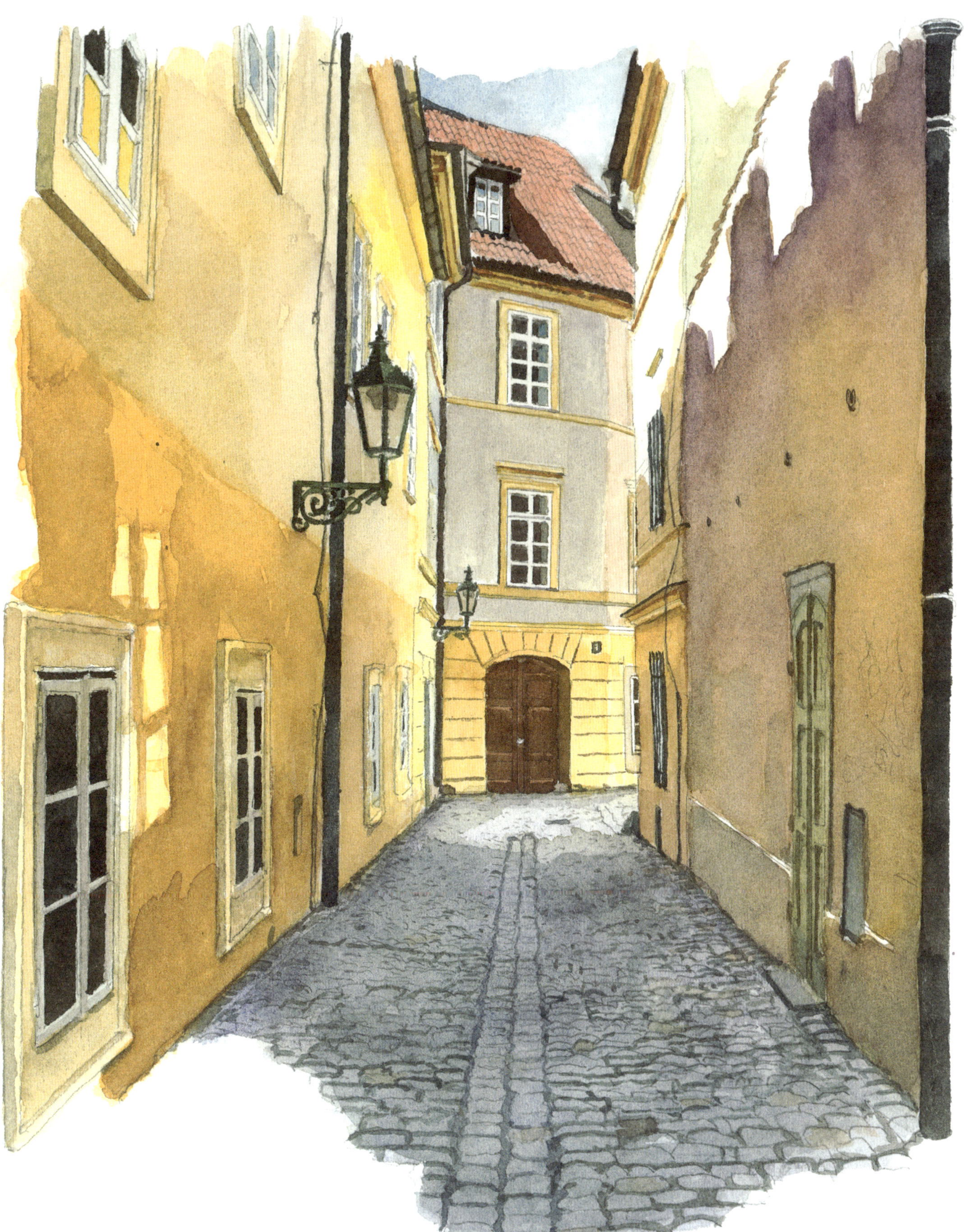
An alleyway
in the Old Town.
Every pedestrian in
Prague knows the
unique feeling of
these small, round
cobblestones on
their exhausted feet.

U zlatého Tygra Pub
(golden tiger pub)
"PRAZDROJ"
PIVO
z Měšťanského pivovaru v Plzni

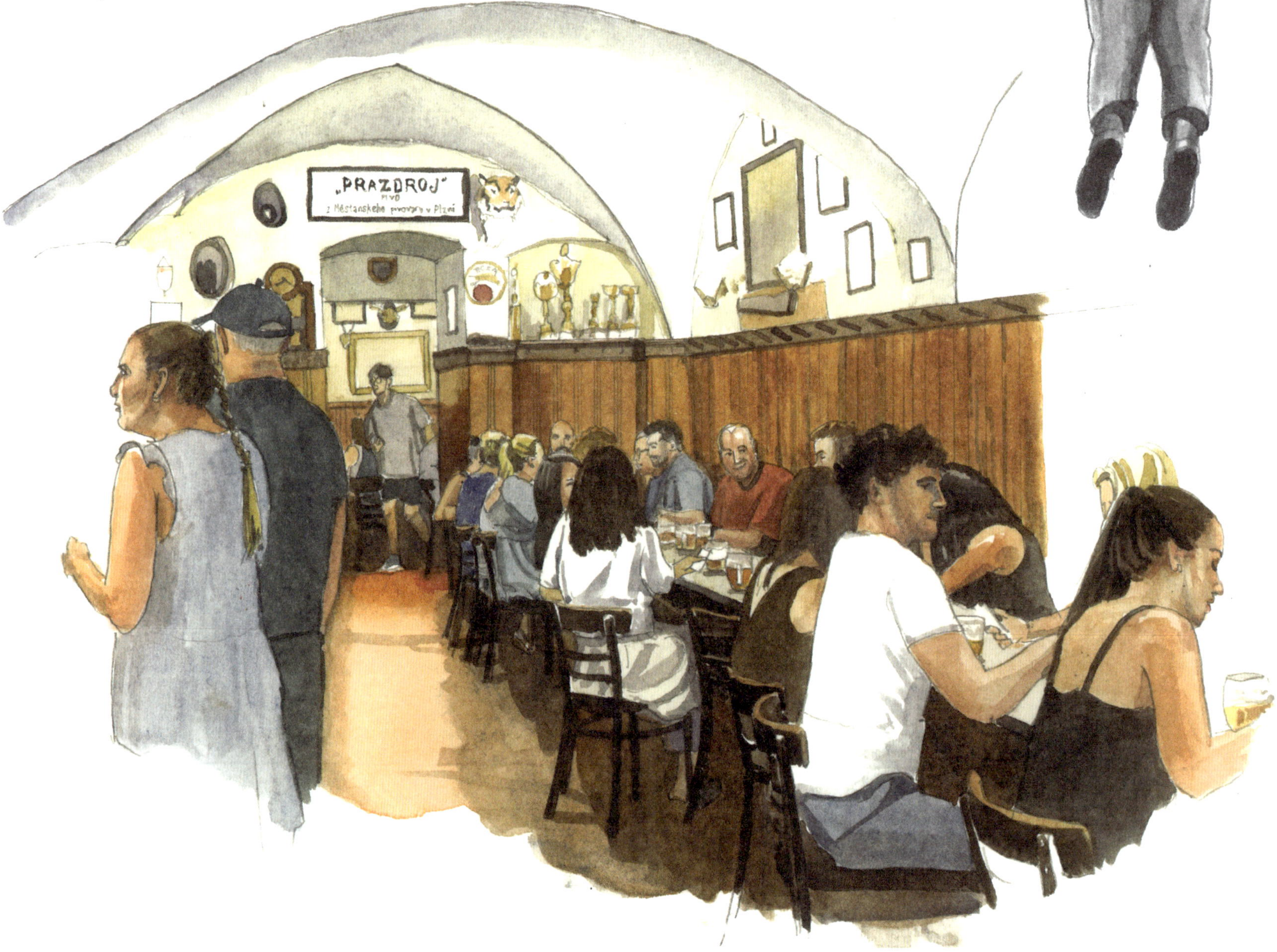

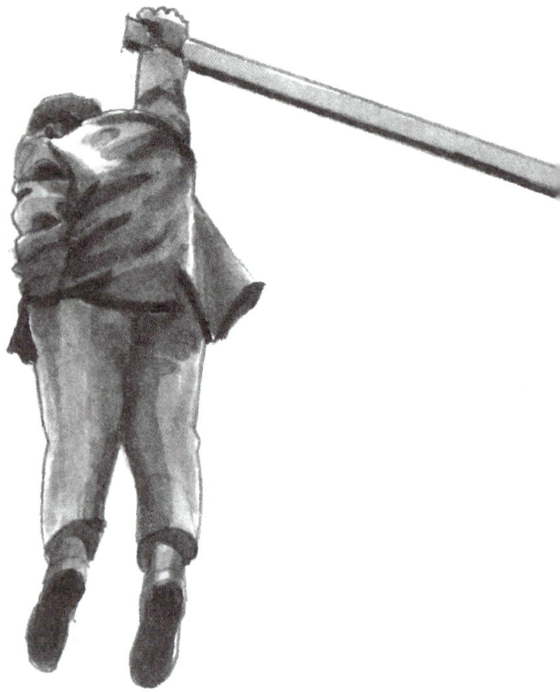

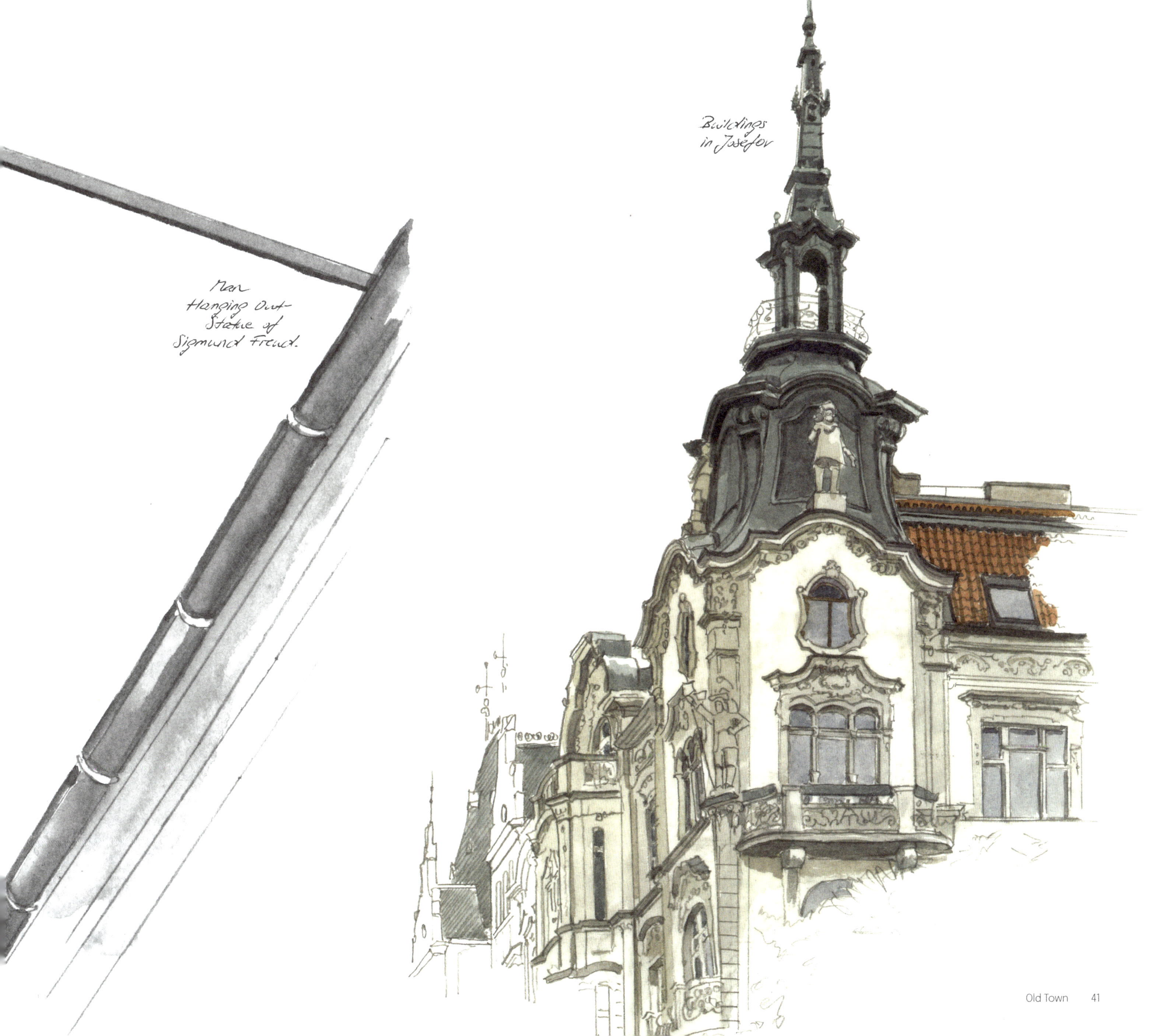

Man
Hanging Out-
Statue of
Sigmund Freud.

Buildings
in Josefov

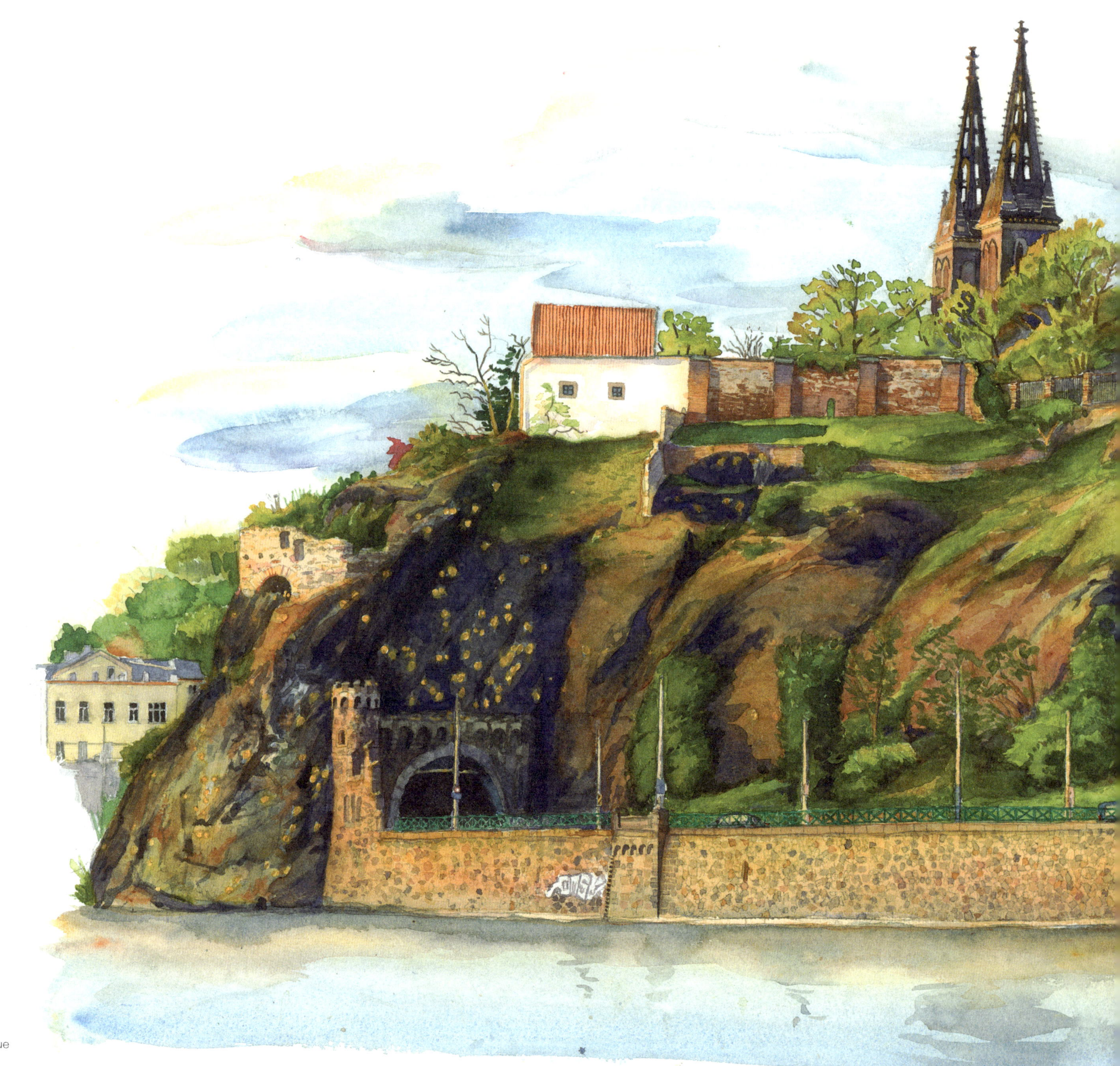

Vyšehrad

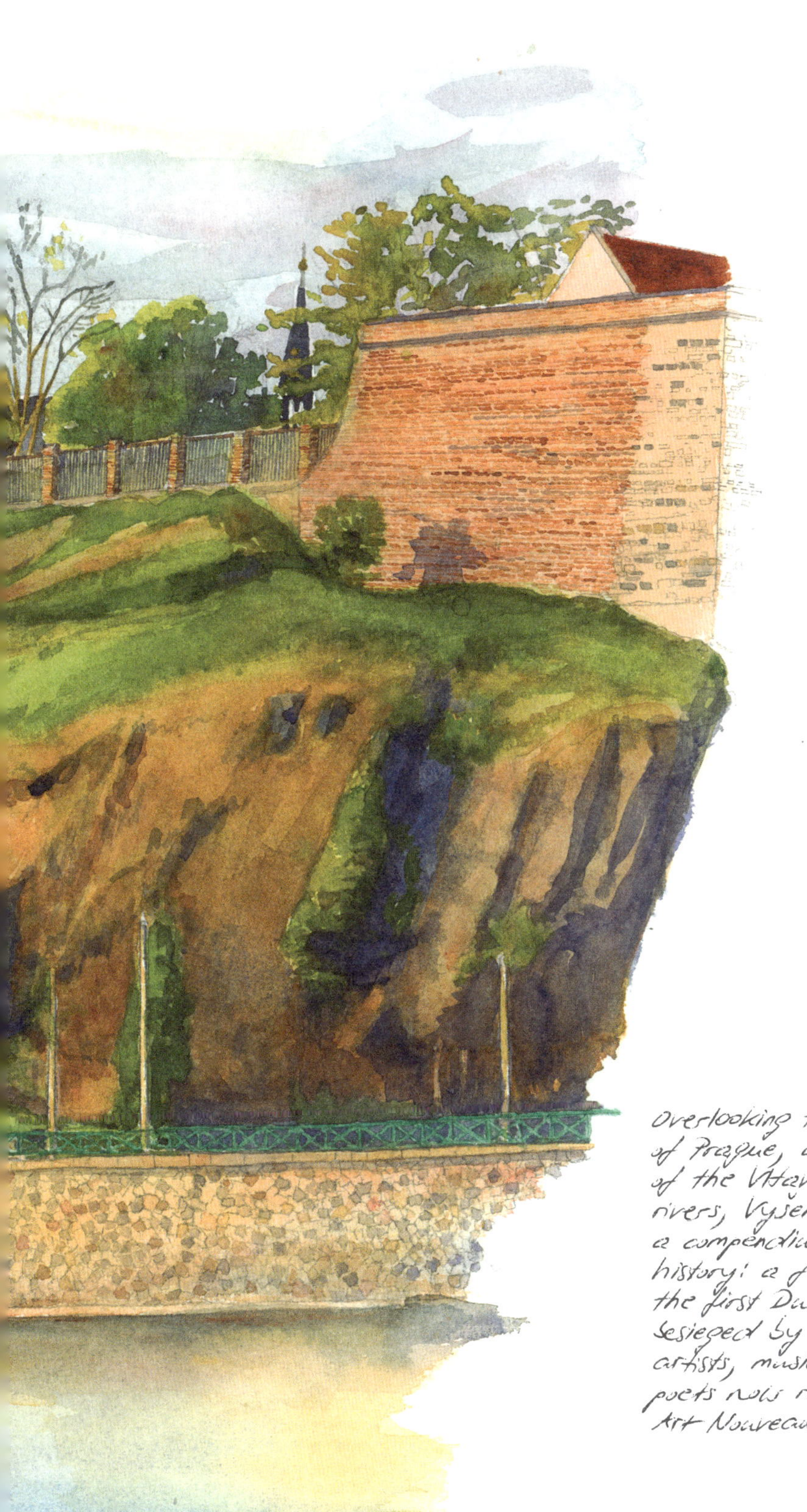

Overlooking the south
of Prague, at the confluence
of the Vltava and Botic
rivers, Vyšehrad Hill is
a compendium of Czech
history: a fortress of
the first Dukes of Bohemia,
besieged by all their enemies,
artists, musicians and
poets now rest there, in its
Art Nouveau cemetery.

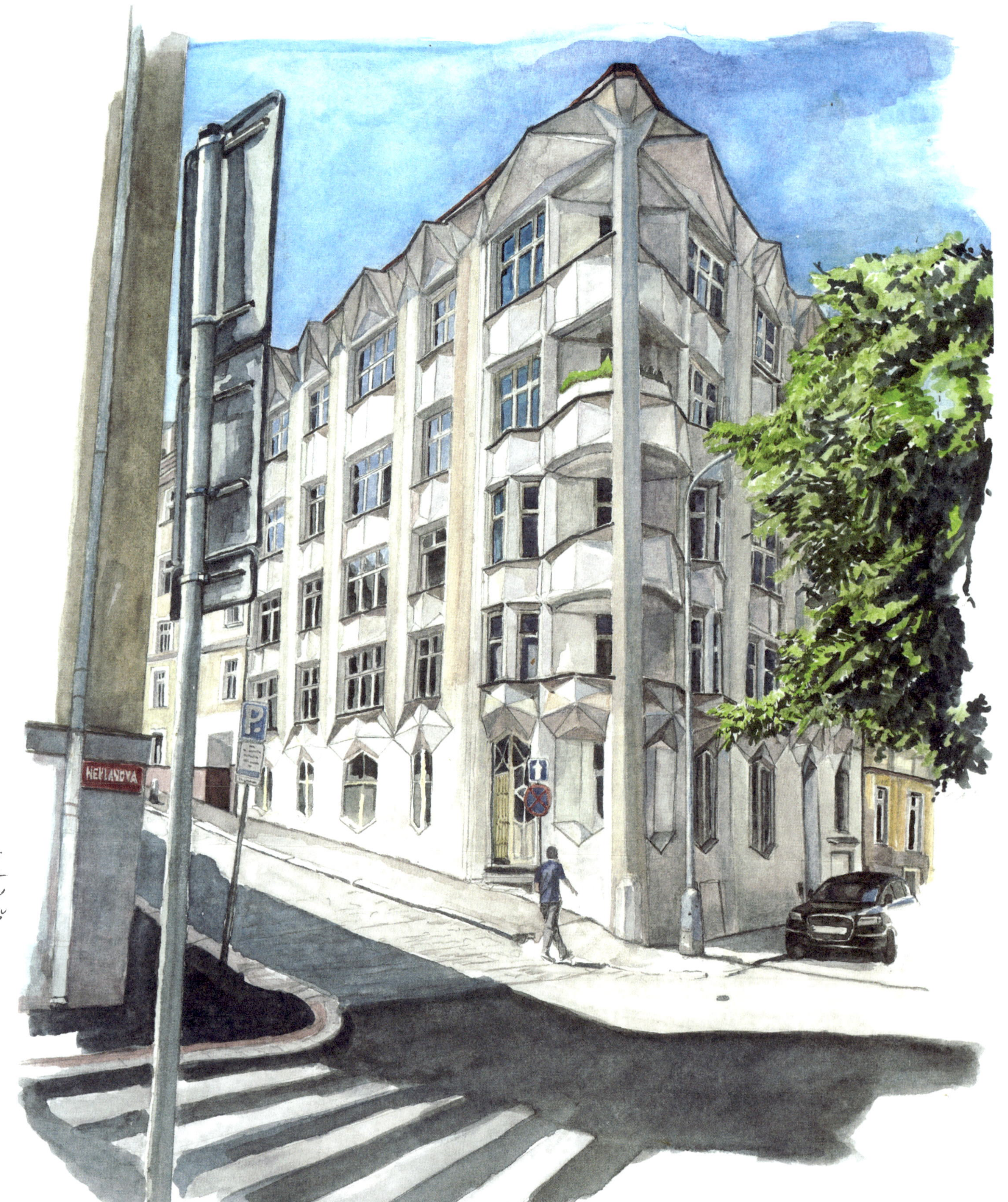

One of the cubist buildings designed by the architect Josef Chochol, a student of Otto Wagner, on Neklanově Street in Vyšehrad.

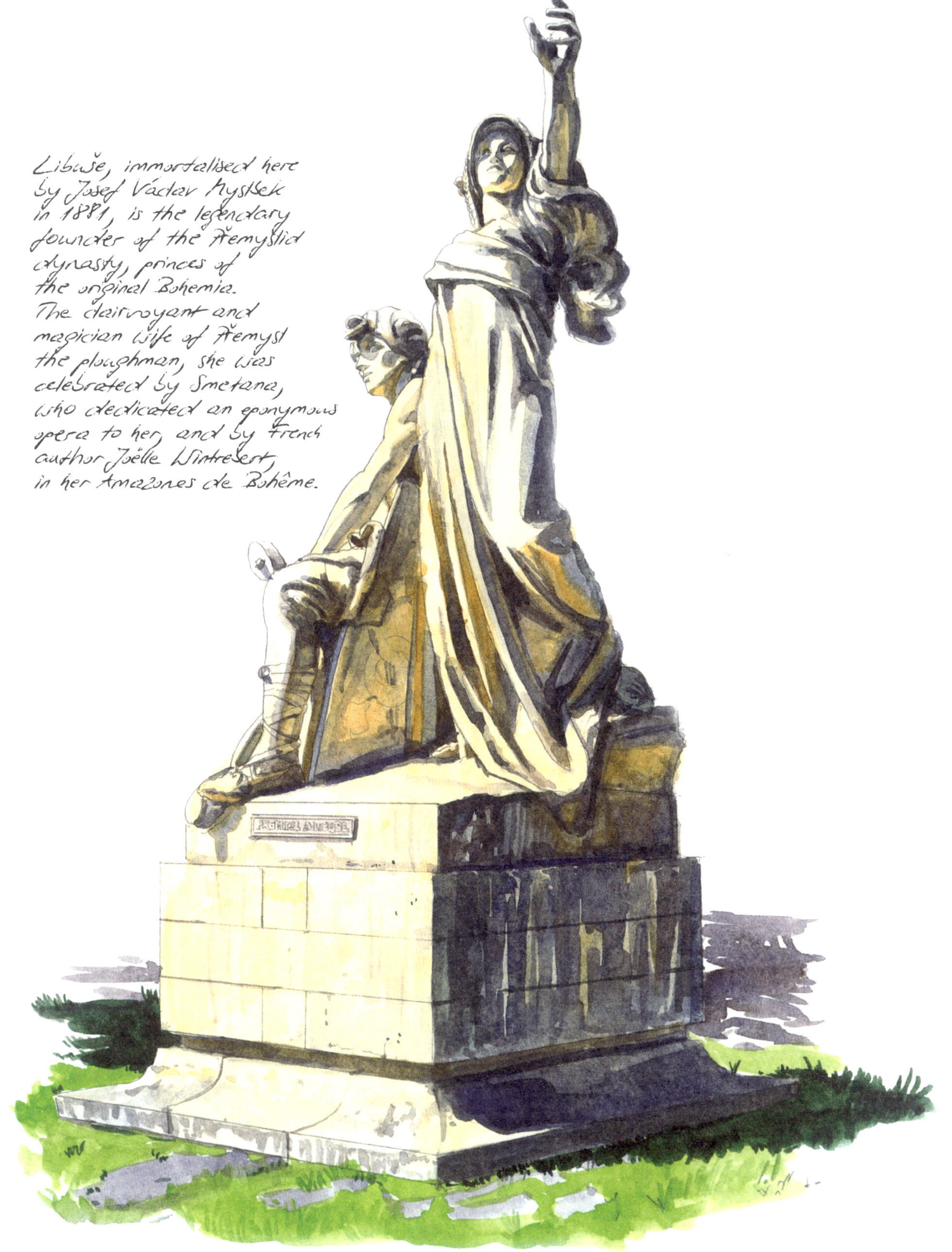

Libuše, immortalised here
by Josef Václav Myslbek
in 1881, is the legendary
founder of the Přemyslid
dynasty, princes of
the original Bohemia.
The clairvoyant and
magician wife of Přemysl
the ploughman, she was
celebrated by Smetana,
who dedicated an eponymous
opera to her, and by French
author Joëlle Wintrebert,
in her Amazones de Bohême.

Malá Strana

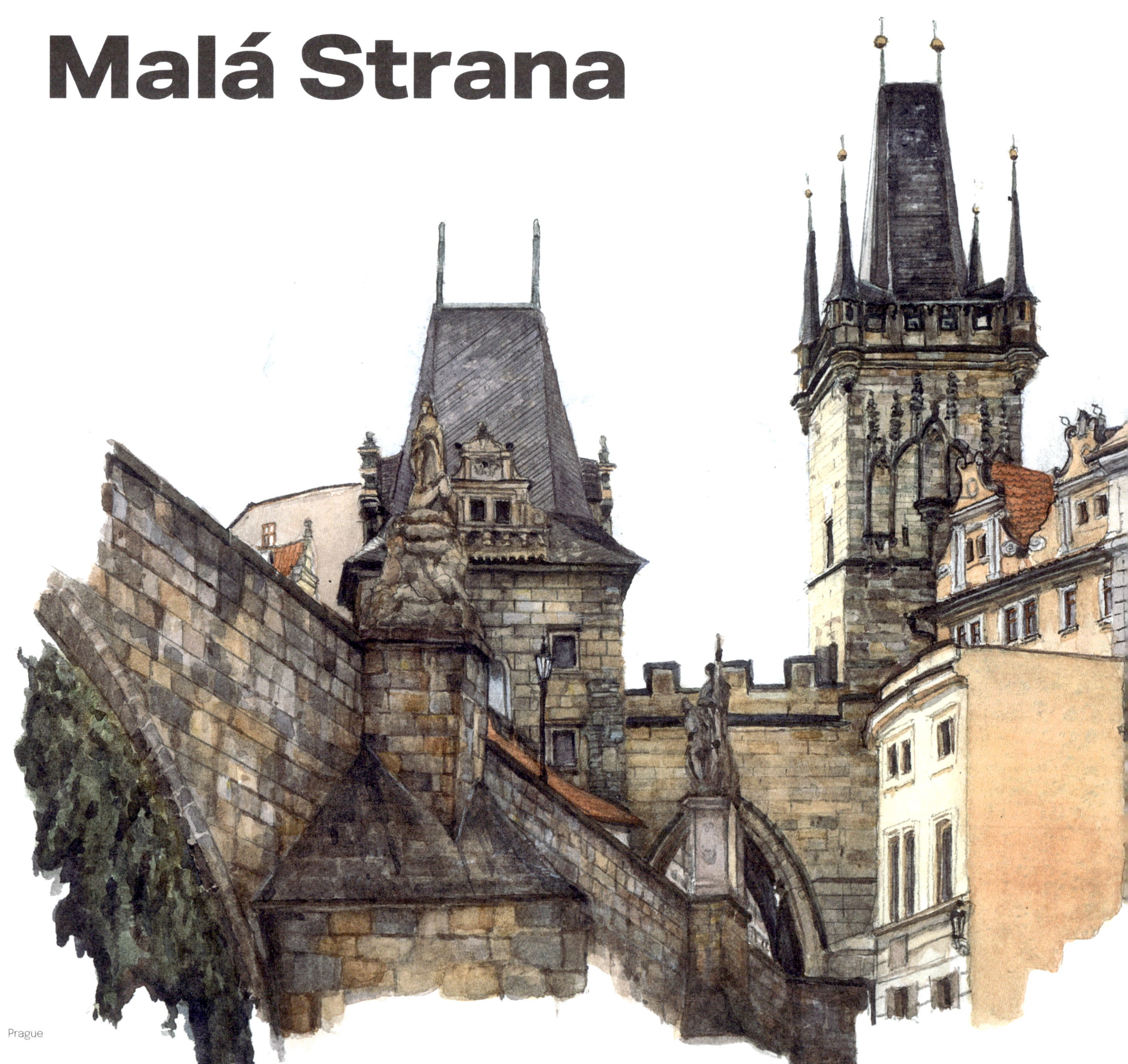

Charles Bridge (Karlův most),
links the Old Town and the
'Lesser Town', Malá Strana.
In 1342, it replaced Judith
Bridge, which had been destroyed
by frost. From 1683, it was
decorated with almost thirty
statues by the greatest Baroque
and Rococo sculptors of the
period, including Matthias Braun.

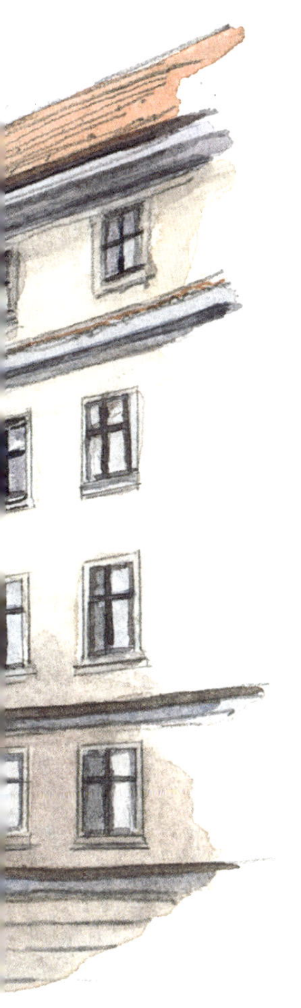

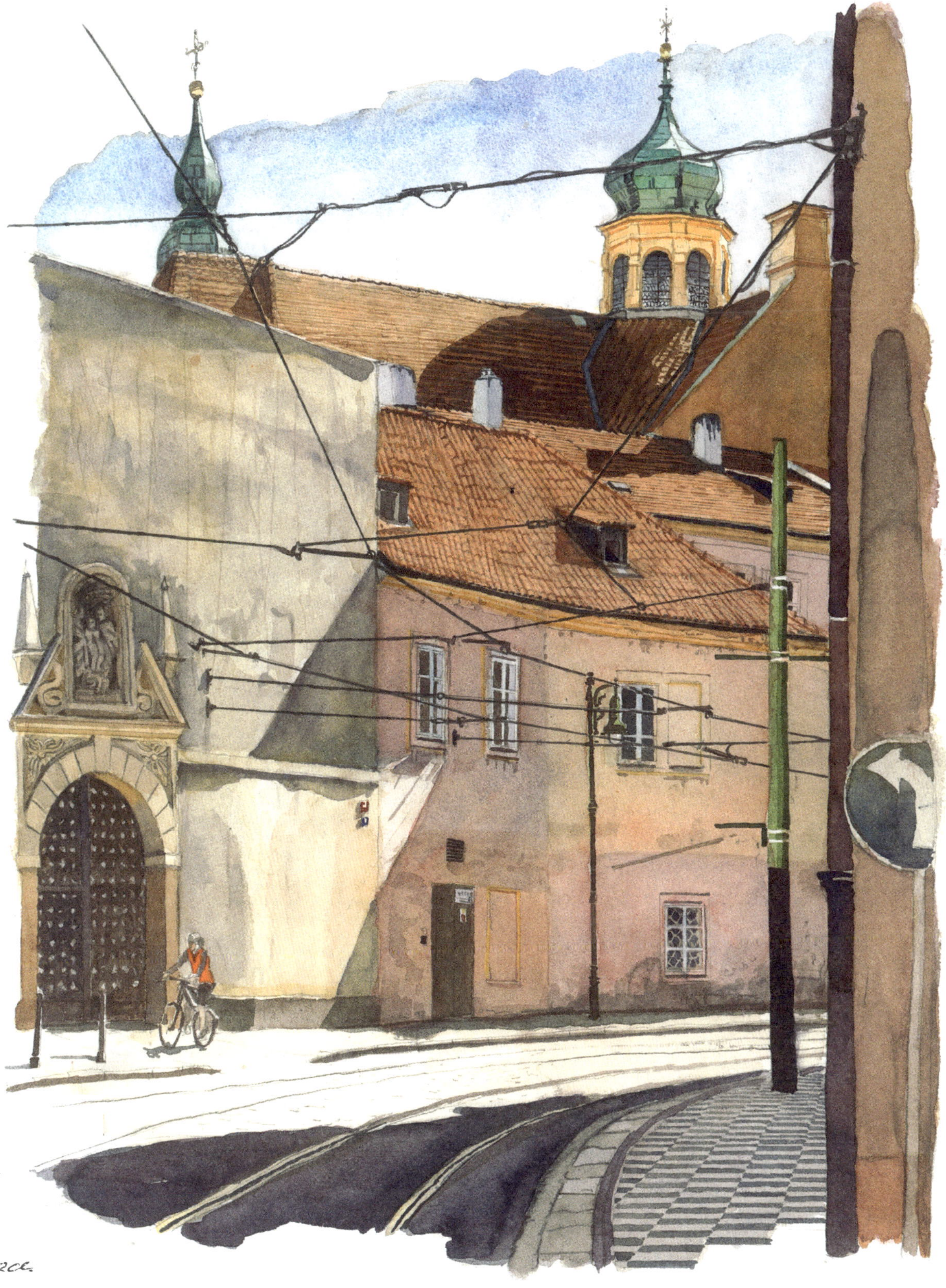

The tramway
track on Letenská
Street, between
the Vojan gardens
and Wallenstein Palace.

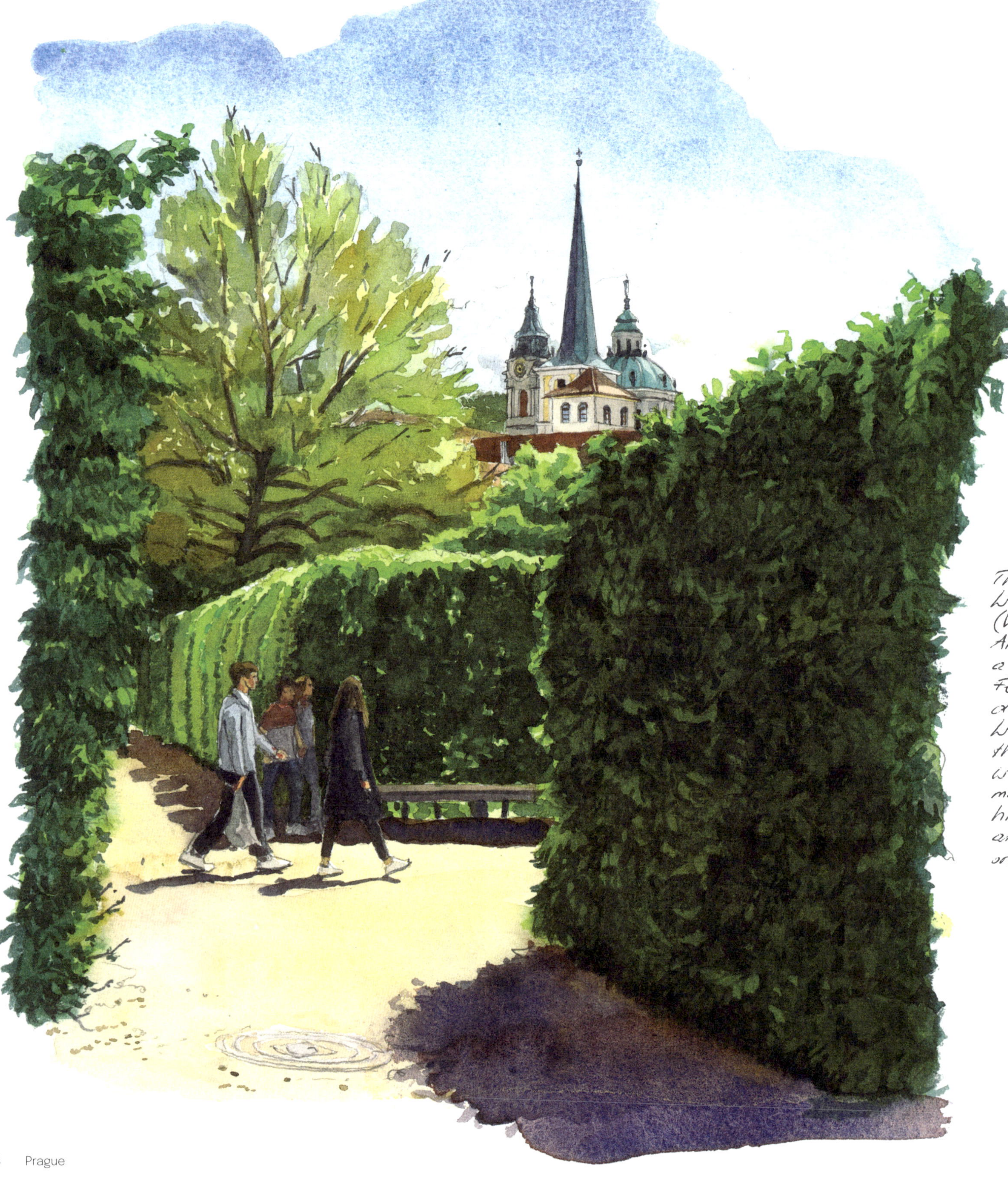

The gardens at Wallenstein Palace (Valdštejnský palác). Albrecht von Wallenstein, a general in Emperor Ferdinand's armies during the Thirty Years' War, was responsible for this splendid structure, where he celebrated many victories before his fall into disgrace and assassination by order of his employer.

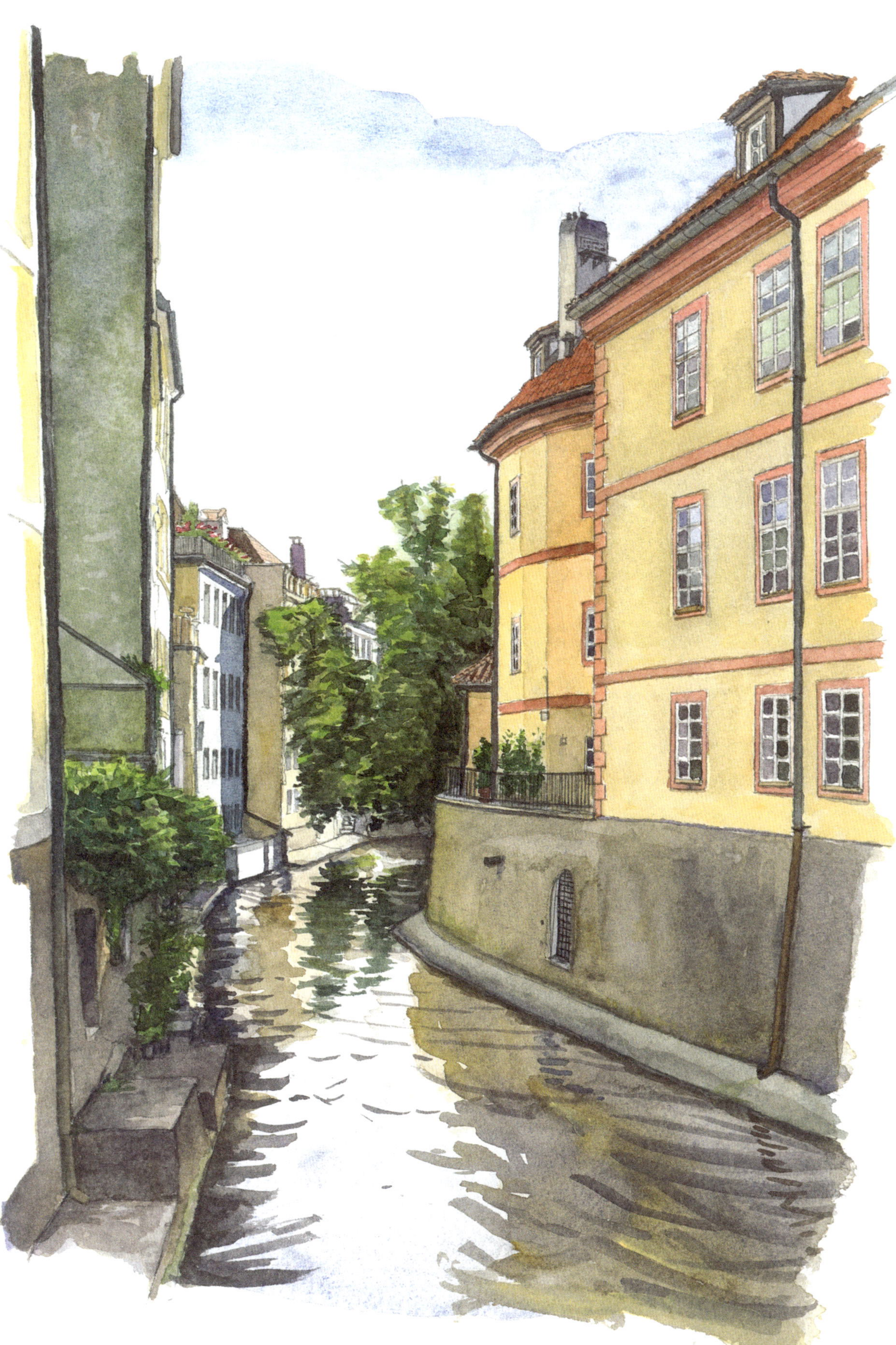

Čertovka ("devil's tongue")
Canal. Together with
the Vltava, it surrounds
Prague's "little Venice",
Kampa Island (Na
Kampě). This charming
neighbourhood was
ravaged by the devastating
floods of August 2002.

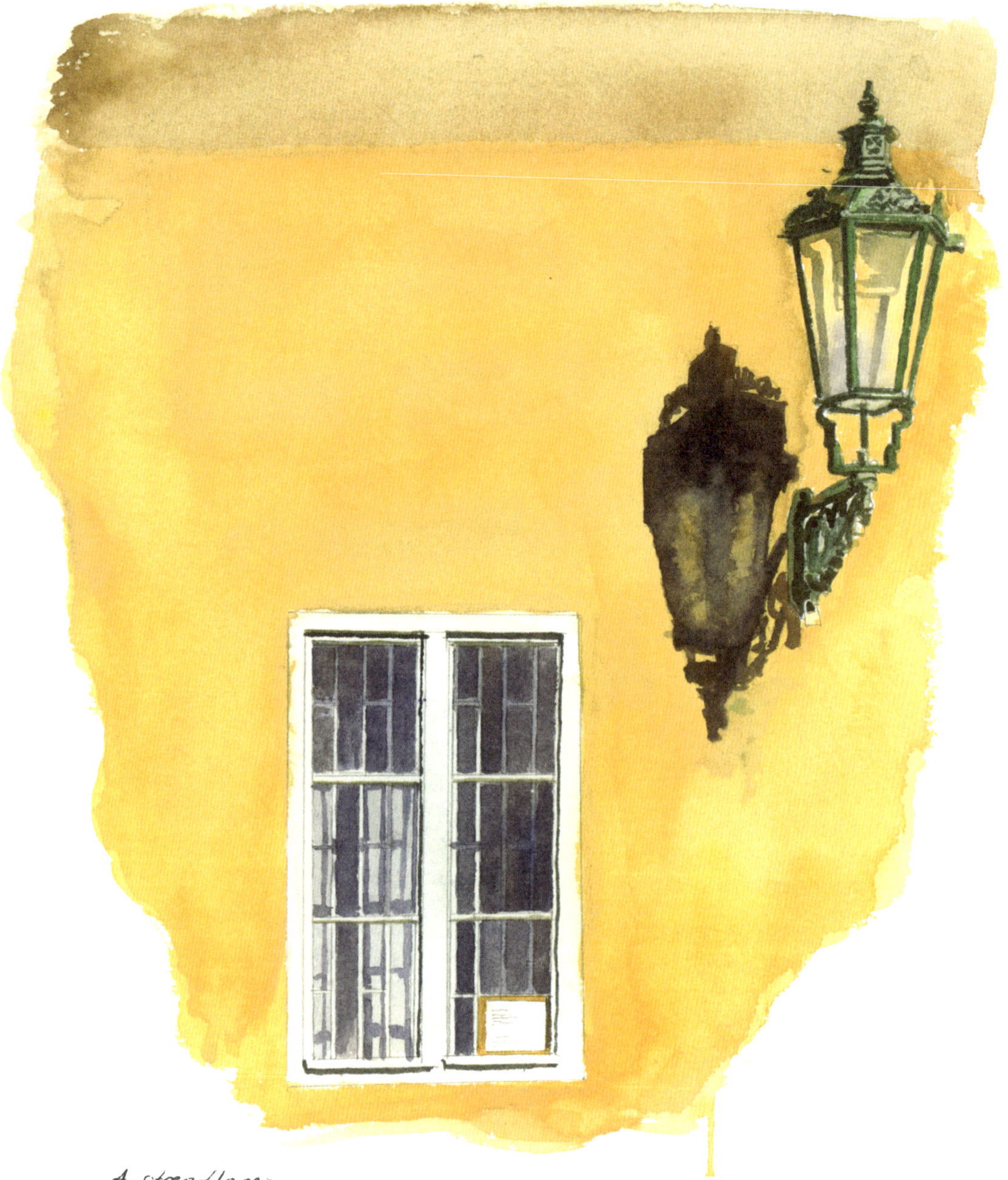

A streetlamp
in Malá strana. And a fine example
of "Maria Theresa yellow", the
yellow ochre colour typical of many
Baroque and Classical buildings from
Central Europe to Northern Italy.

In the streets of Kampa,
graffiti dedicated to Václav
Havel (1936–2011), playwright,
poet, resistance fighter, rock
fan and politician, a pivotal
figure in Czechoslovakia's
return to democracy.

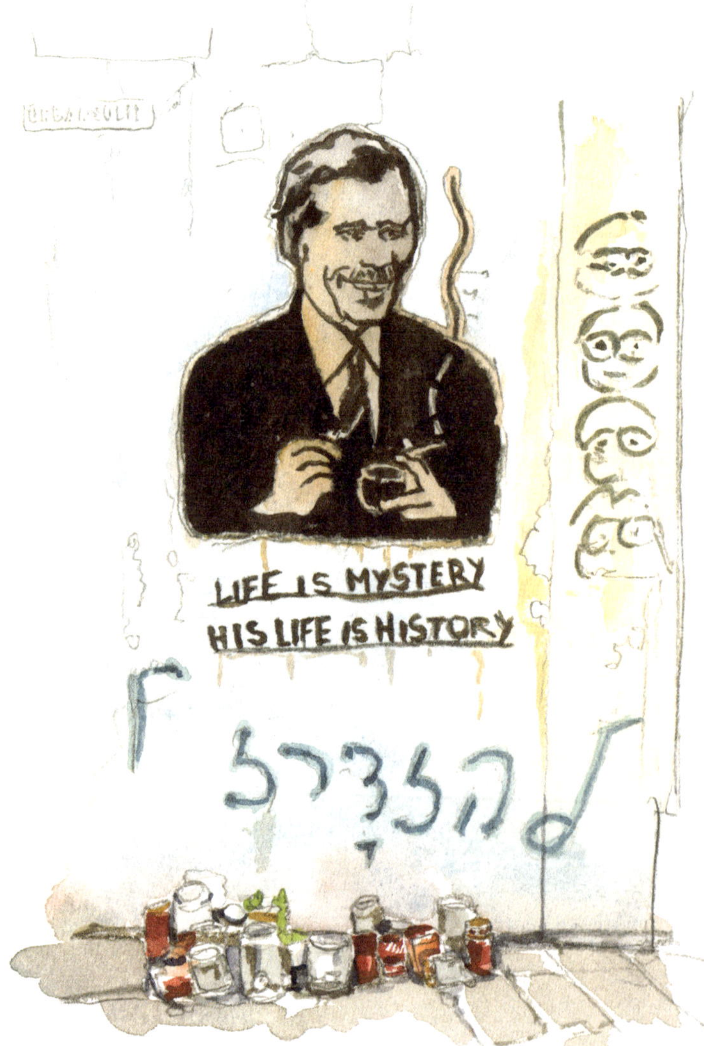

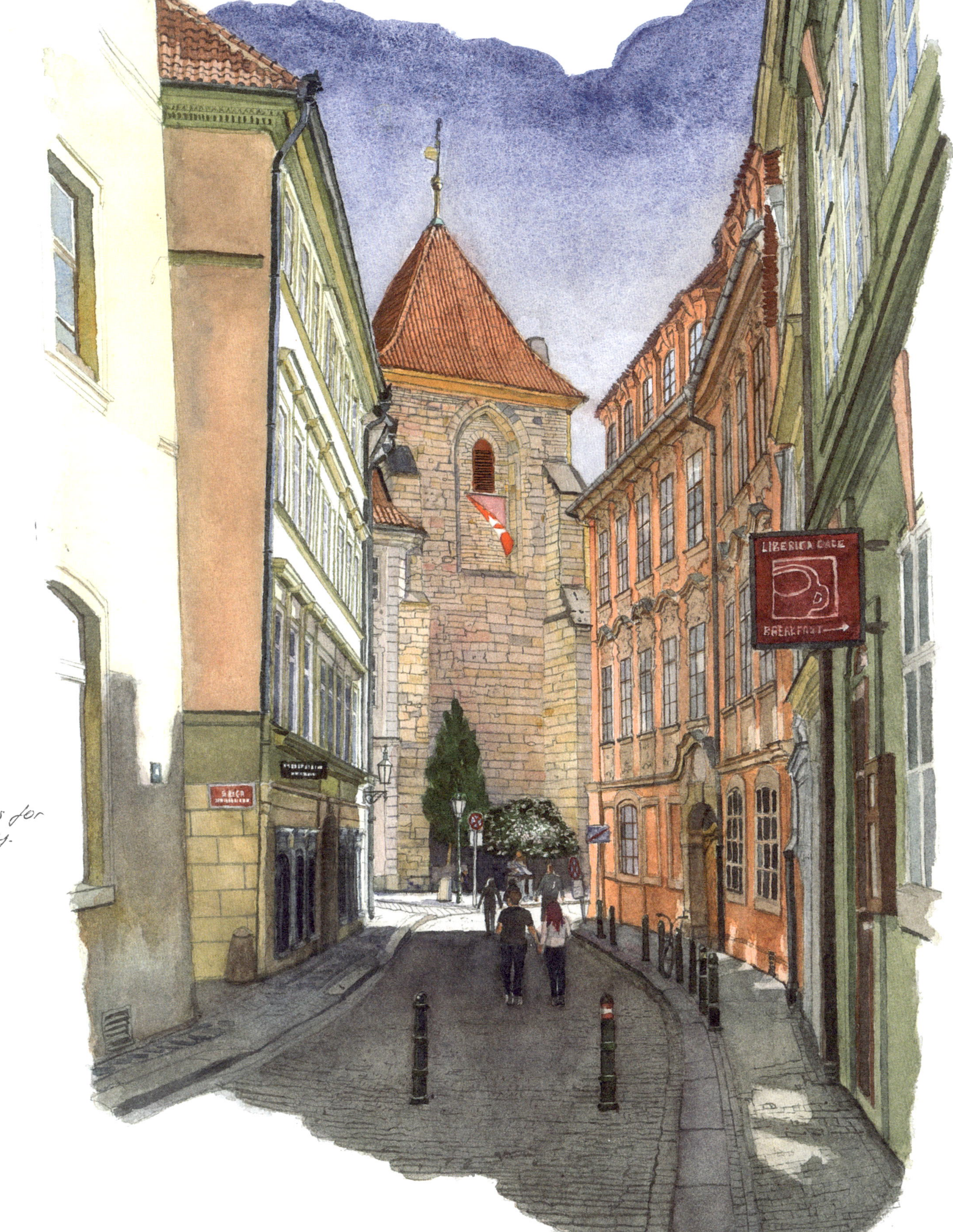

Lázeňská Street.
Beethoven lived here for a few months in 1796 and composed a number of pieces for mandolin for Countess Clary.

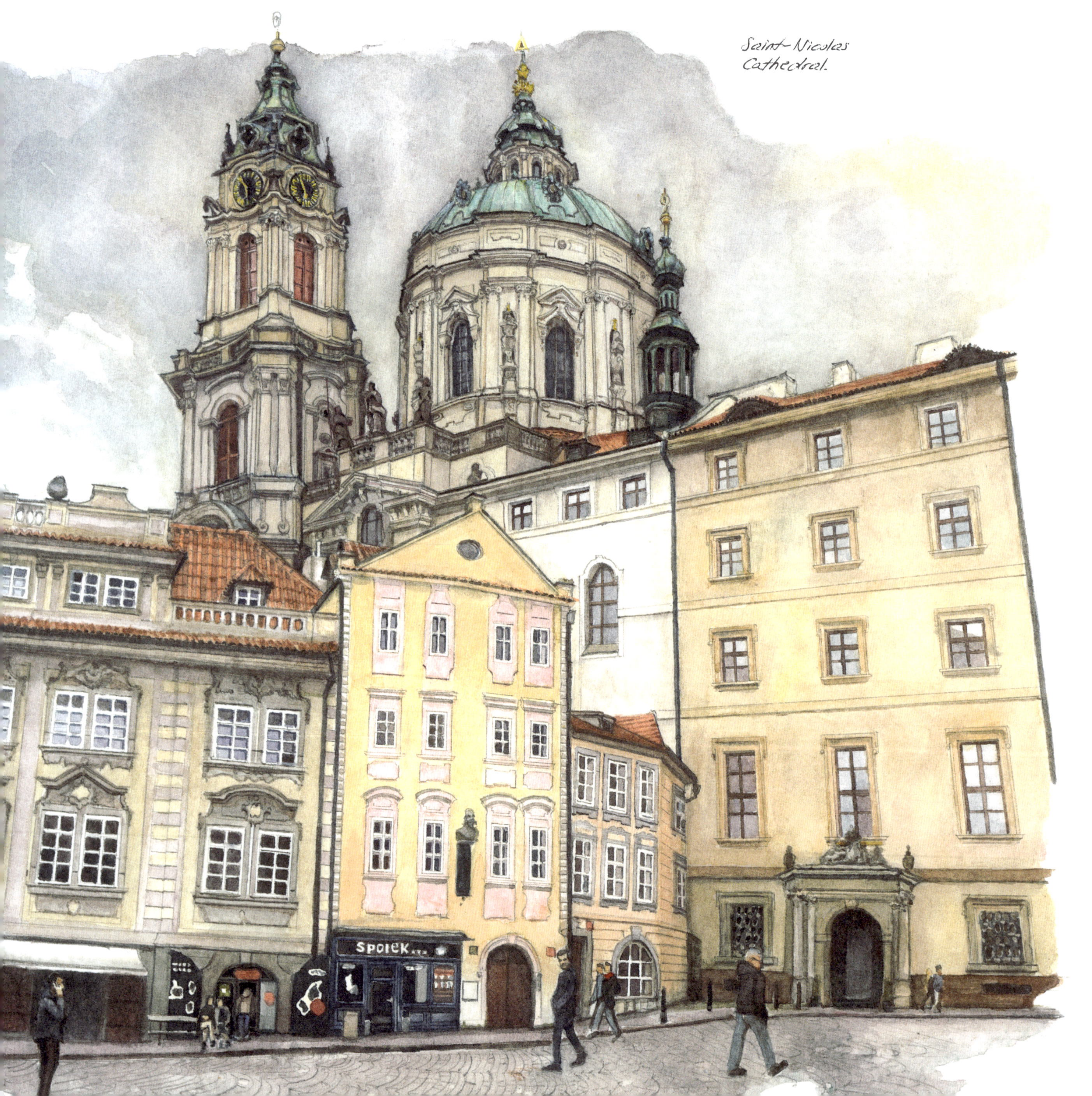
Saint-Nicolas
Cathedral.
Spolek

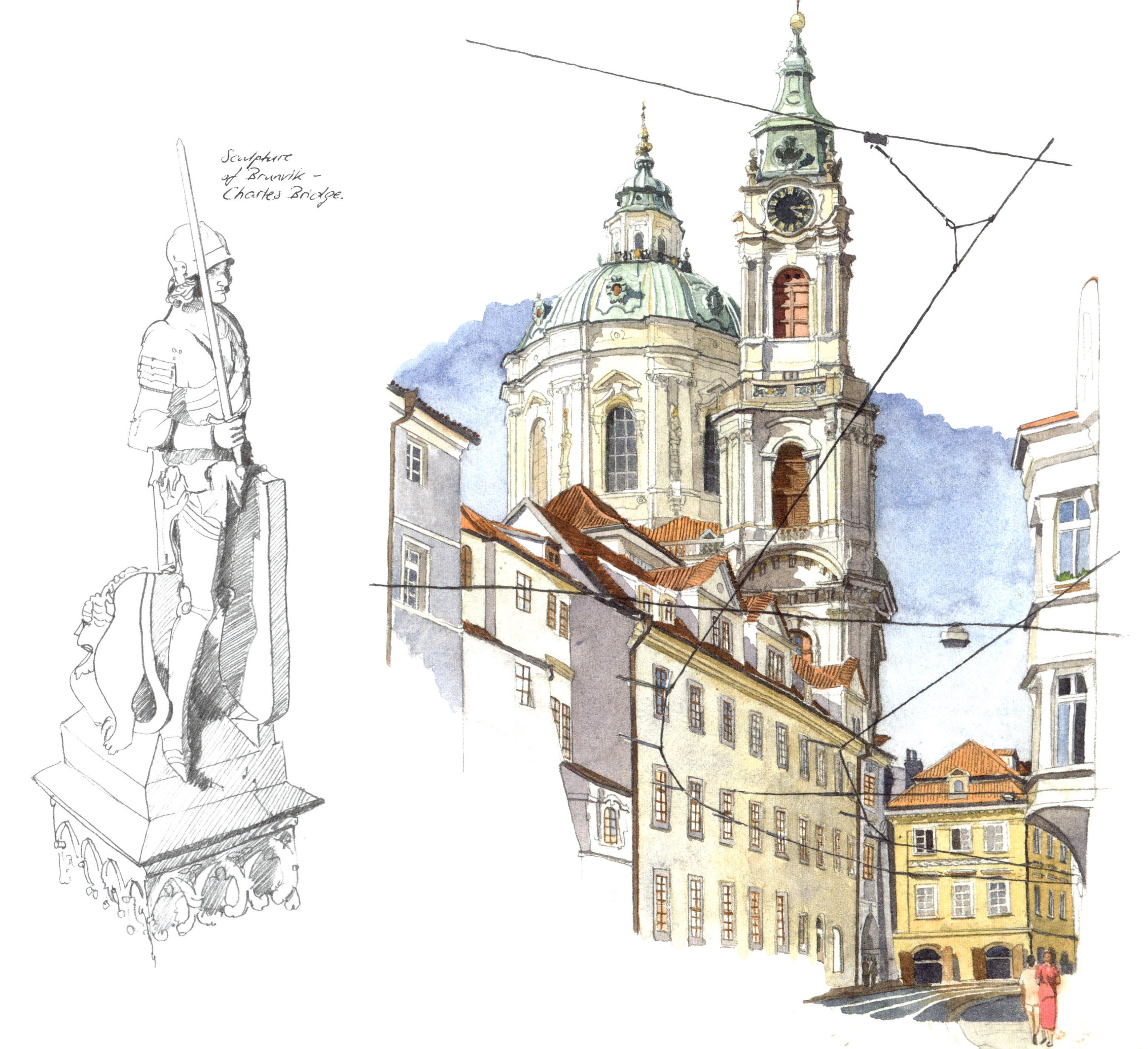

Sculpture
of Brunvik -
Charles Bridge.

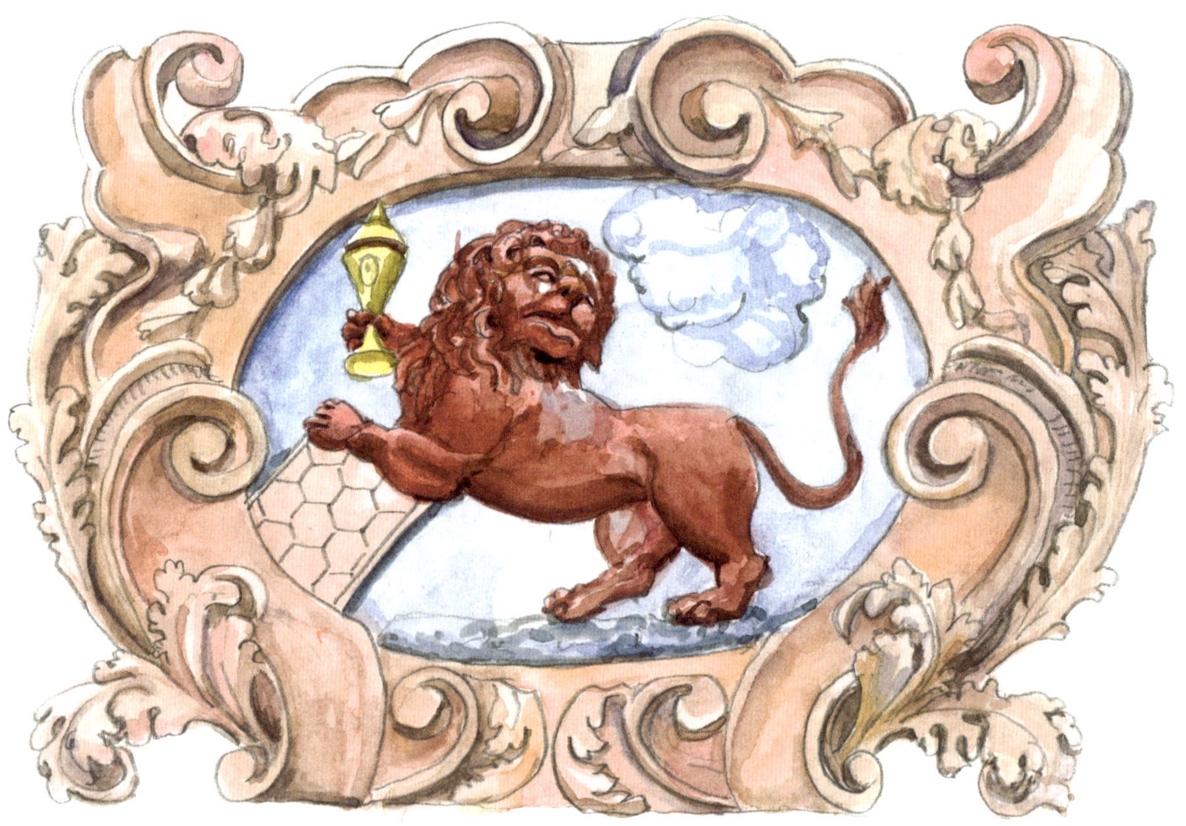

The House
of the Red Lion
on Neruda Street
is now a hotel.

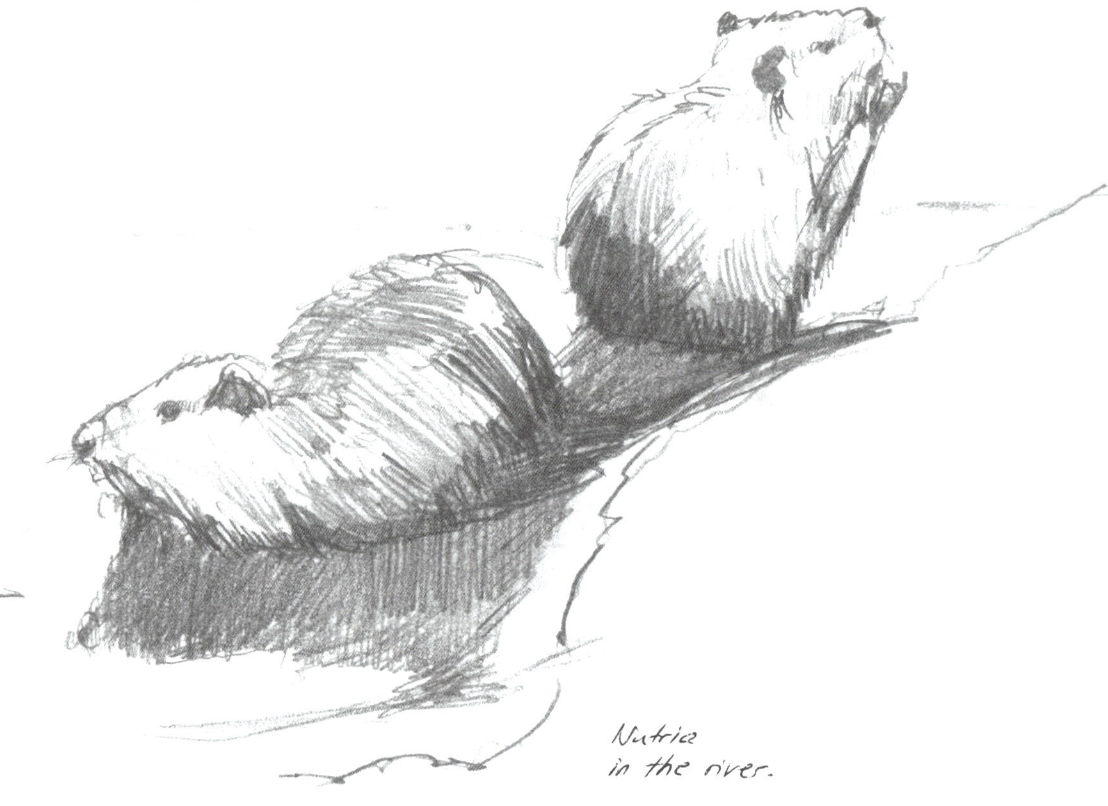

Nutria
in the river.

Nový Svet
(New World).
To the north
of Prague Castle, this
once-poor district, which
was joined to Prague
in the 14th century,
is now a quiet village
within the city, and
popular with artists.

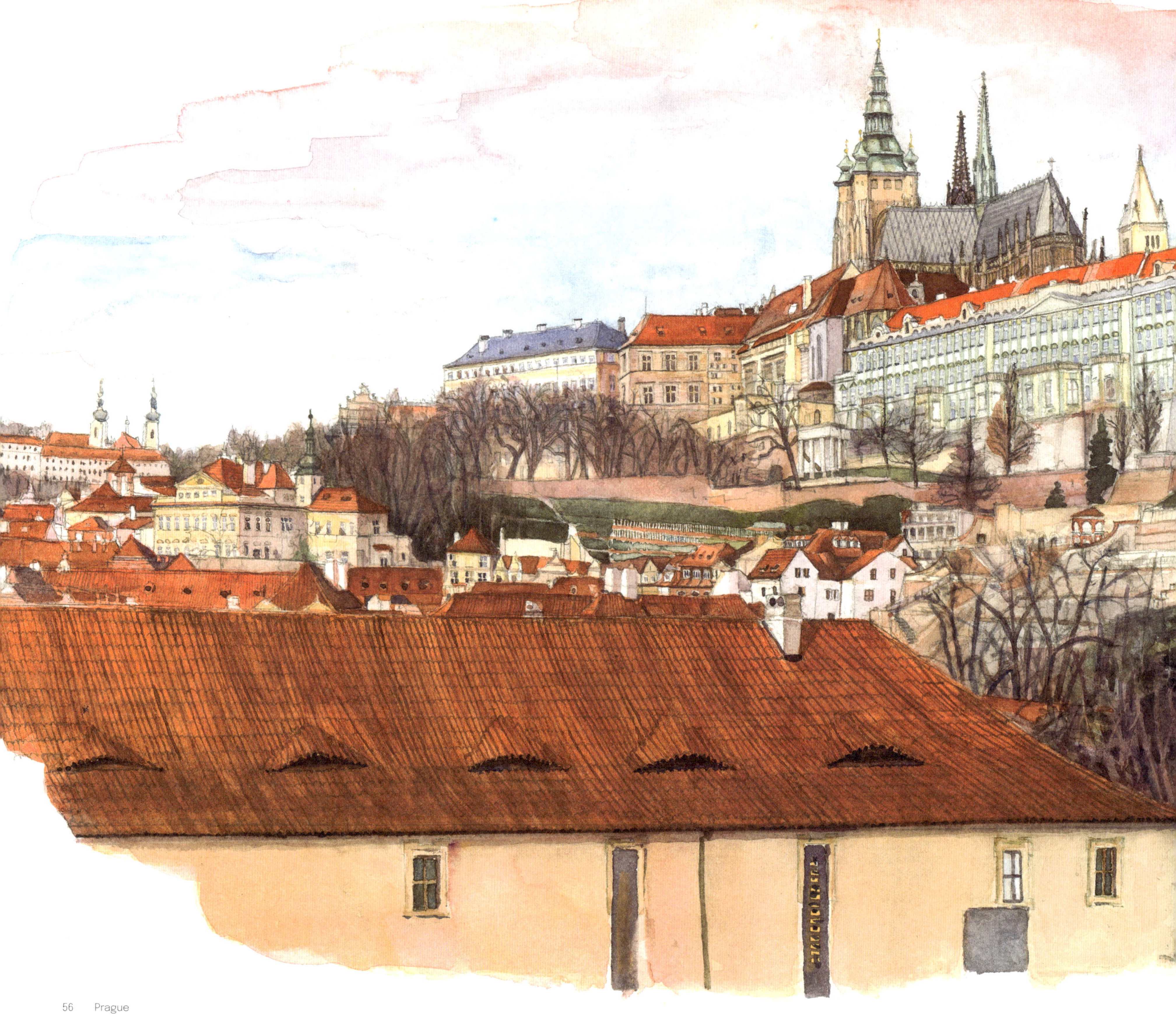

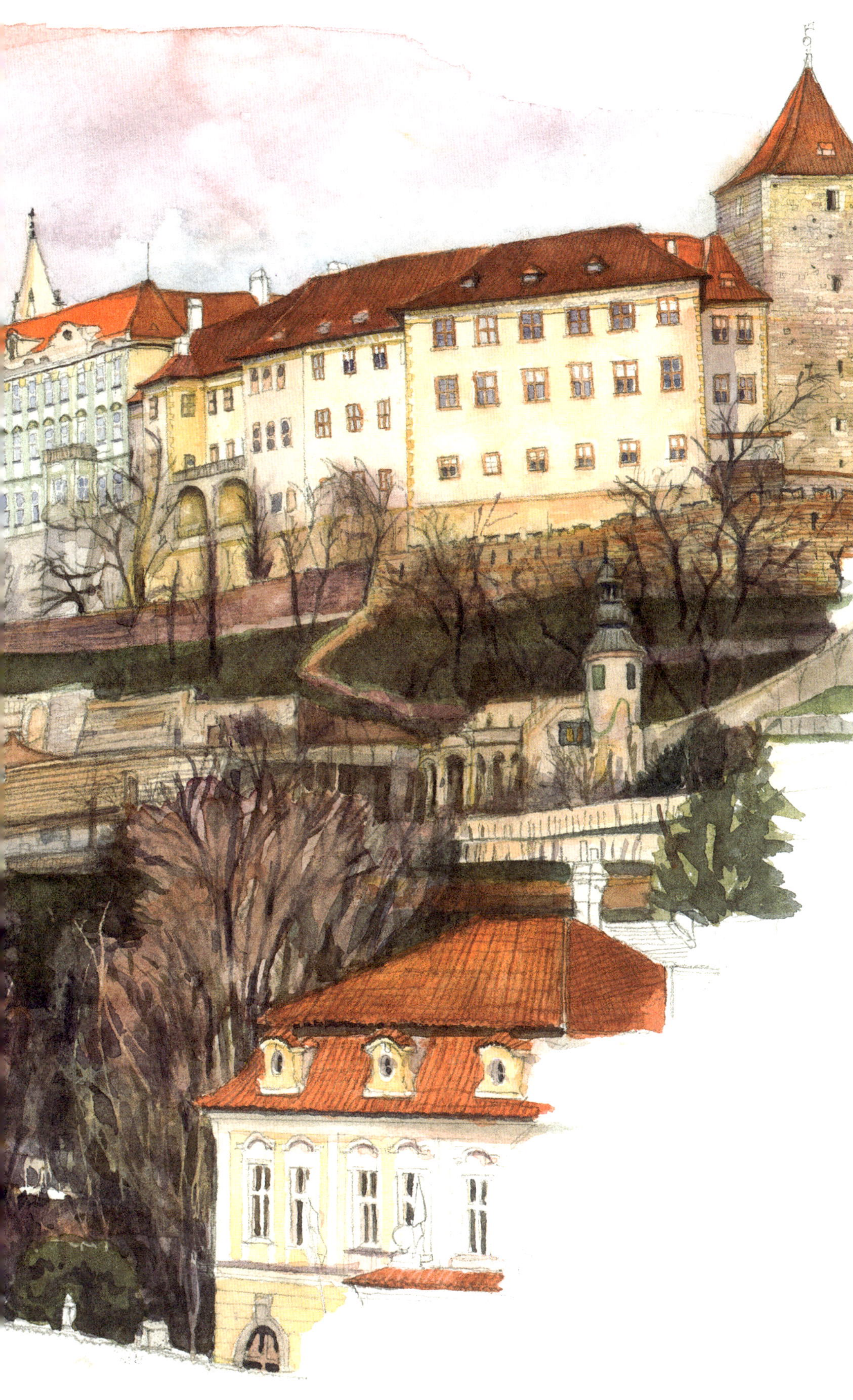

Prague Castle (Pražský hrad).
Massive and majestic, it has looked
out over the city for nearly a thousand years;
its walls, spires and changes reflect the country's
turbulent history. The young Czechoslovakia of
1918 reclaimed it, the Communists were wary
of it and Václav Havel had it restored.

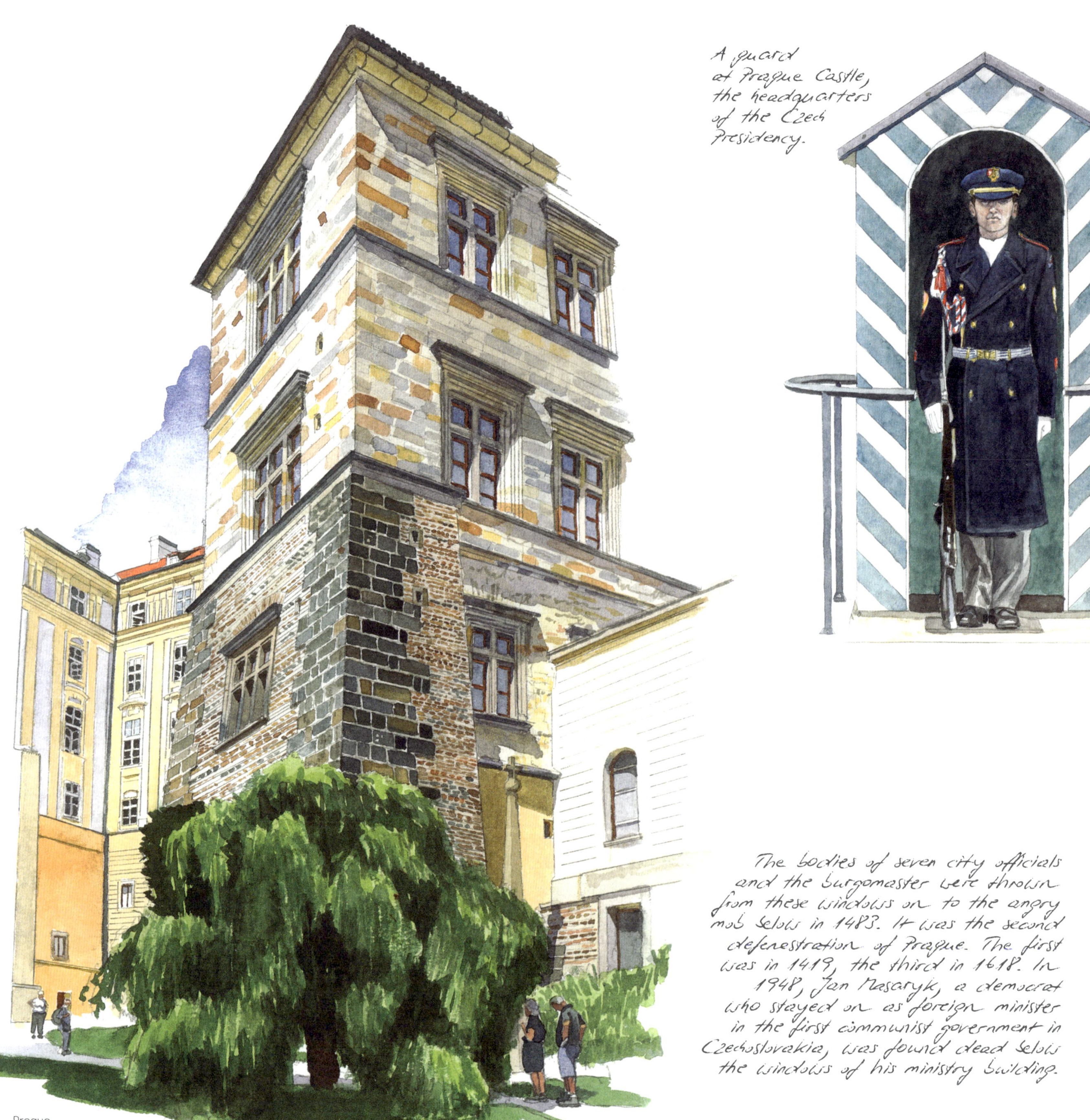

A guard at Prague Castle, the headquarters of the Czech Presidency.

The bodies of seven city officials and the burgomaster were thrown from these windows on to the angry mob below in 1483. It was the second defenestration of Prague. The first was in 1419, the third in 1618. In 1948, Jan Masaryk, a democrat who stayed on as foreign minister in the first communist government in Czechoslovakia, was found dead below the windows of his ministry building.

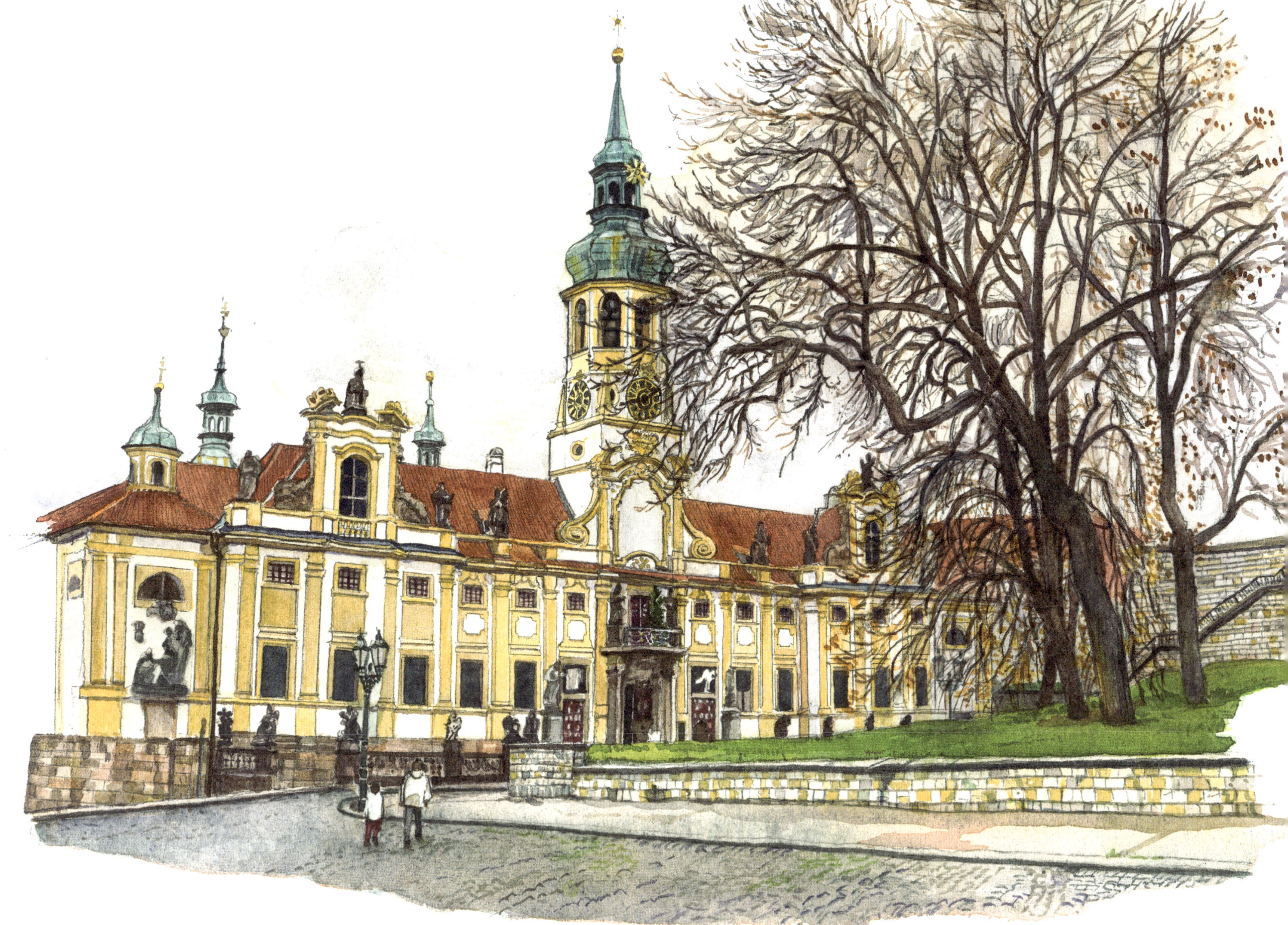

Our Lady of Loreto, a copy of
the Loreto church by the Italian architect
Orsi, is famous for its carillon. It is one of
the many chapels dedicated to Marian worship
in Europe, which was particularly prevalent
from the Renaissance to the Classical Age.

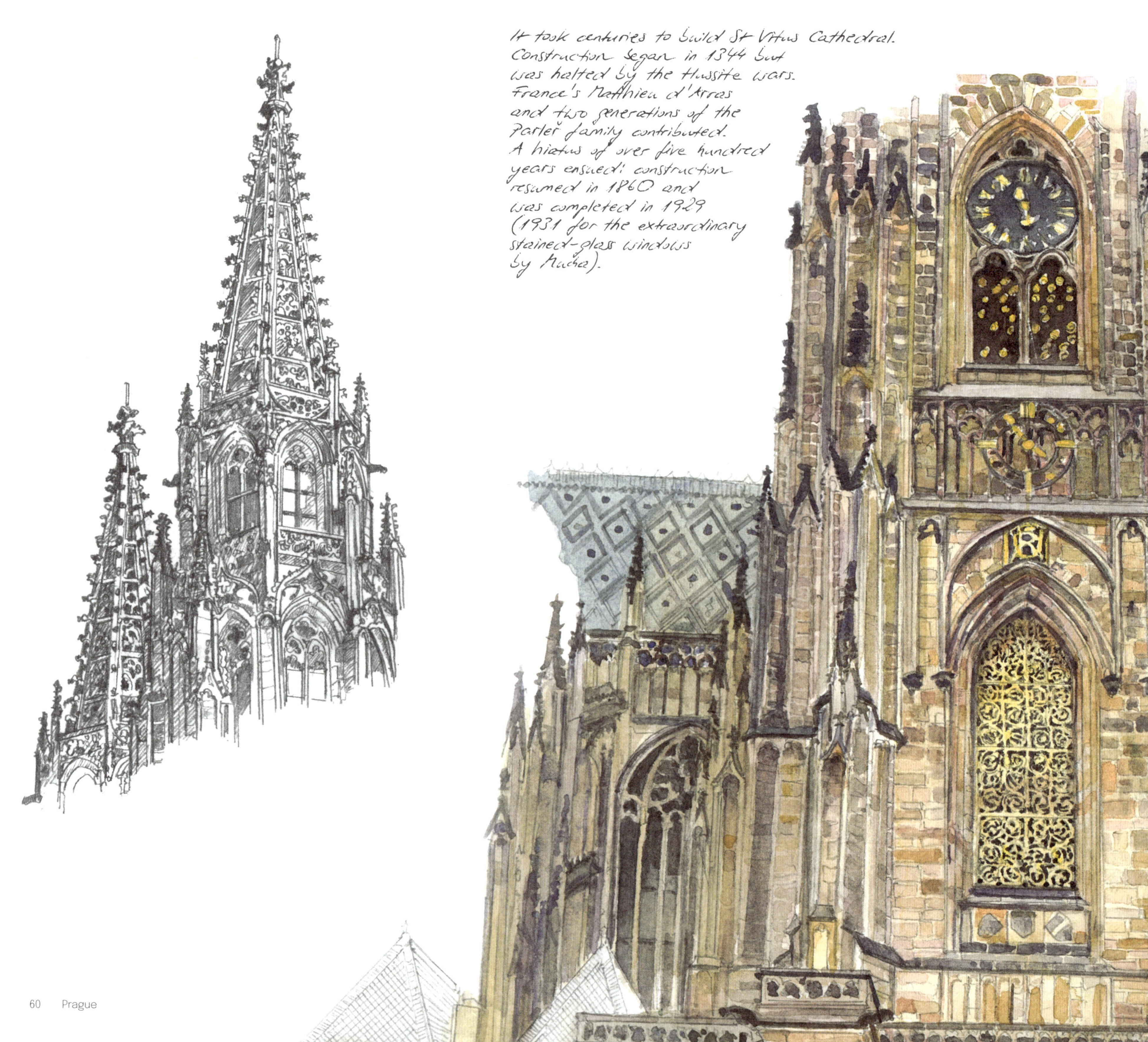

It took centuries to build St Vitus Cathedral.
Construction began in 1344 but
was halted by the Hussite wars.
France's Matthieu d'Arras
and two generations of the
Parléř family contributed.
A hiatus of over five hundred
years ensued: construction
resumed in 1860 and
was completed in 1929
(1931 for the extraordinary
stained-glass windows
by Mucha).

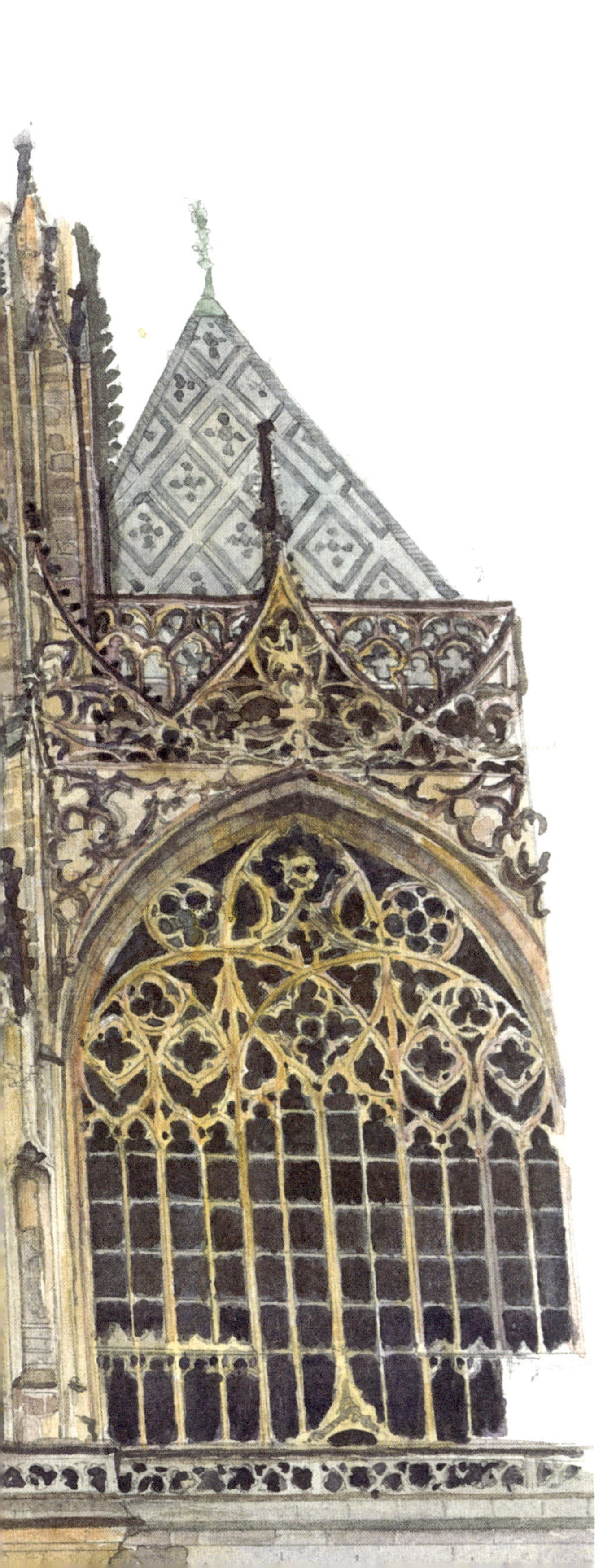

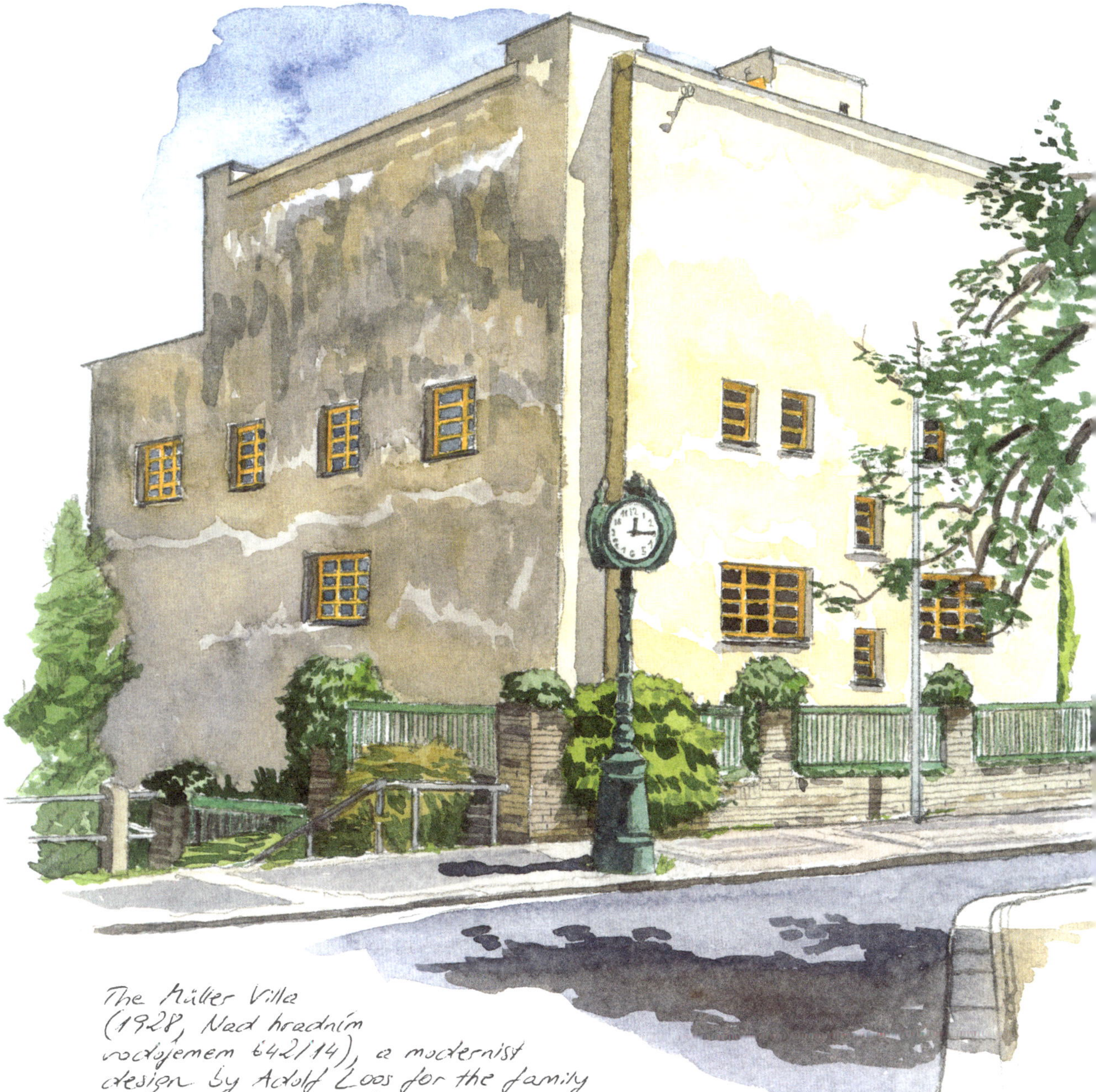

The Müller Villa
(1928, Nad hradním
vodojemem 642/14), a modernist
design by Adolf Loos for the family
of engineer František Müller. Returned
to the descendants of its owners in
1989 after the fall of communism,
the residence with its simple, pure lines
now belongs to the city of Prague.

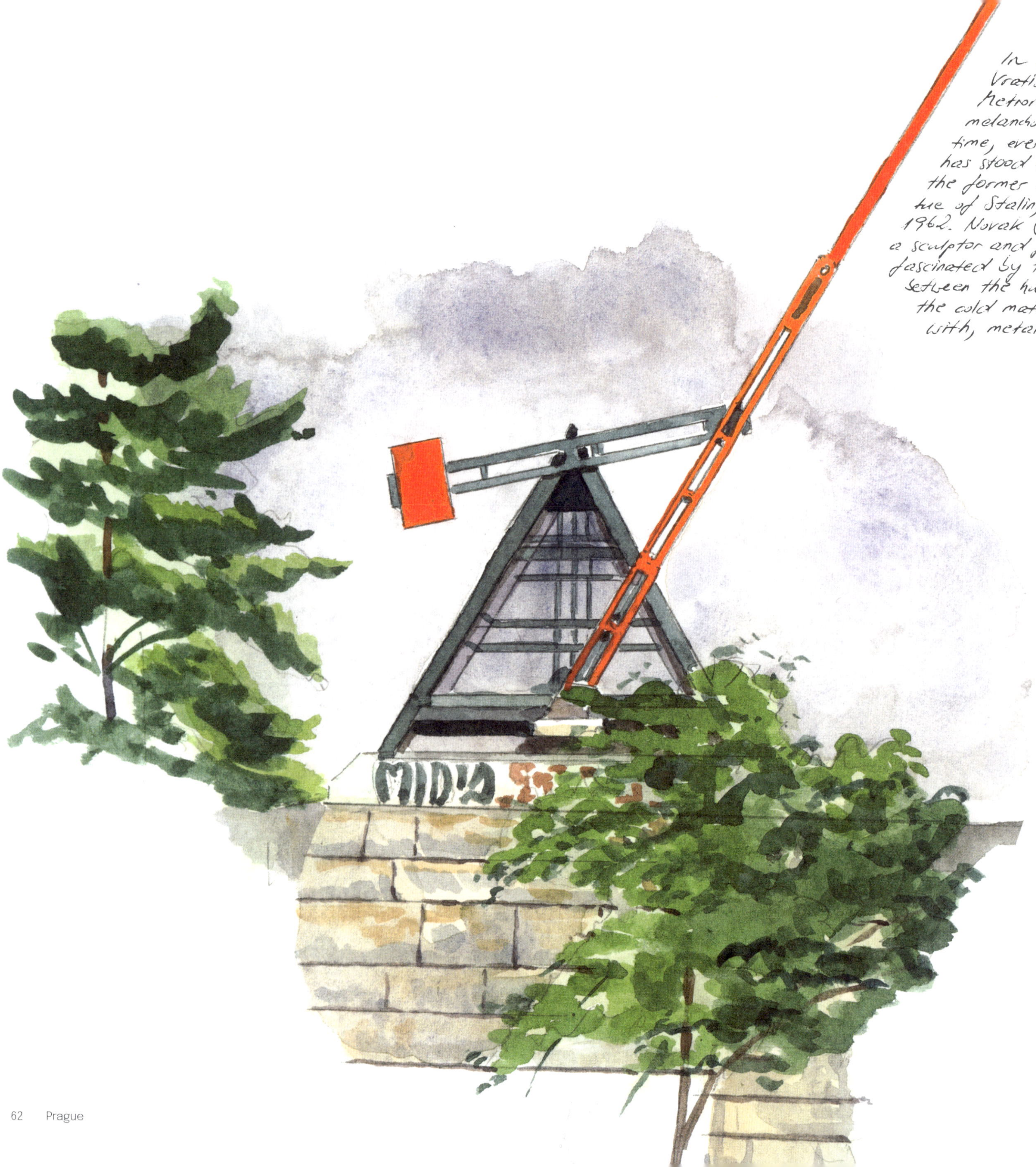

In Letna Park,
Vratislav Novak's
Metronome (with its
melancholy warning: "With
time, everything passes")
has stood since 1991 on
the former site of a sta-
tue of Stalin, destroyed in
1962. Novak (1942-2014),
a sculptor and jeweller, was
fascinated by the contrasts
between the human body and
the cold materials he worked
with, metal and glass.

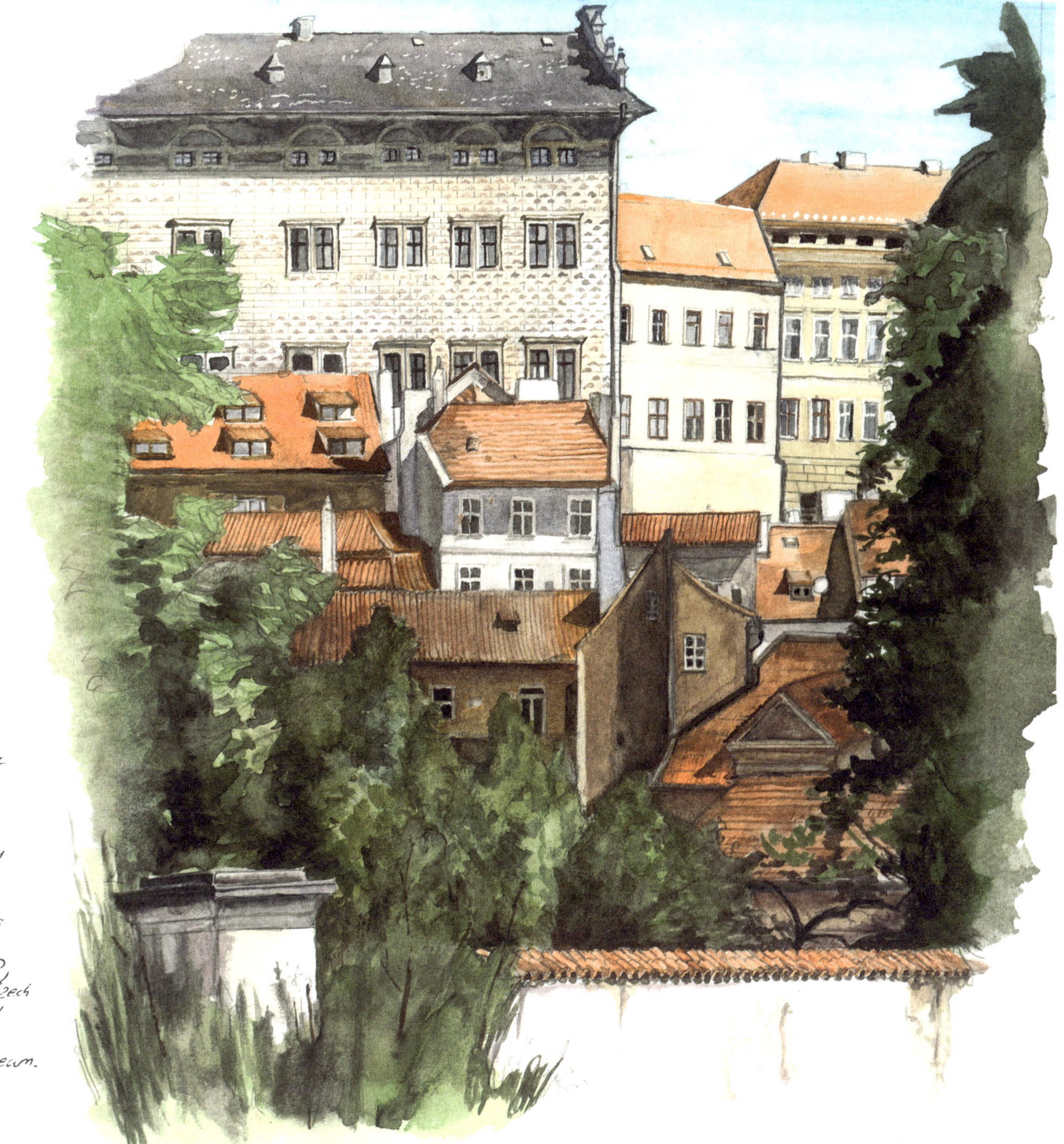

The Schwarzenberg Palace (Schwarzenberský palác), with its distinctive geometric sgraffiti, was built in the 16th century for the Burgrave of Prague, Jan Lobkovitz. It bears the name of its subsequent owners, the Schwarzenbergs. In 1910, they leased it to the Czech government, who turned it into a technical, then military, then art museum.

Nové Město

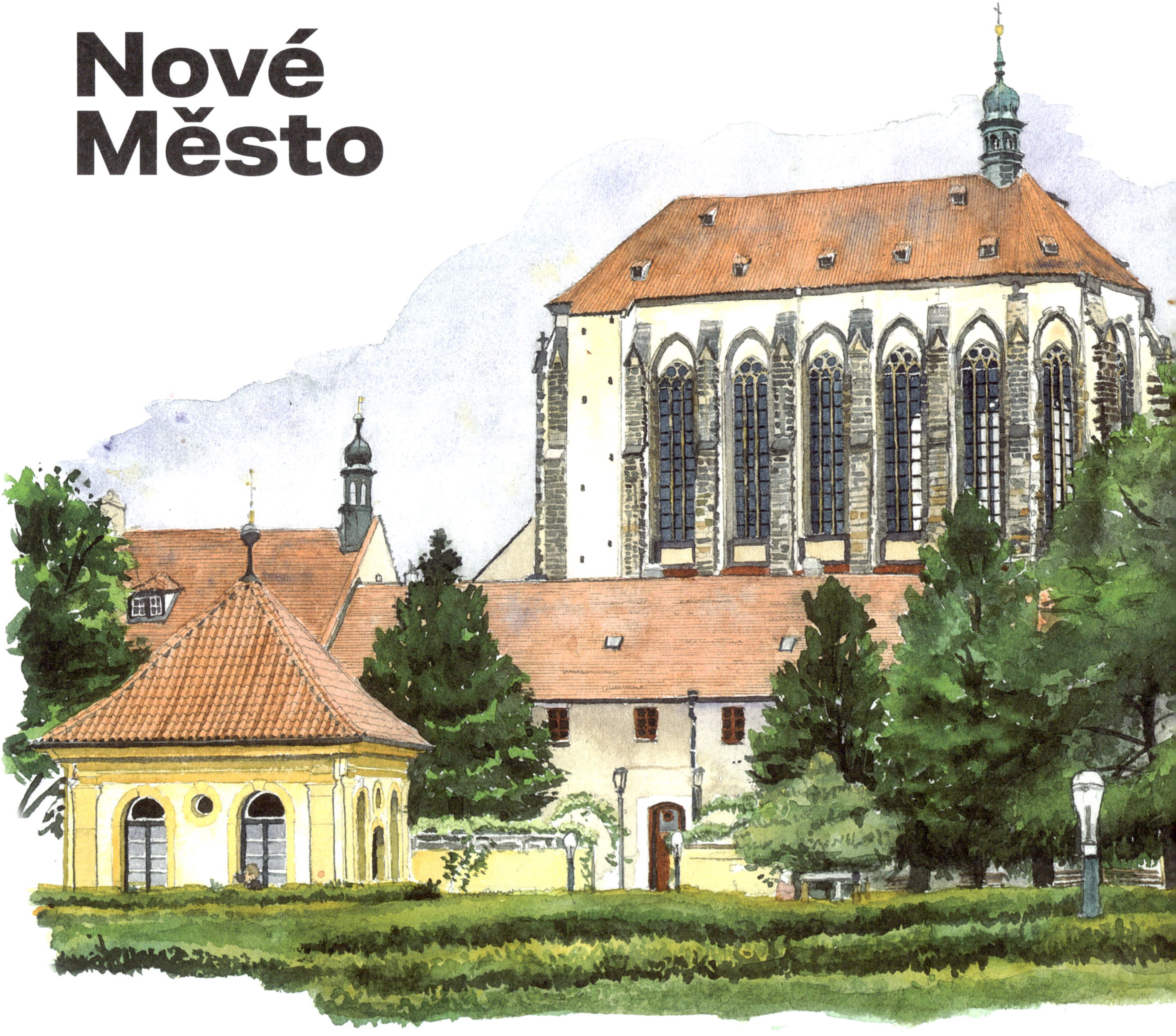

Our Lady of the Snows was the result
of an ambitious project: to build a
huge basilica that would make Prague
the second Rome. As a result of the
Hussite wars, Our Lady of the Snows
was more modest in size. It is, however,
famed for its imposing Baroque altar,
the highest (over thirty metres)
in the entire Holy
Roman Empire.

Four Seasons Market,
22 Vodičkova Street,
in front of the former
girls' high school
(now a primary school).

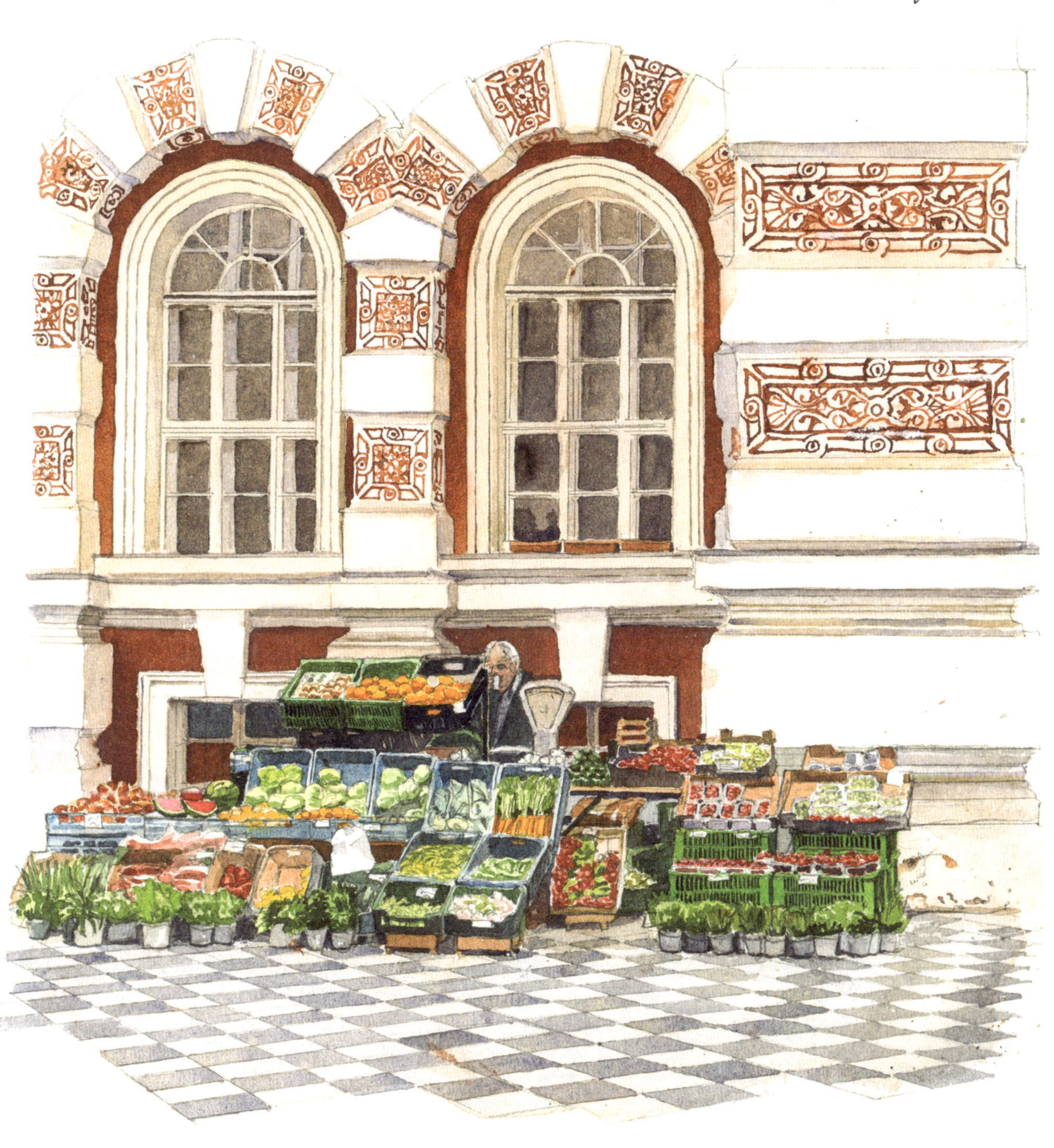

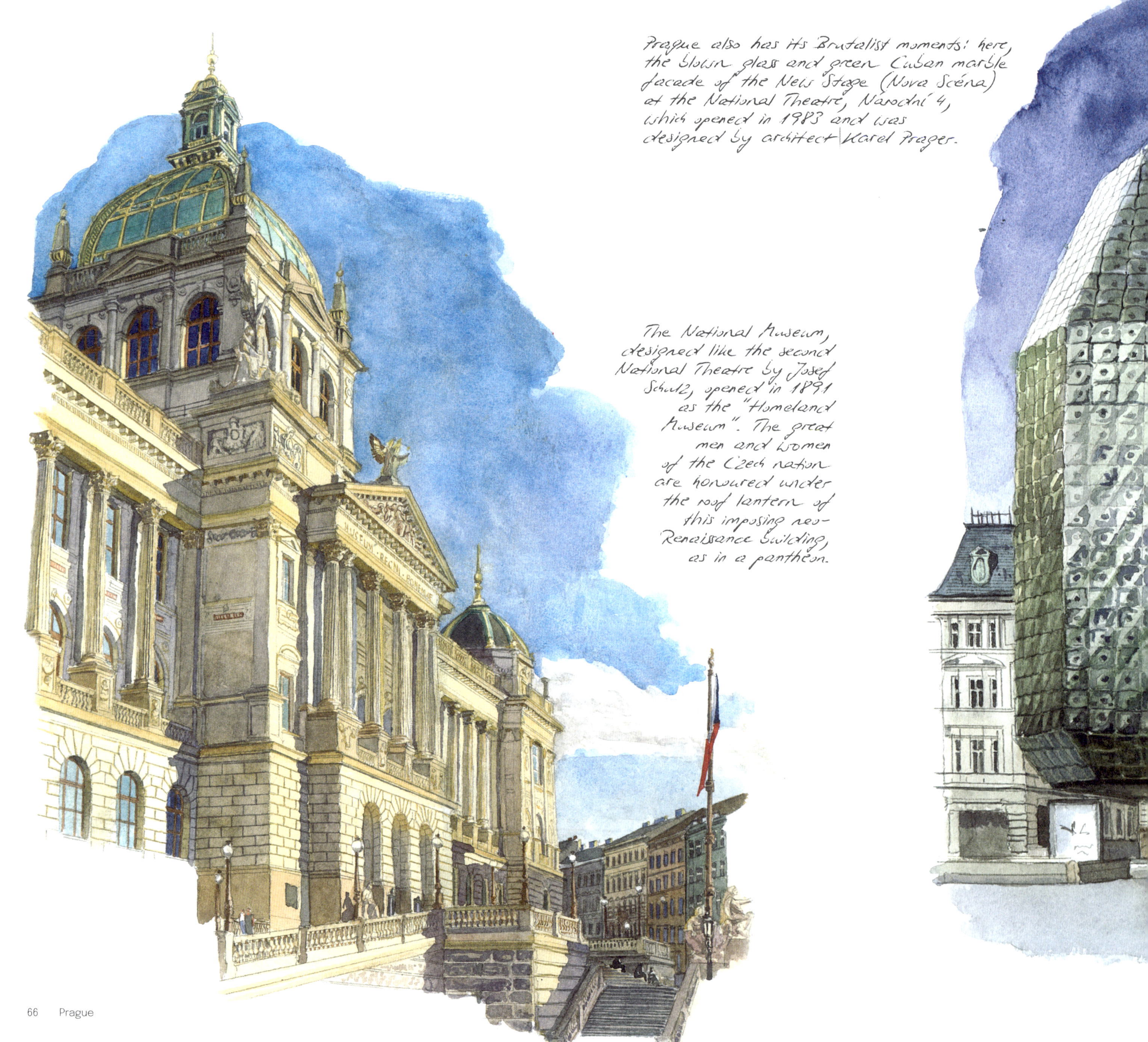

Prague also has its Brutalist moments: here,
the blown glass and green Cuban marble
facade of the New Stage (Nova Scéna)
at the National Theatre, Národní 4,
which opened in 1983 and was
designed by architect Karel Prager.

The National Museum,
designed like the second
National Theatre by Josef
Schulz, opened in 1891
as the "Homeland
Museum". The great
men and women
of the Czech nation
are honoured under
the roof lantern of
this imposing neo-
Renaissance building,
as in a pantheon.

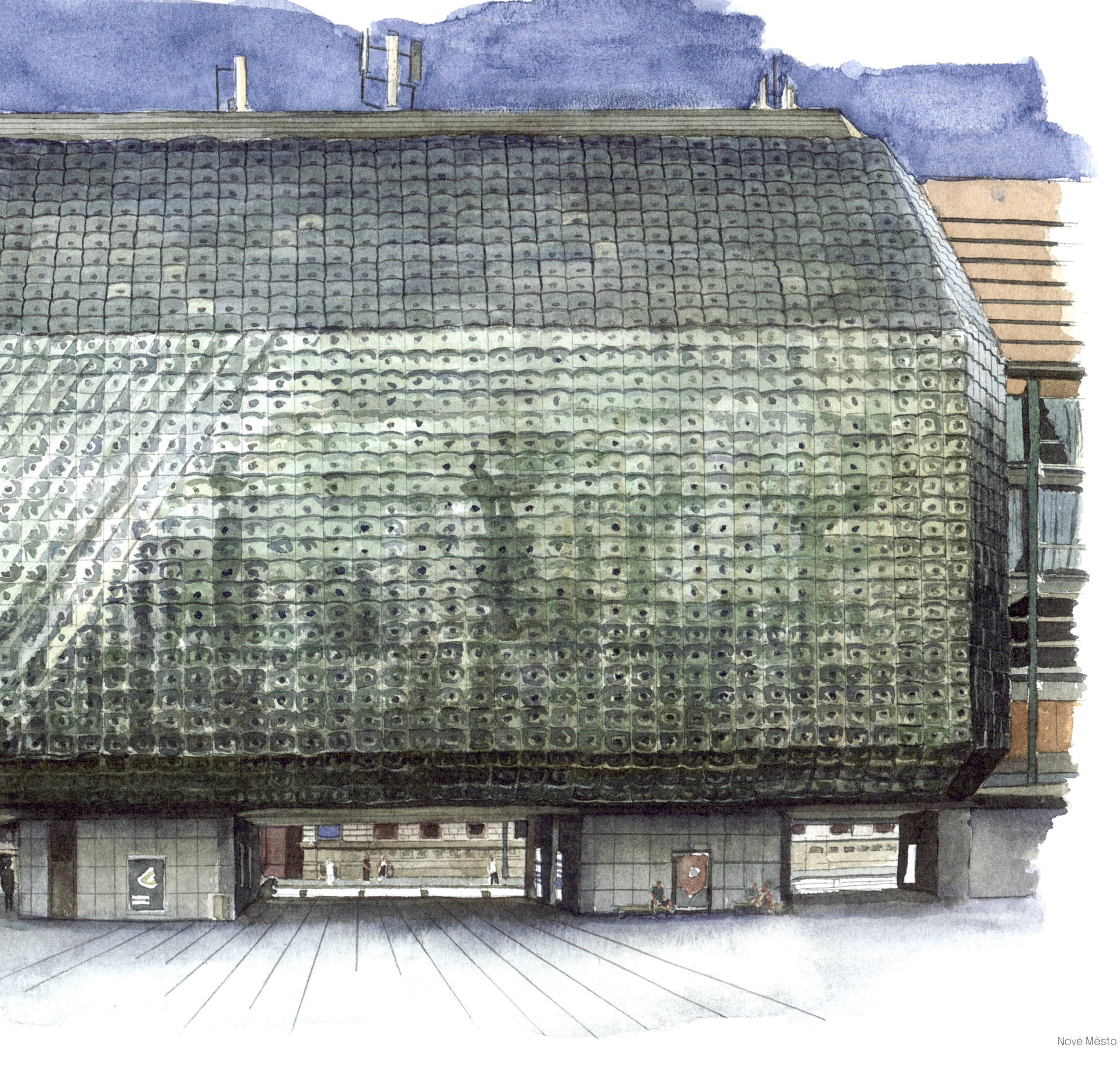

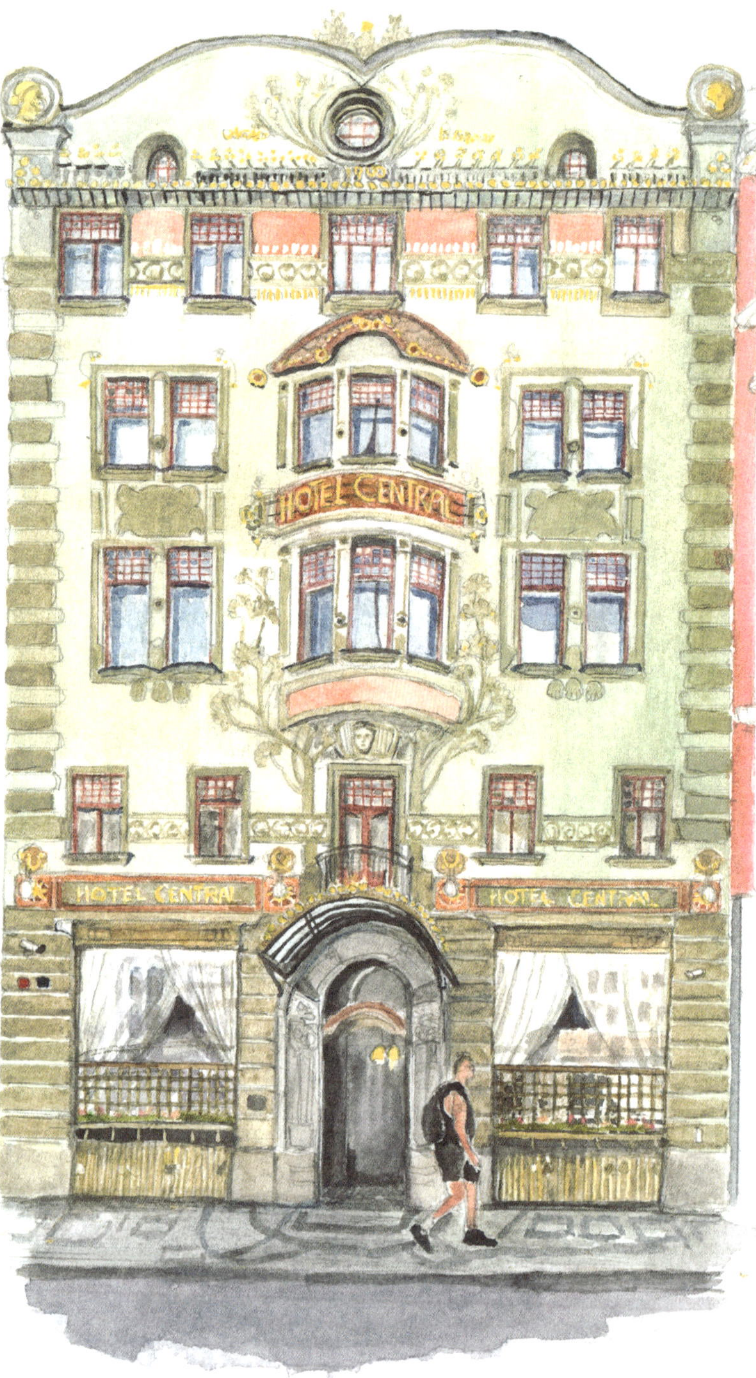

The Hotel Central (Hybernská 10) opened in 1901 (architects: Ohmann, Dryak, Bendelmayer and Bělský) and the graceful ginkgo branches that adorn its green façade - Prague, like all European capitals at the turn of the century, embraced Japonism.

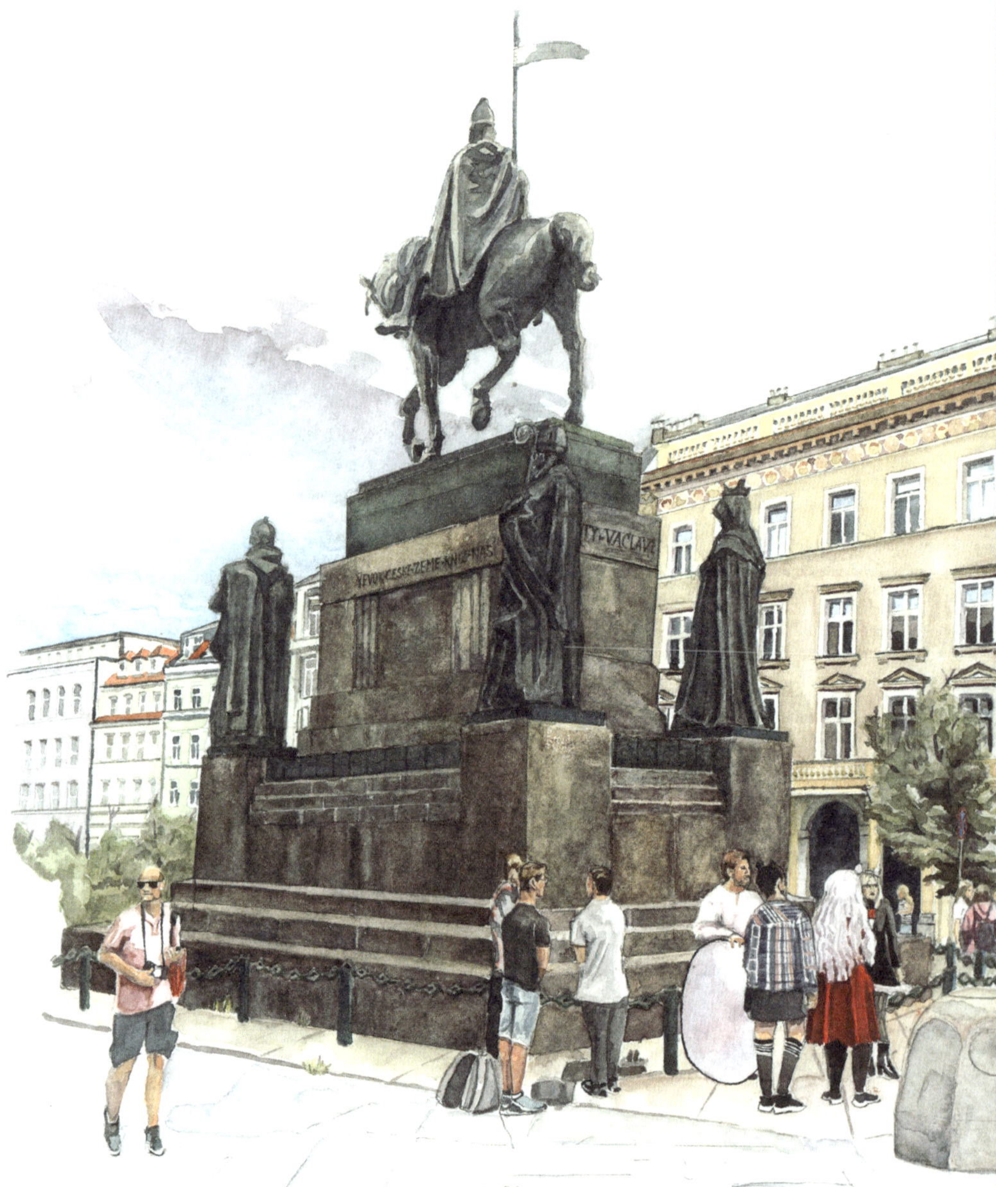

Below the National Museum, Wenceslas Square and the equestrian statue of the prince, saint and martyr of the same name. Wenceslas (Václav in Czech) was Prince of Bohemia from 921 to 935, until he was assassinated by his brother Boleslaus the Cruel.

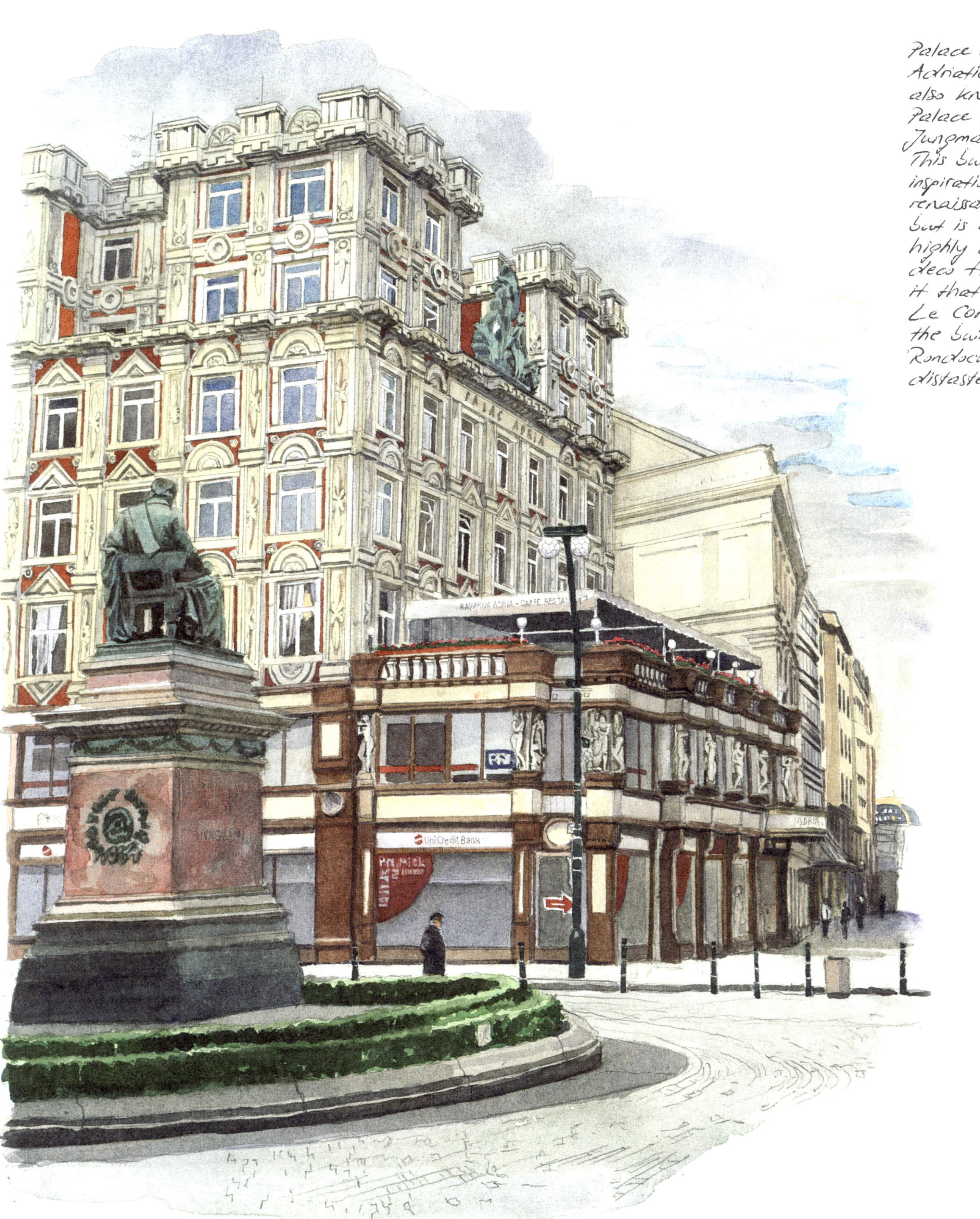

Palace of the Riunione Adriatica di Sicurtà, also known as Adria Palace (1922-1925) Jungmannovo náměstí. This building takes inspiration from Italian renaissance palaces, but is amplified into a highly decorative art deco twist. Rumor has it that Modernist architect Le Corbusier found the building's lavish Rondocubist details distasteful.

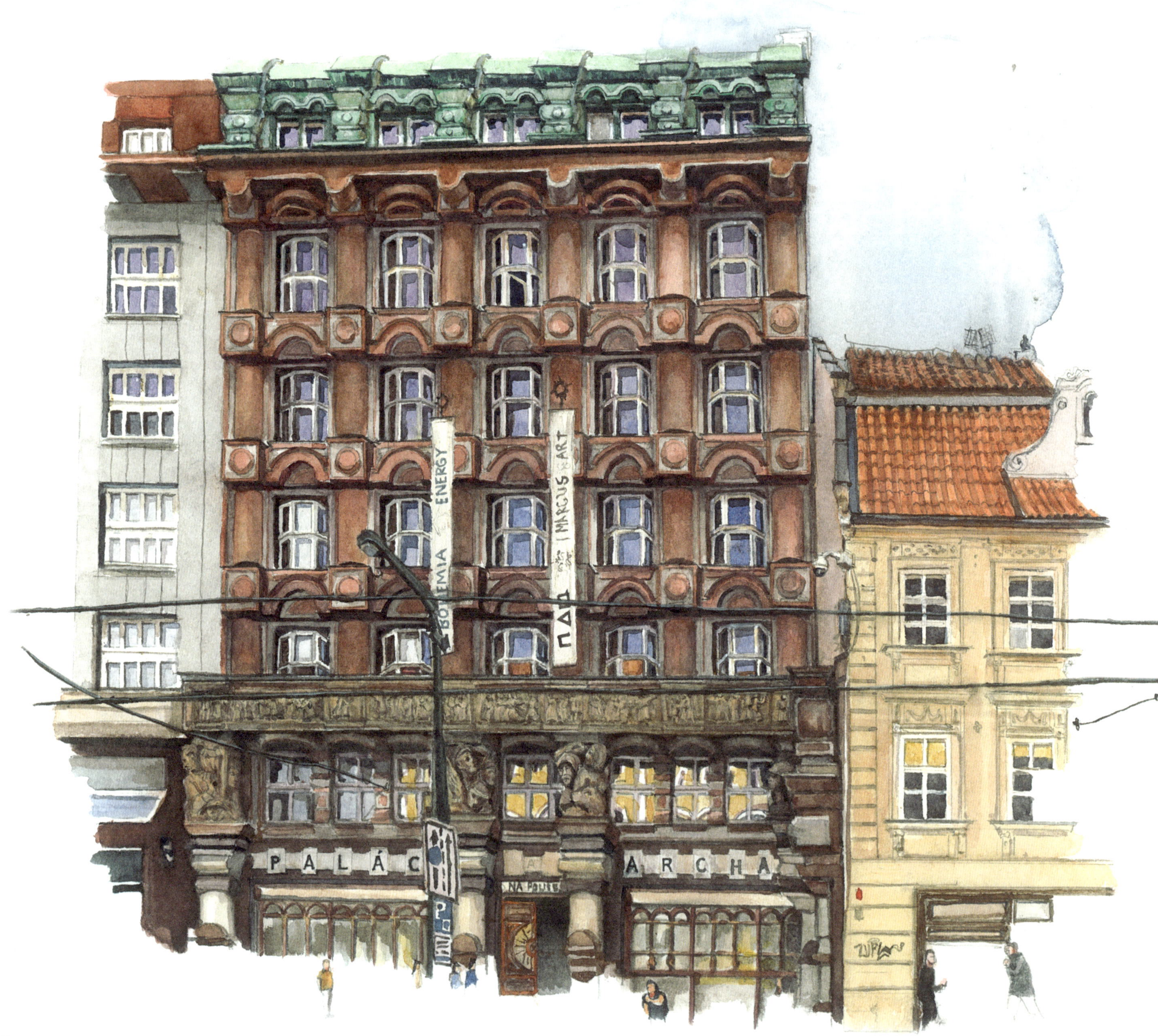

BOHEMIA ENERGY
I MARCUS ART
PALÁC
NA PORÍČÍ
ARCHA

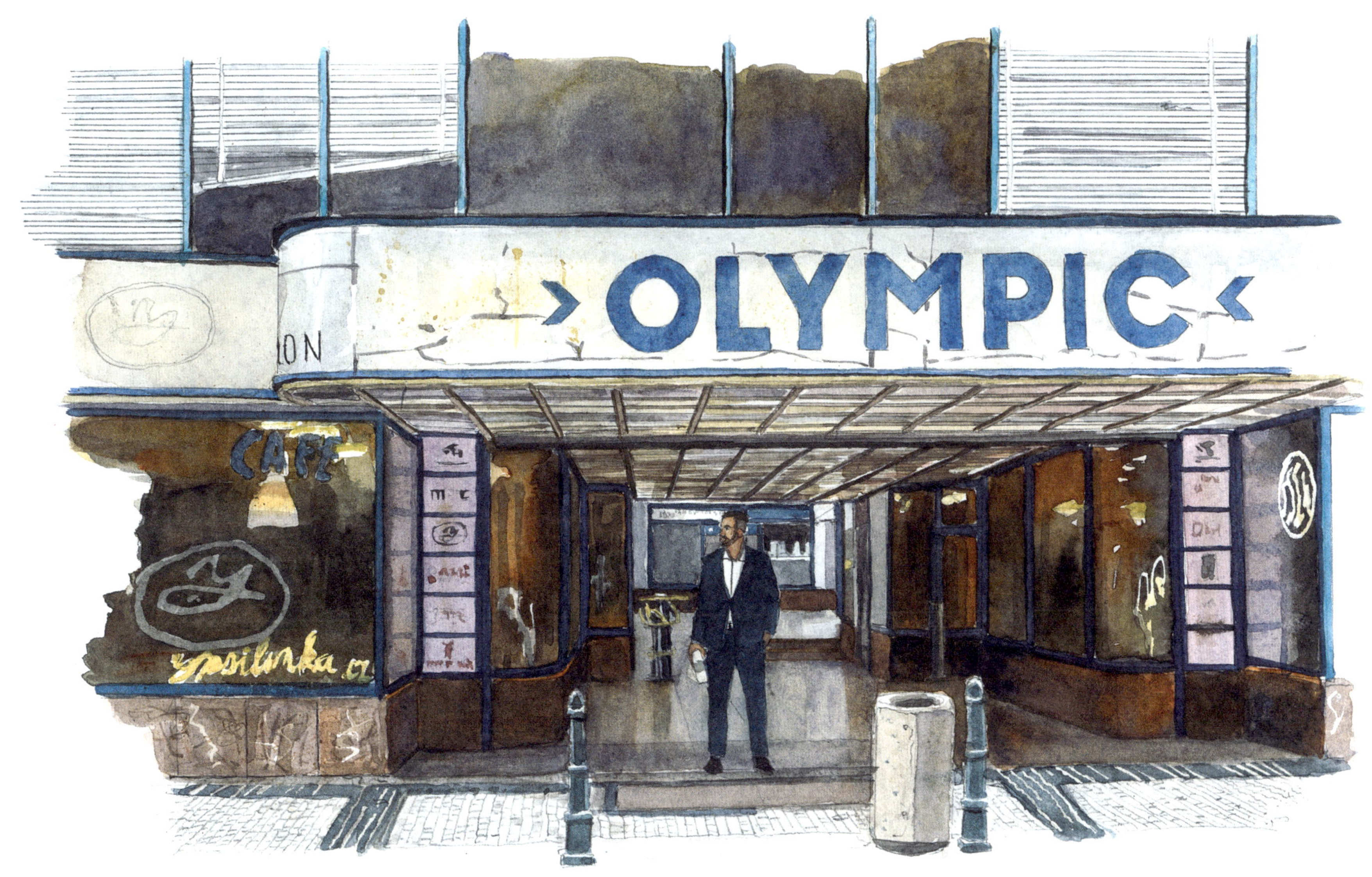

Bank of the Czechoslovak Legion
1921–1923
Bank of the Czechoslovak
Legion cylinder and circular
geometric patterns has cubist
elements, but what is most
striking is the cast stone
facade. It depicts the
Czech legion returning from
the first World War and
starting their future lives.

Passage of the Olympic Palace
(1923–1926)
Prague is famous for its
many passages, linking many
buildings to each other.
The Olympic Palace passage
offers many hidden surprises,
including a shortcut to
the Ypsilon Theater.

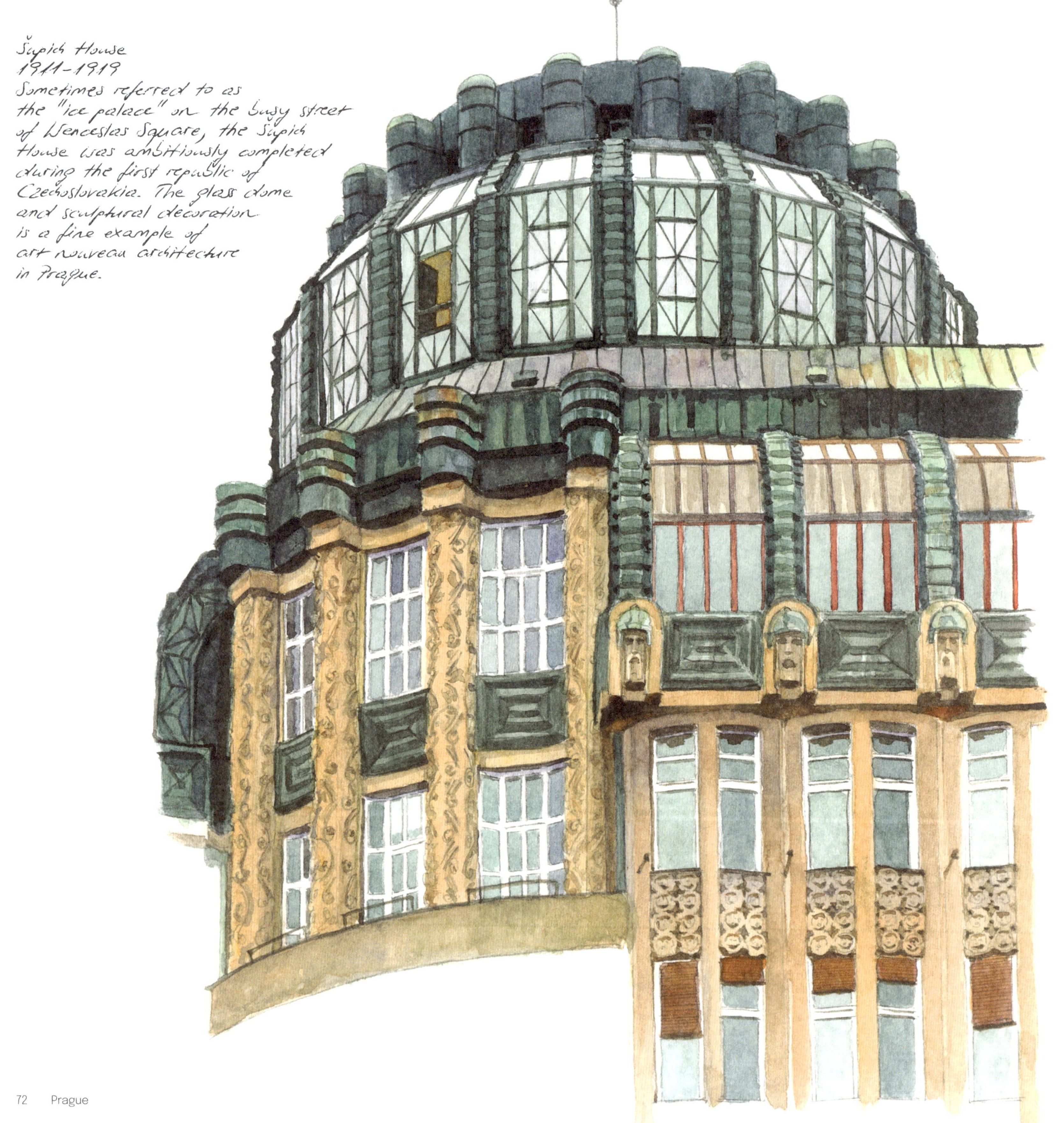

Šupich House
1911-1919
Sometimes referred to as
the "ice palace" on the busy street
of Wenceslas Square, the Šupich
House was ambitiously completed
during the first republic of
Czechoslovakia. The glass dome
and sculptural decoration
is a fine example of
art nouveau architecture
in Prague.

Diamond House
1912–1913
Prague offers many
examples of the
geometrical style
of cubist architecture.
The Diamond House
was controversial when
it was completed
in 1913, but, like
many cubist structures
within the city,
is celebrated.

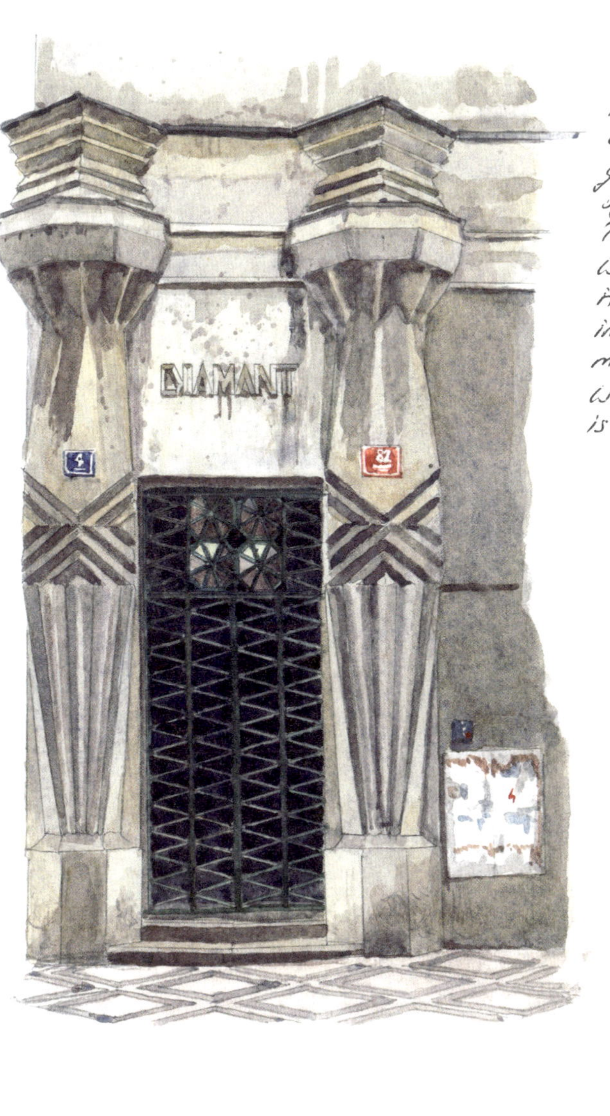

Koruna Palace
(1911–1913, architects Antonín Pfeiffer
and Matěj Blecha, Václavské náměstí 846/1)
With its strict lines, this splendid building
heralds the advent of Art Deco. It owes its
name, Koruna, to the crown on its tower. You
should visit its gallery, but you will no doubt
rue the passing of Automat, the fully automated
cafeteria designed in 1931 by Ladislav Machoň.

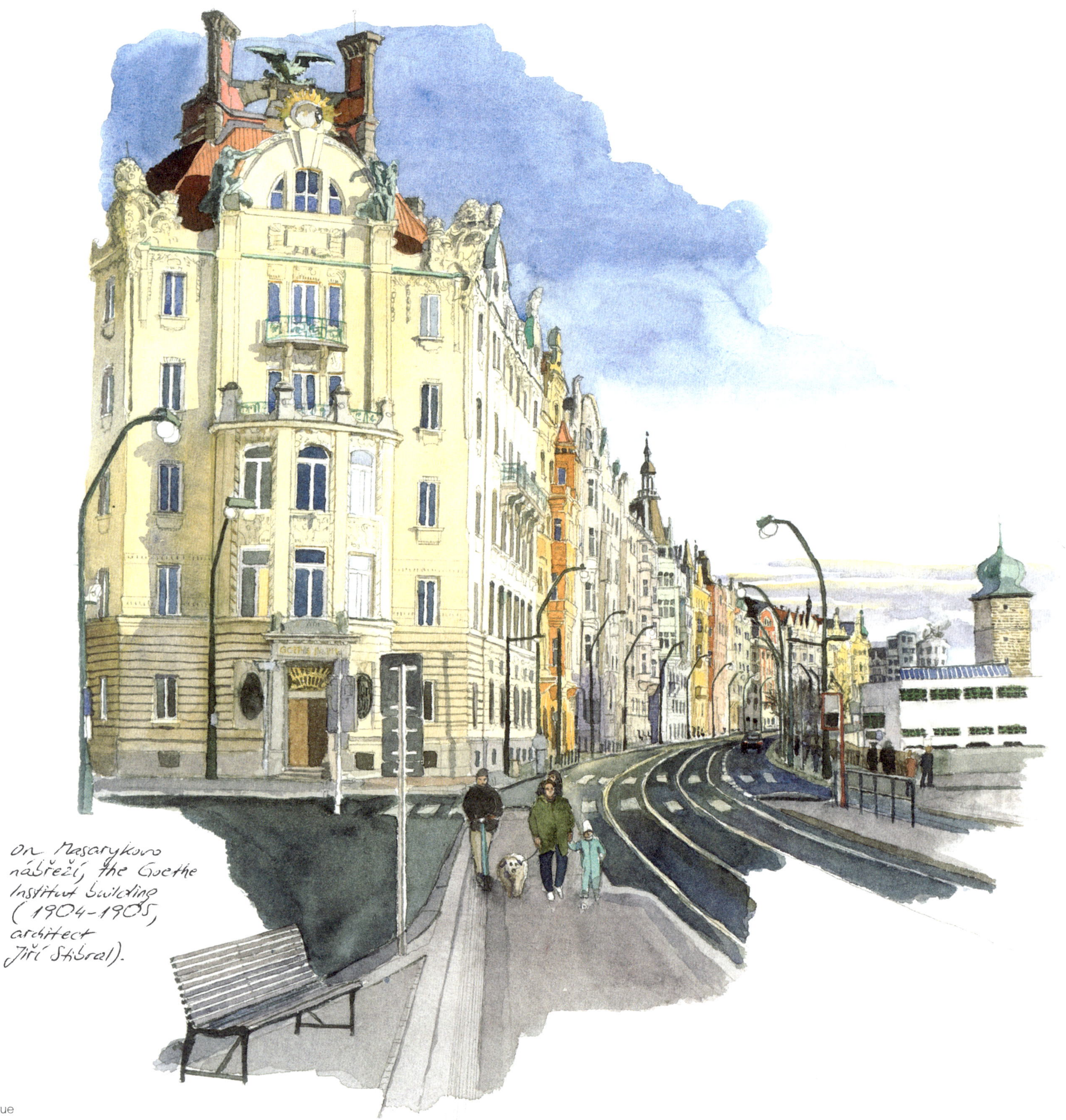

on Masarykovo
nábřeží, the Goethe
Institut building
(1904-1905,
architect
Jiří Stibral).

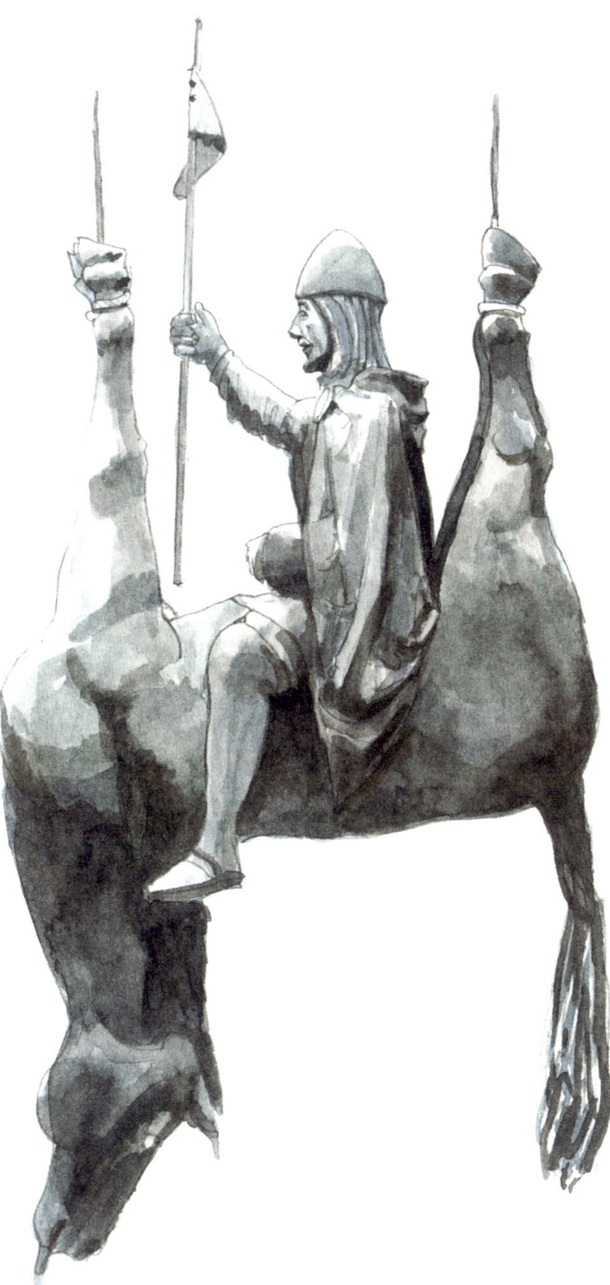

Statue from the Lucerna Palace
(1907–1921, architect Stanislav
Bechyně, Štěpánská 704/61 and
Vodičkova 704/36). This 'urban
palace', which houses concert halls,
restaurants, a cinema and two galleries,
belongs to the widow of Václav Havel,
the grandson of the entrepreneur
who designed it, Václav Havel.

On the side of Saints Cyril and Methodius cathedral,
this plaque commemorates the members of Operation
Anthropoid. Sent to Prague by the British secret
service to assassinate the Nazi leader Heydrich, these
Czech resistance fighters took refuge in the cathedral
crypt after the attack but were discovered and
killed by the Germans three weeks later.

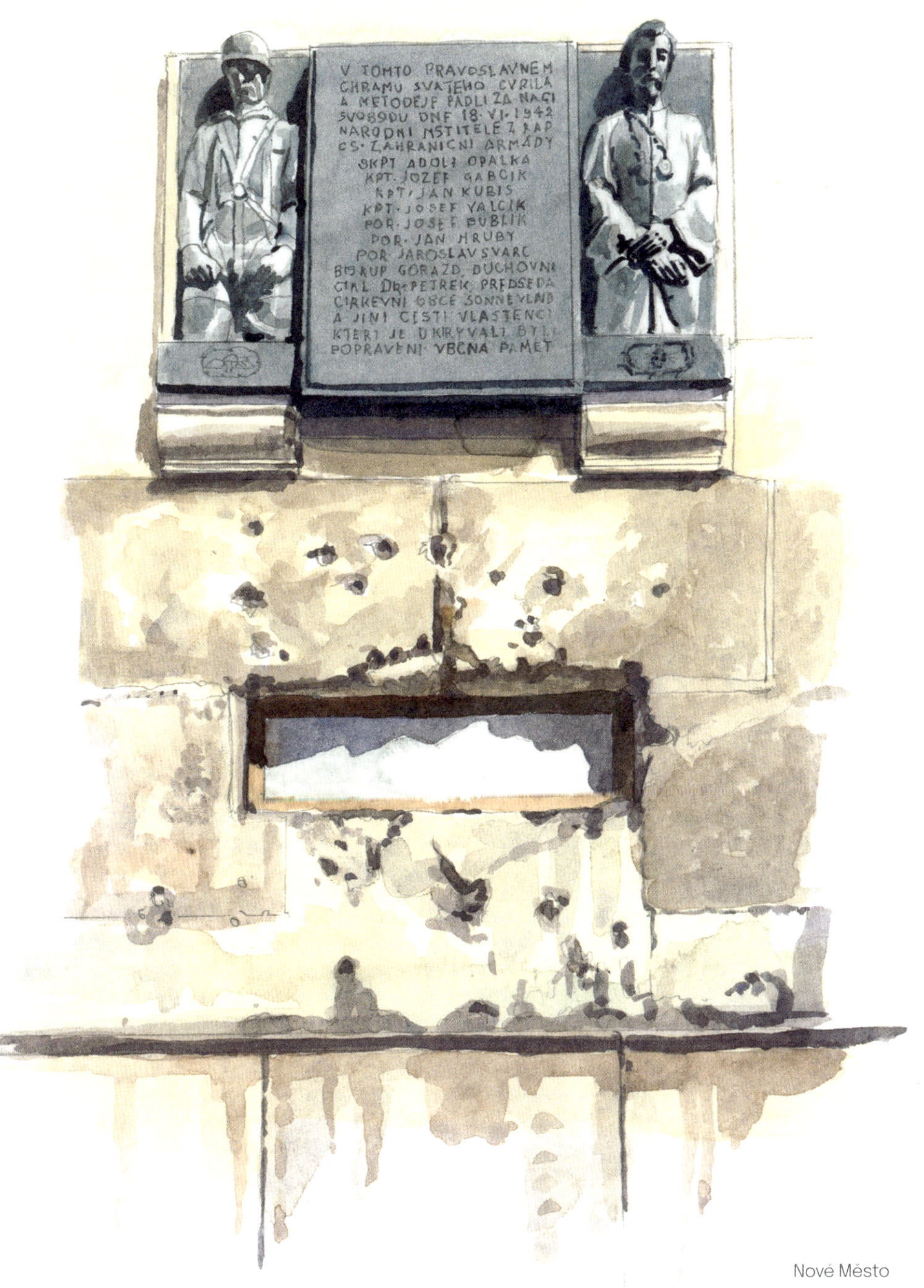

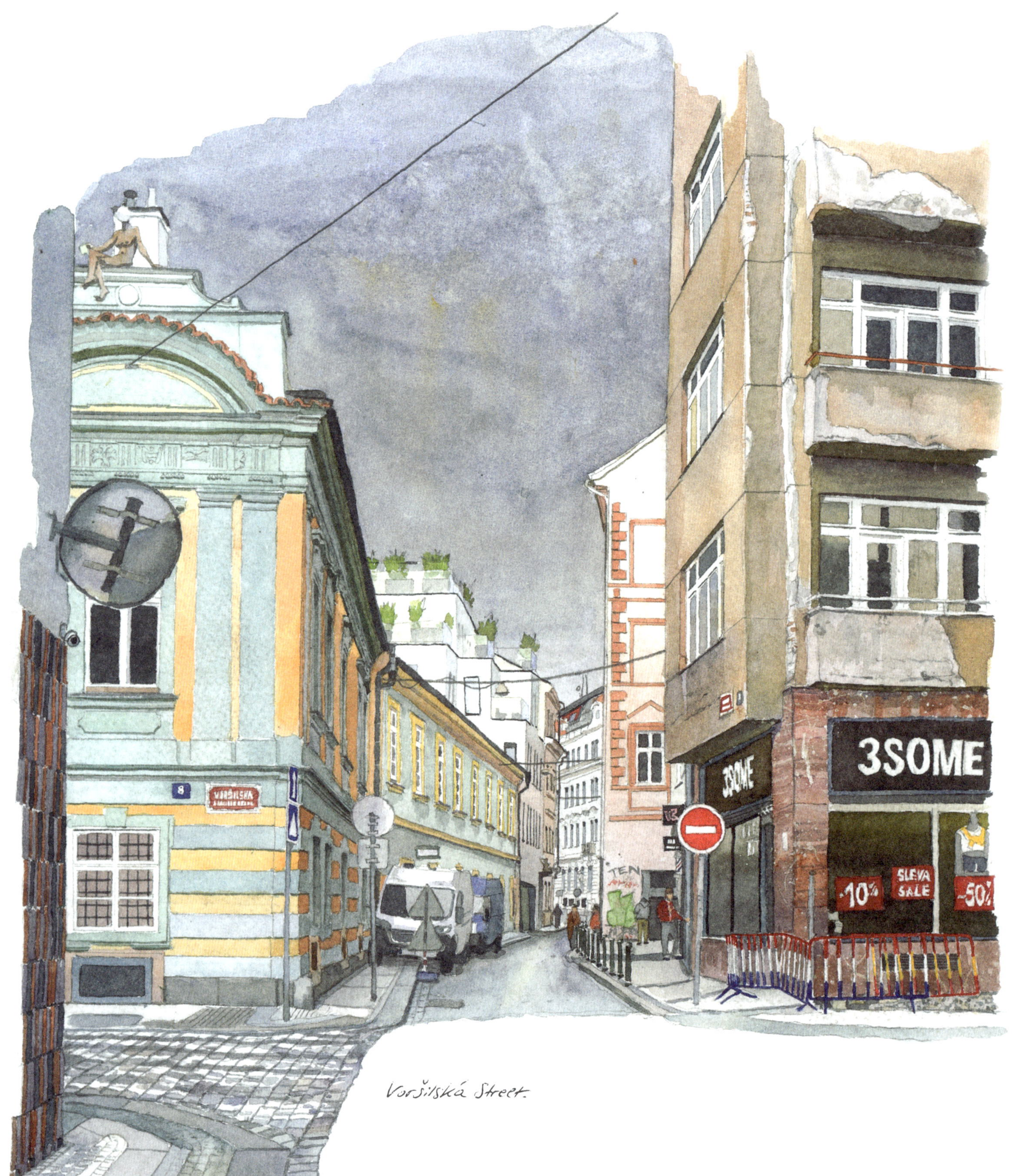

Voršilská Street.

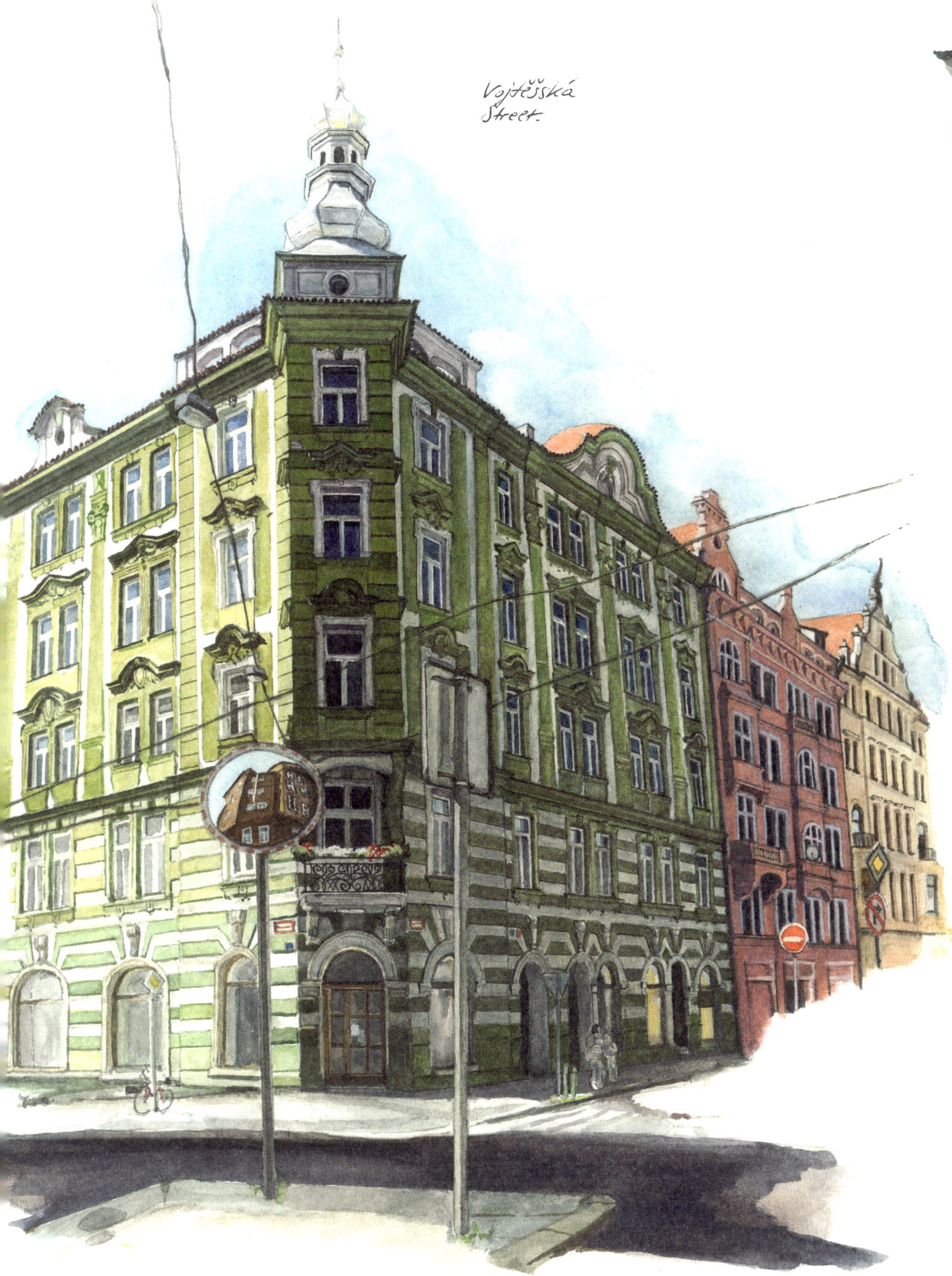

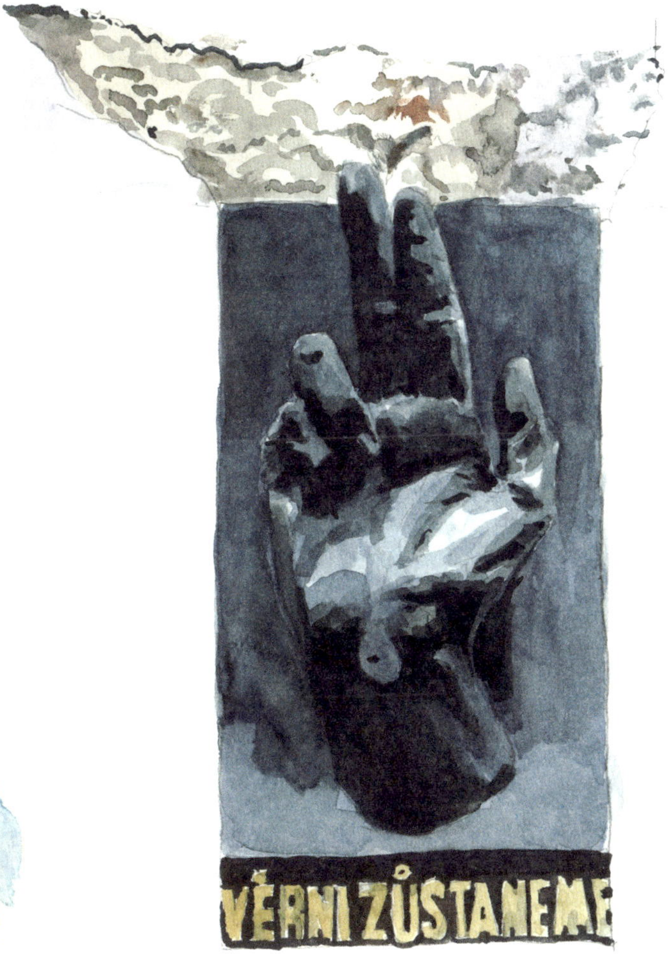

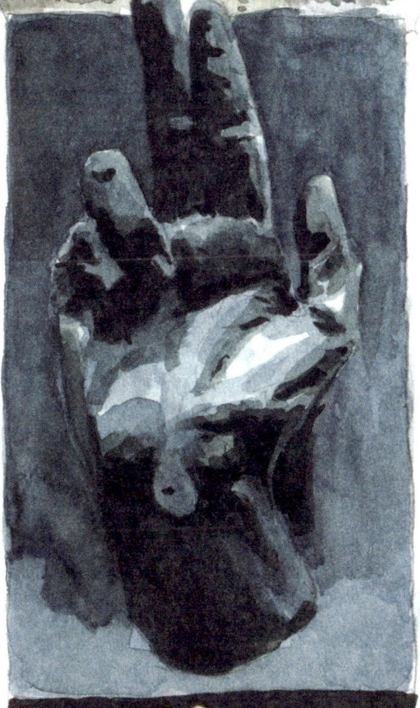

Betlémská 331/1,
"We will stay
faithful" a monument
to Luboš Jeřábek,
a lawyer who died
during the defence
of Prague, 1945

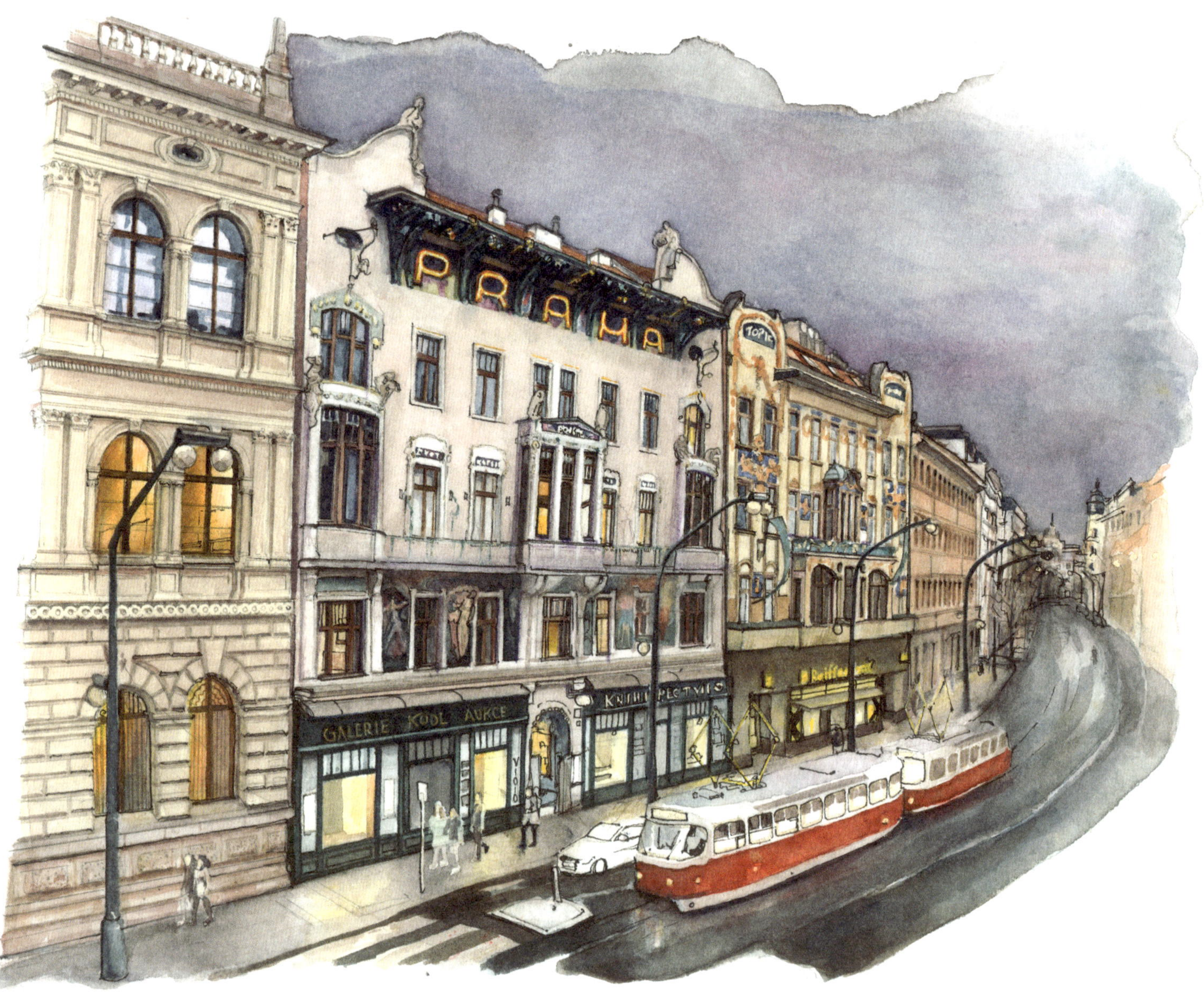

Národní třída, the Praha insurance company building and Topič House, named after a famous Prague publisher and bookseller, František Topič. The beautiful façade is the work of Osvald Polívka.

Cubist Lamp

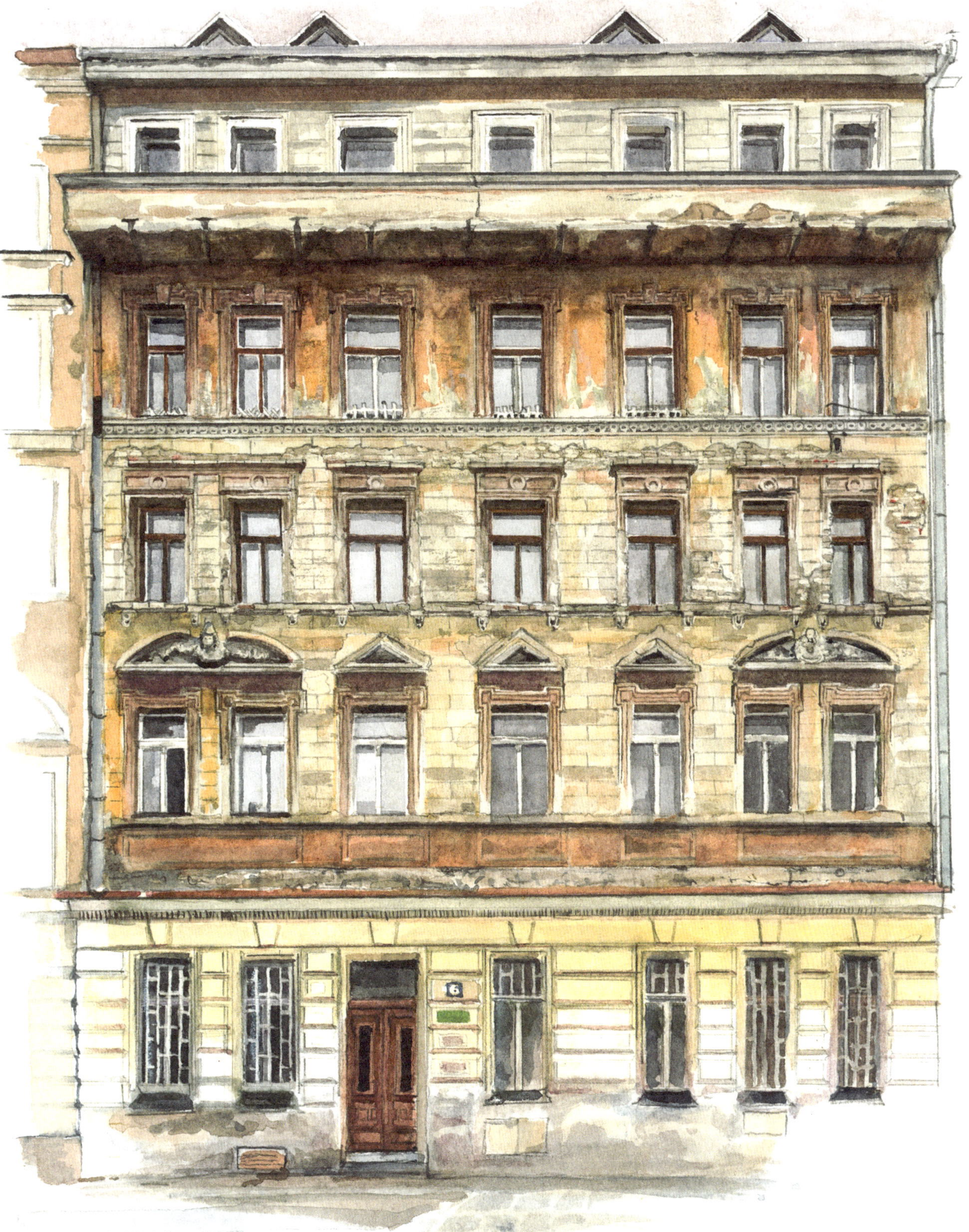

Letná

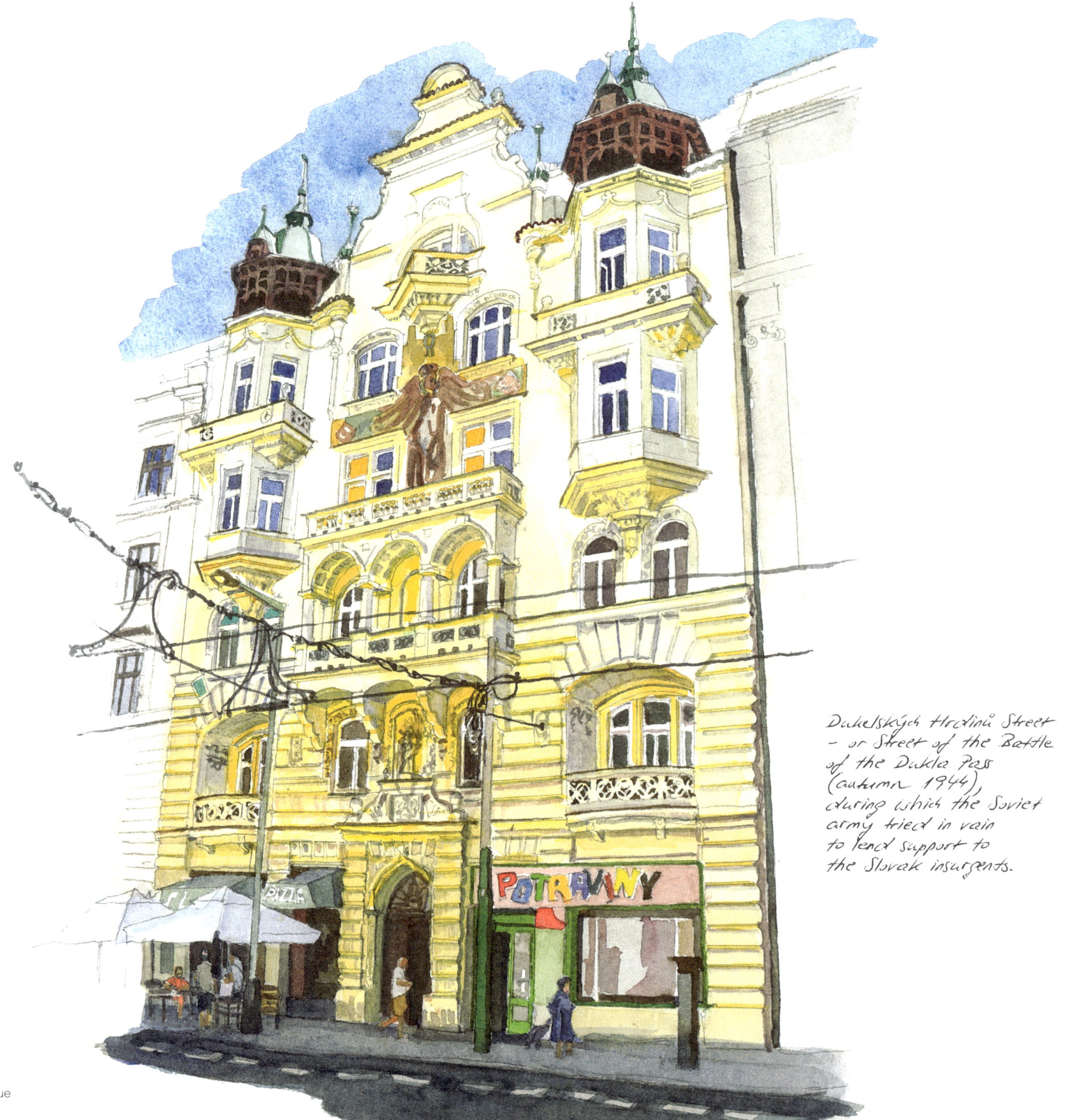

Dukelských Hrdinů Street
– or Street of the Battle
of the Dukla Pass
(autumn 1944),
during which the Soviet
army tried in vain
to lend support to
the Slovak insurgents.

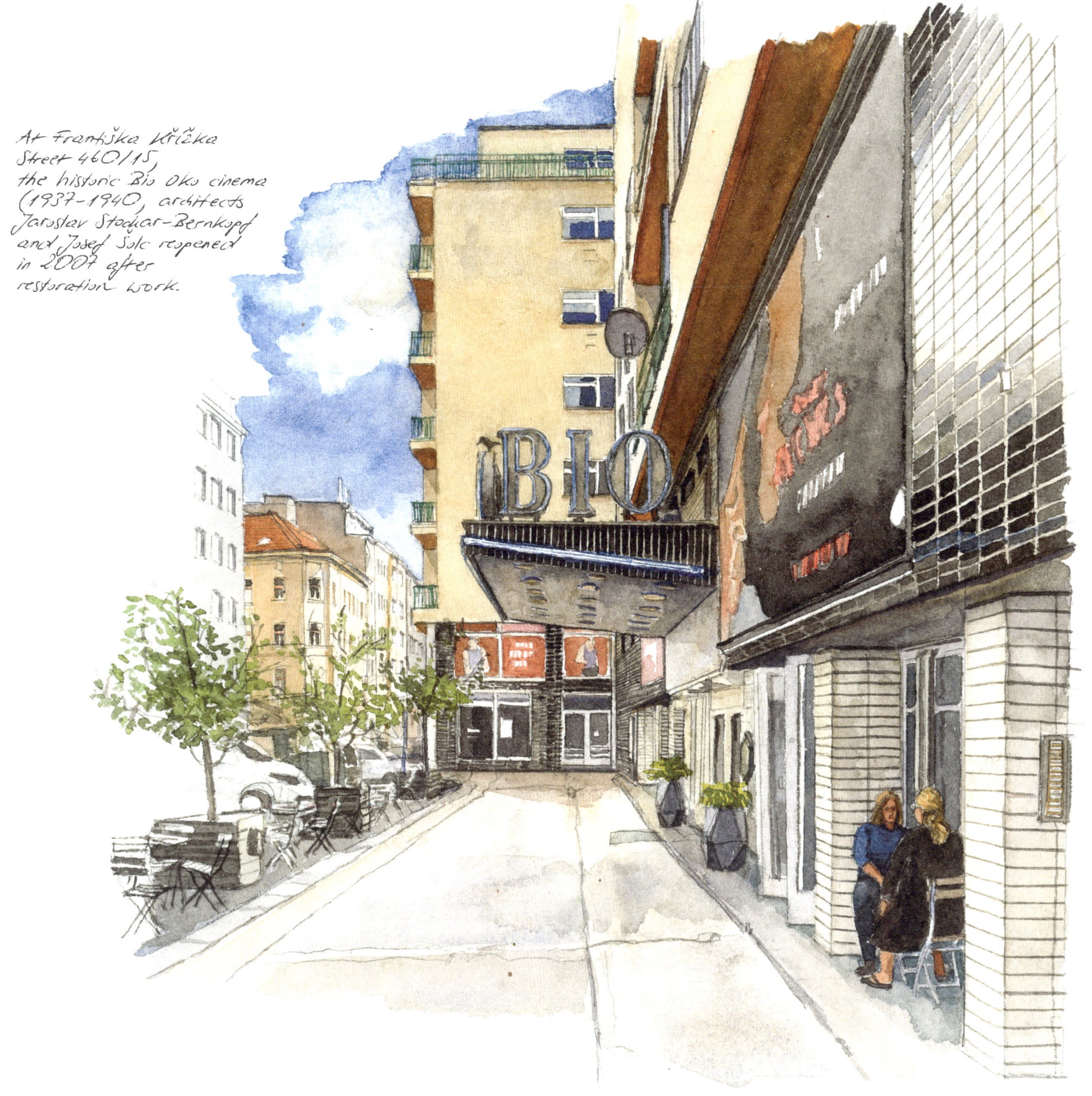

At Františka Křička
Street 460/15,
the historic Bio Oko cinema
(1937–1940, architects
Jaroslav Stockar-Bernkopf
and Josef Šolc reopened
in 2007 after
restoration work.

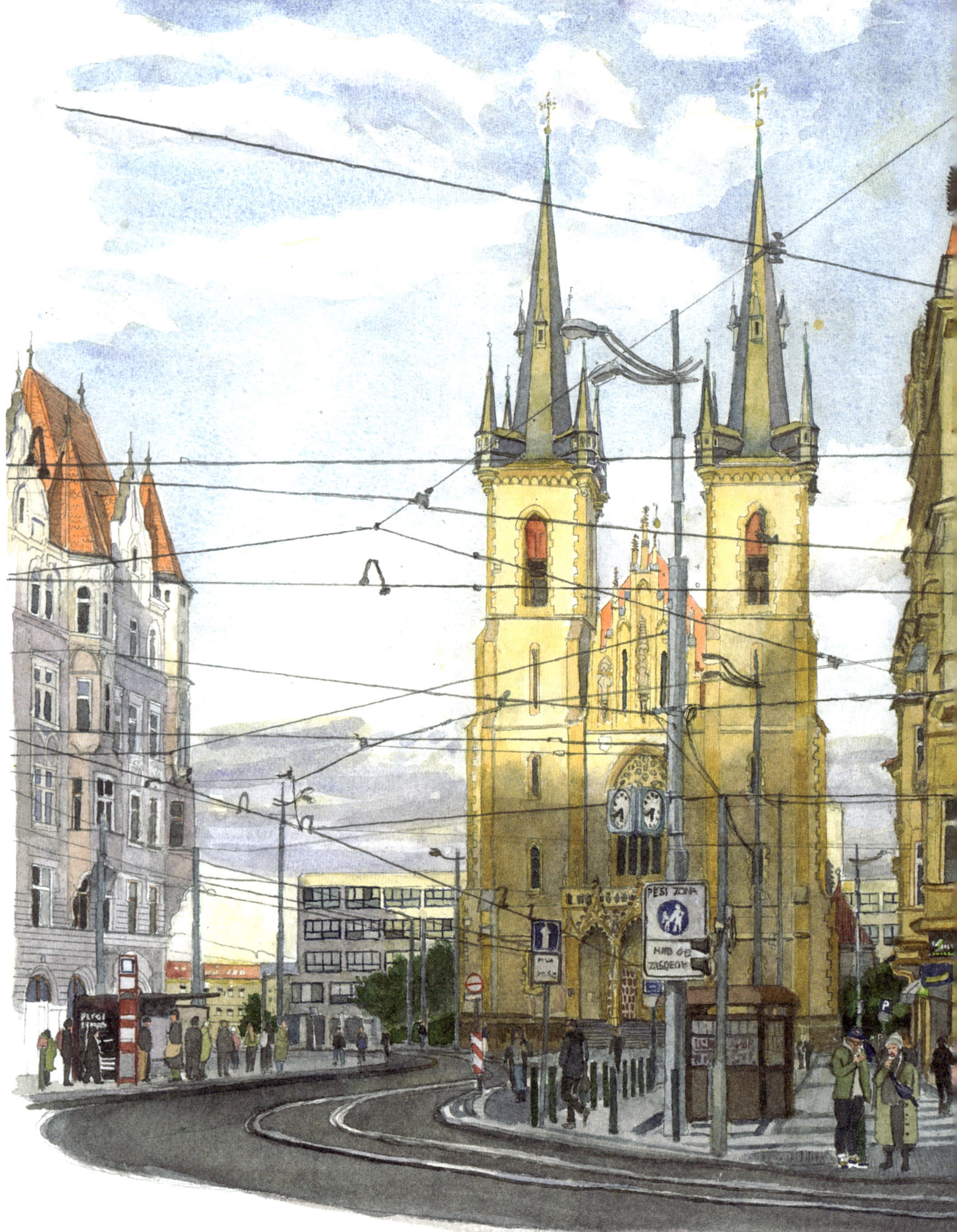

On Place Strassmayer, the towers of the neo-Gothic church of St Anthony of Padua.

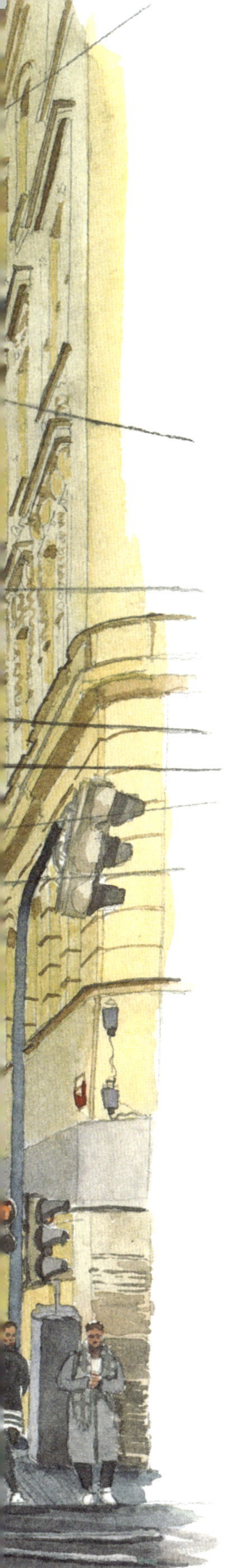

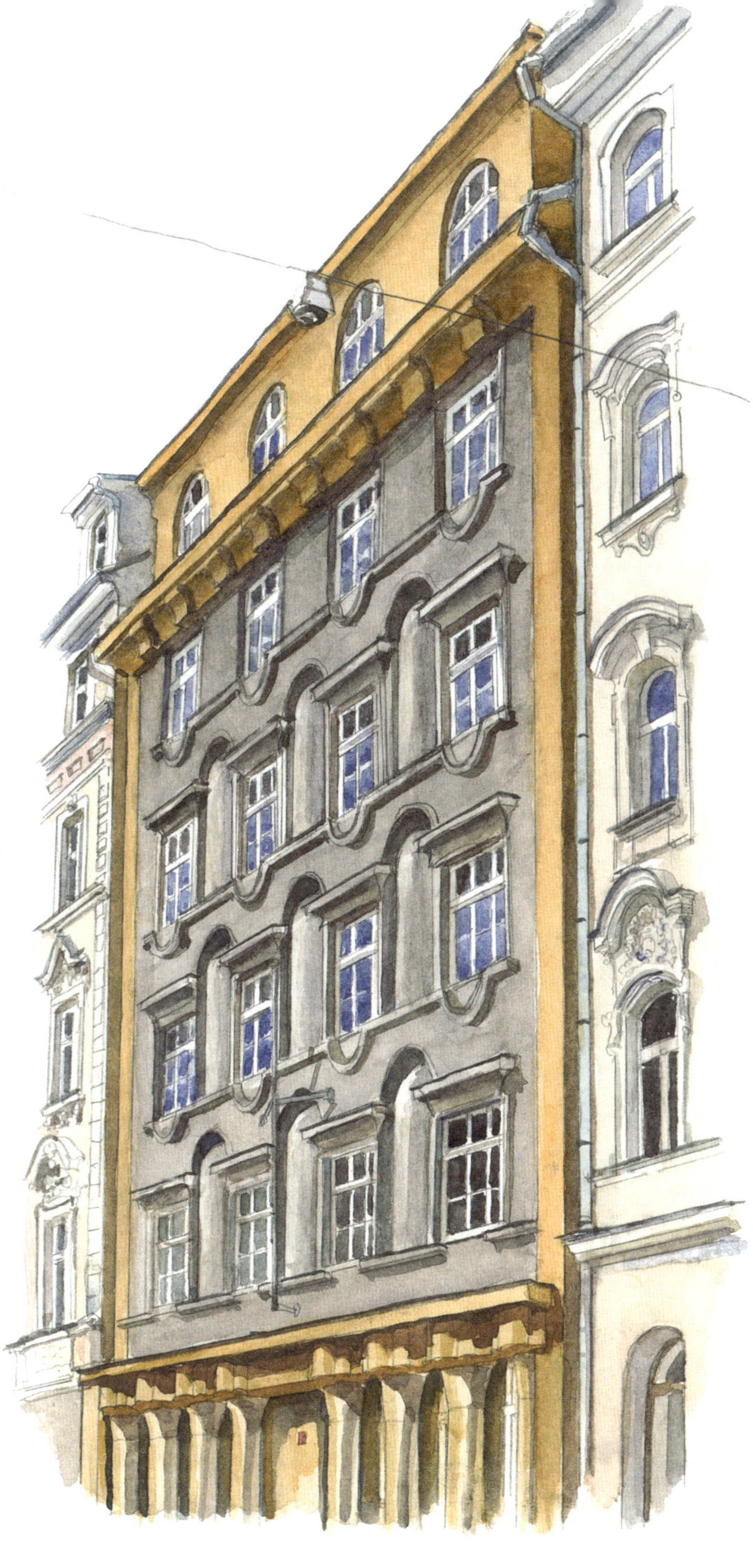

Rondocubist
residential building
at 35 Kamenická
Street (1922–1923,
architect:
Otakar Novotný).

Žižkov

The Žižkov tunnel and its 'neboj'
- Don't be afraid (work by artist
Timo, 2017). This 300-metre-
long pedestrian and cycle tunnel
connects the Karlin district to
Žižkov. On the other side
of one of its steel doors are
the premises of the accelerator
department at the Czech
Institute of Nuclear Physics.

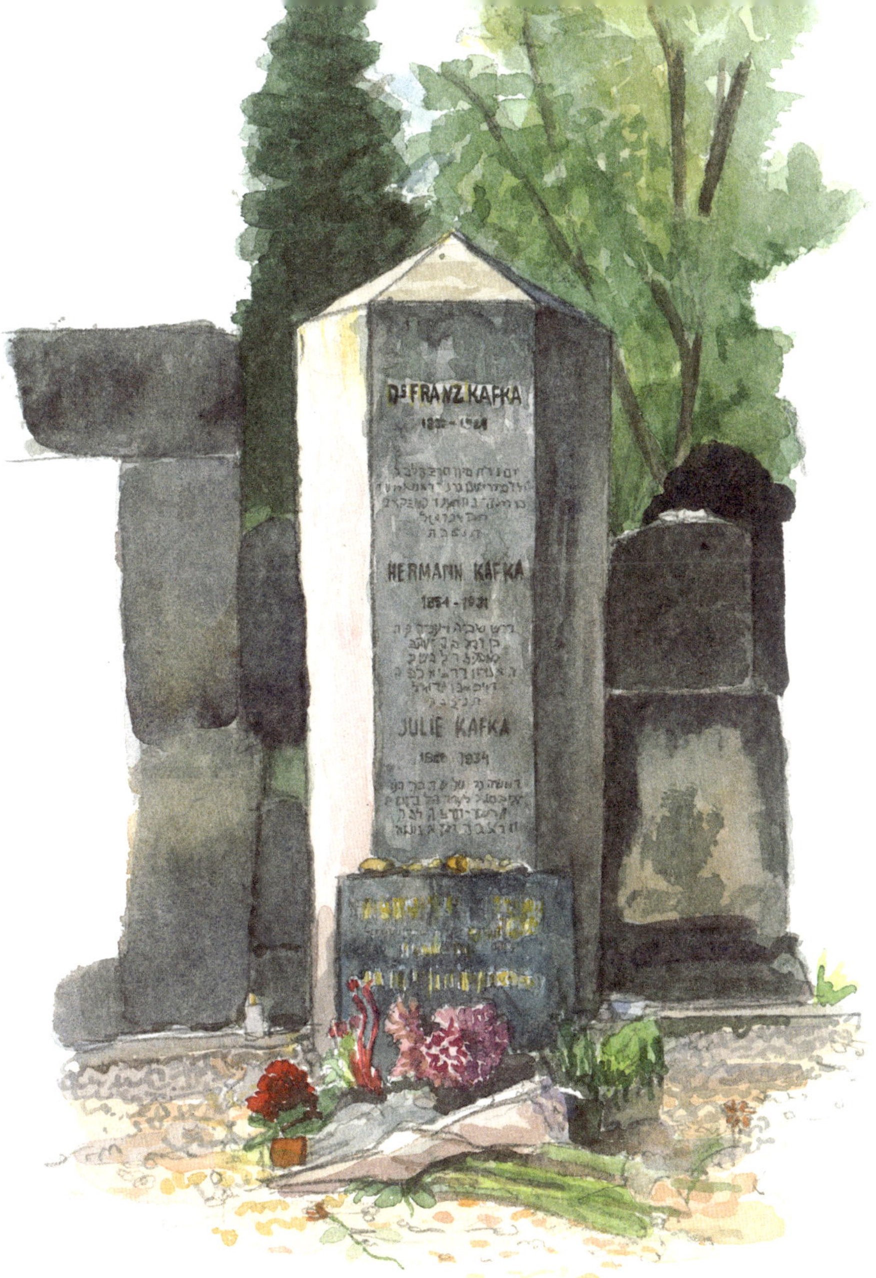

Izraelská 1, the new Jewish cemetery, where you can visit Franz Kafka's grave. The family monument also recalls the names of his sisters, Gabriele, Ottilie and Valerie, who were all murdered by the Nazis.

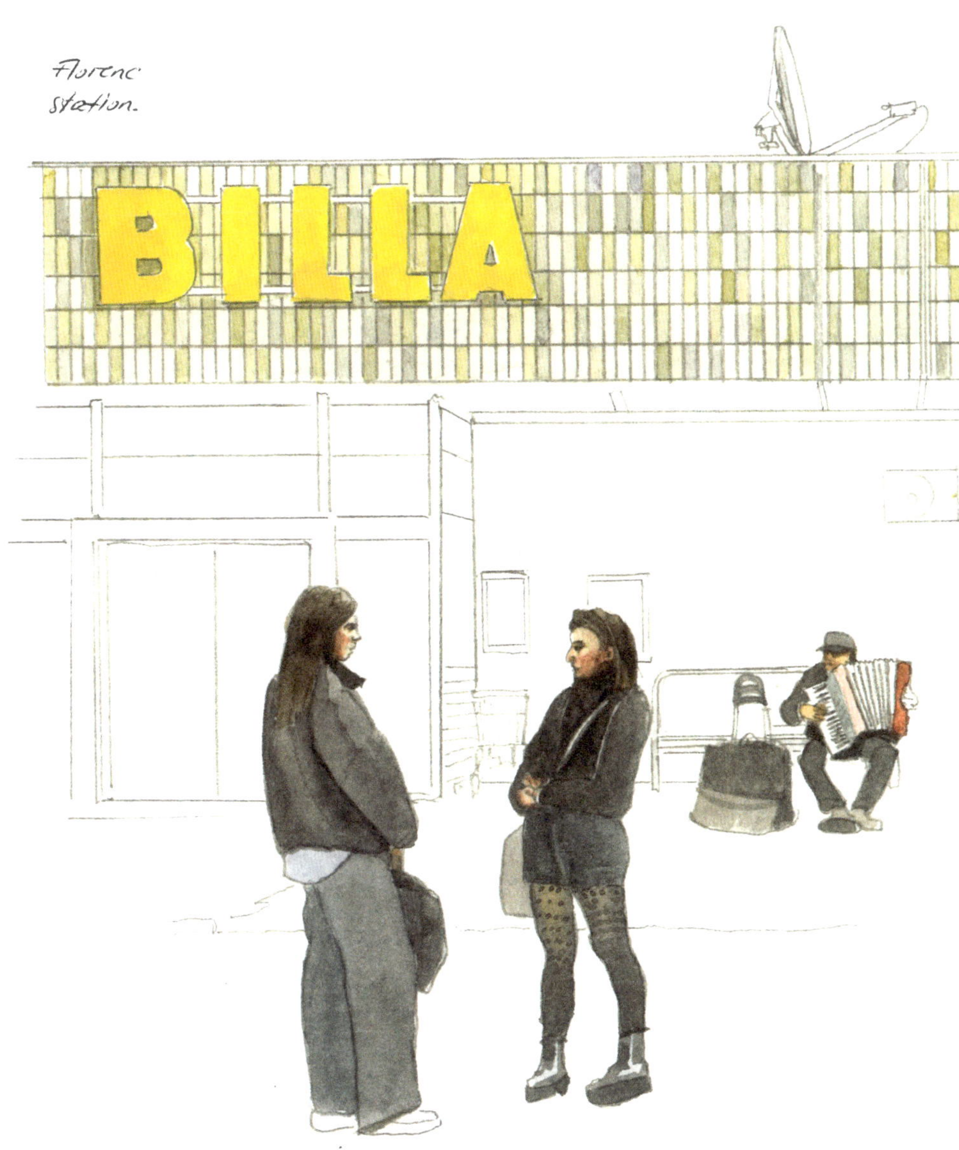

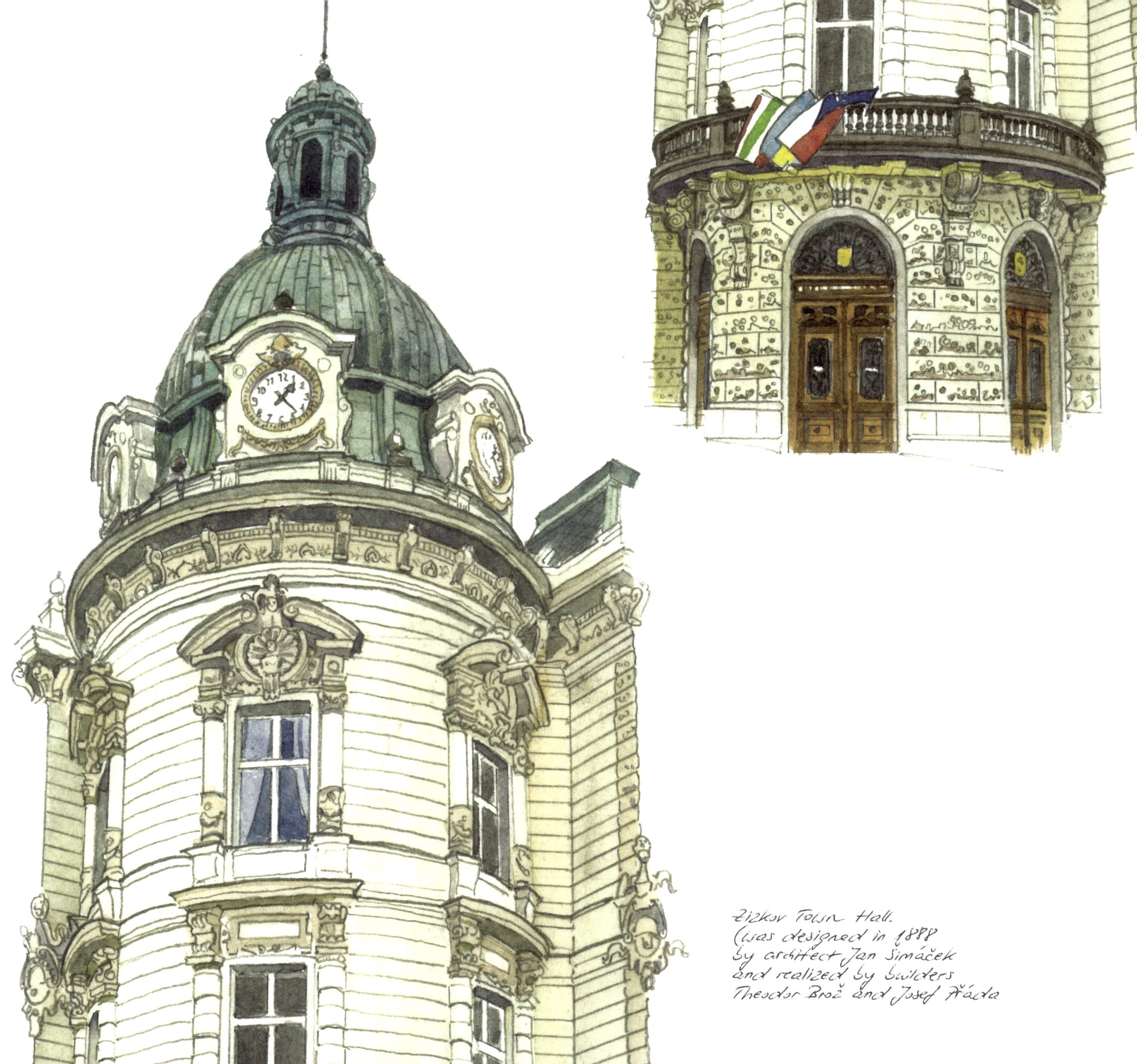

Žižkov Town Hall.
(was designed in 1888
by architect Jan Šimáček
and realized by builders
Theodor Brož and Josef Přáda

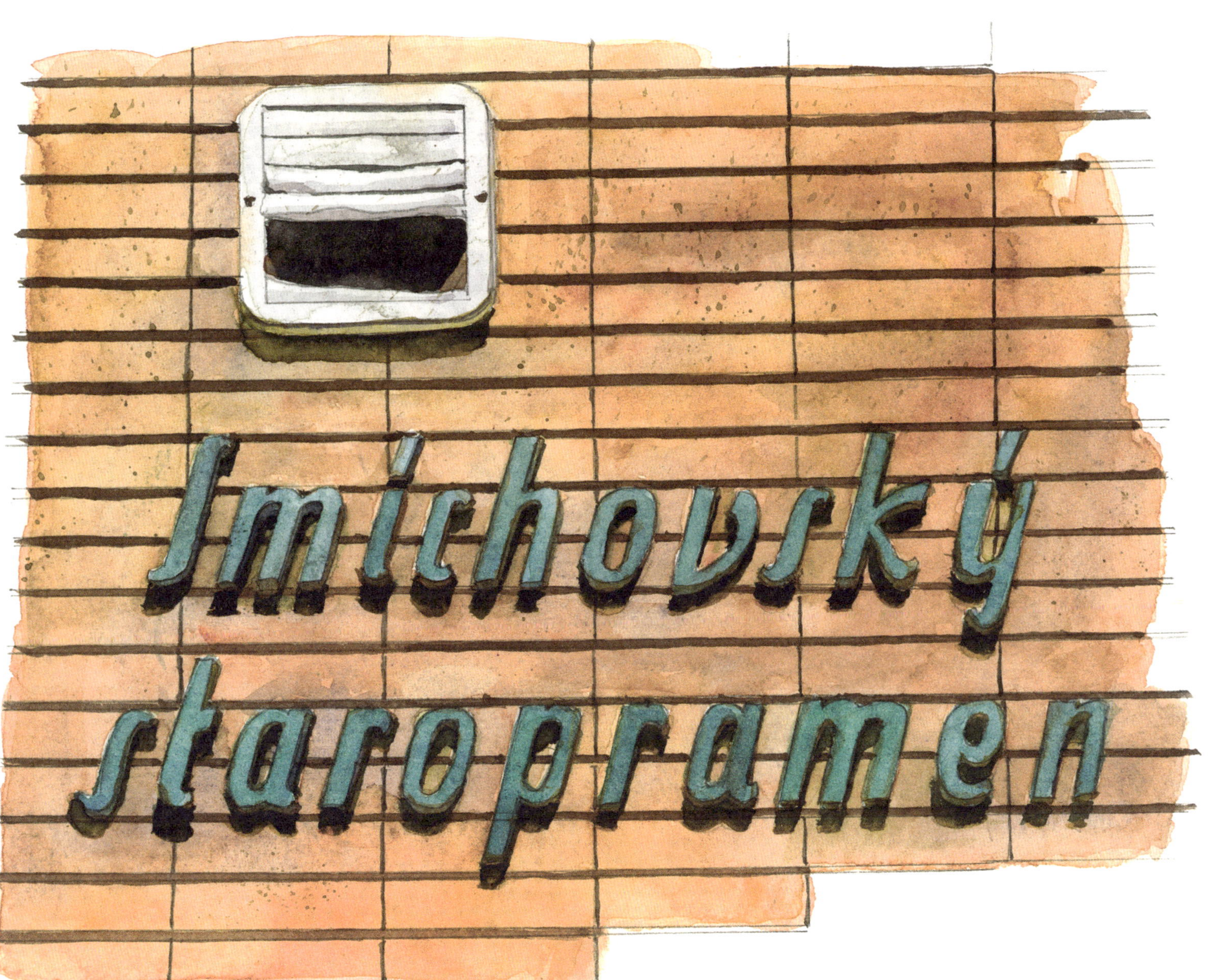

On the facade
of a tavern
in Karlin,
this 1970s
advertisement for
a brand of beer.

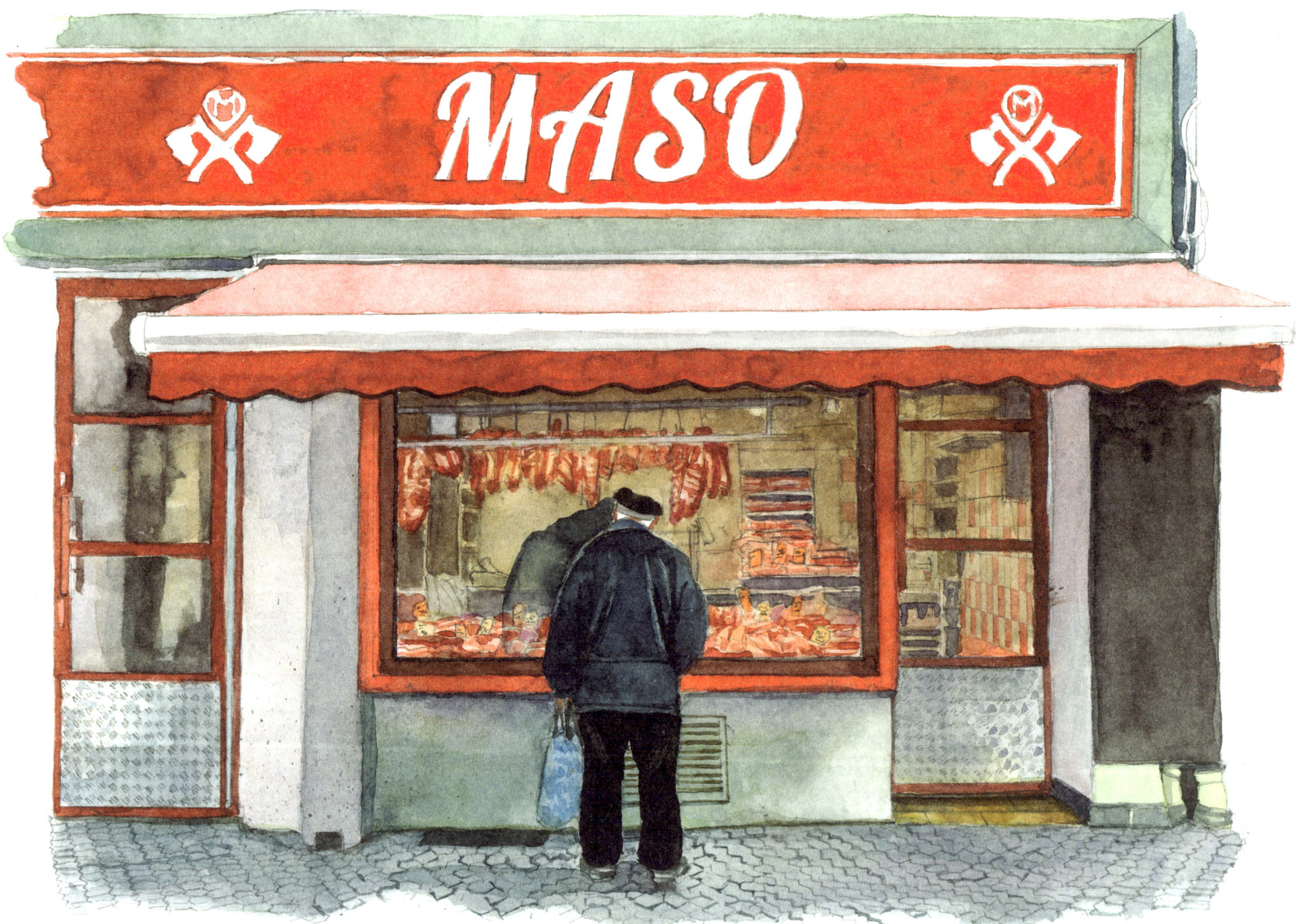

A butcher's shop
on Thámova Street.

Vinohrady

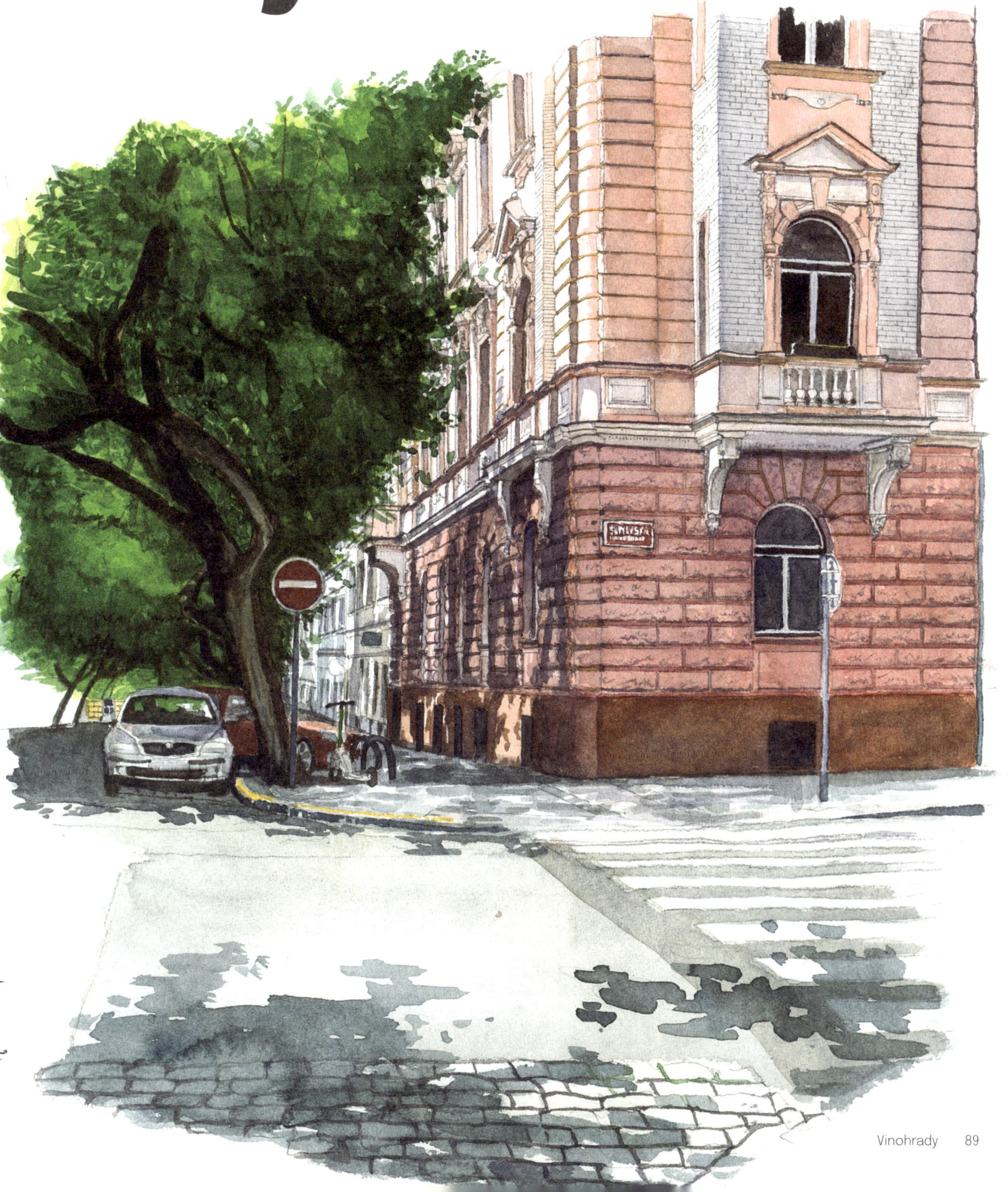

Šumavská Street
is a quiet, leafy street
named after one of
Bohemia's most beautiful
regions, Šumava, on the
border with Germany.

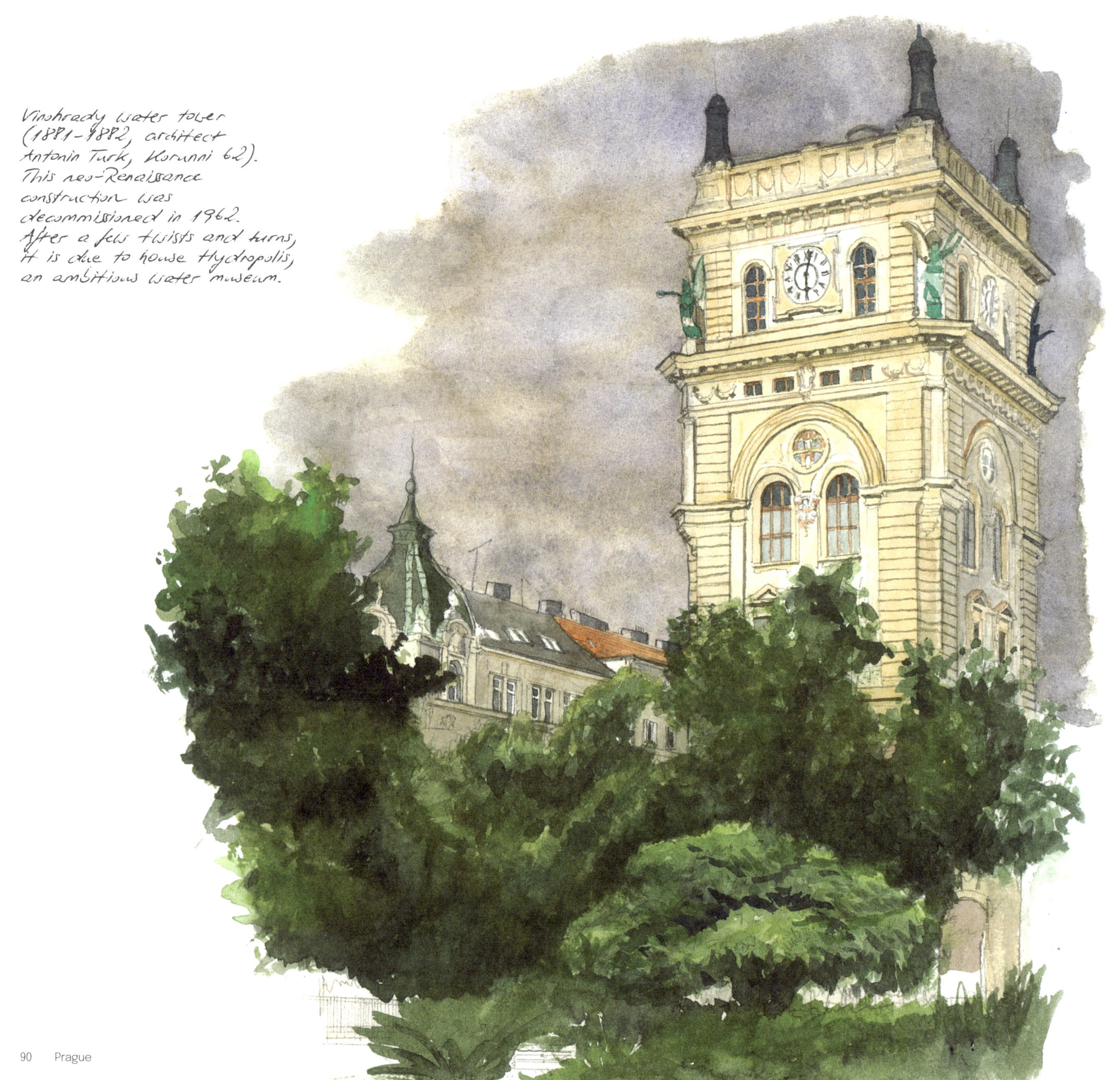

Vinohrady water tower
(1881-1882, architect
Antonin Turk, Korunni 62).
This neo-Renaissance
construction was
decommissioned in 1962.
After a few twists and turns,
it is due to house Hydropolis,
an ambitious water museum.

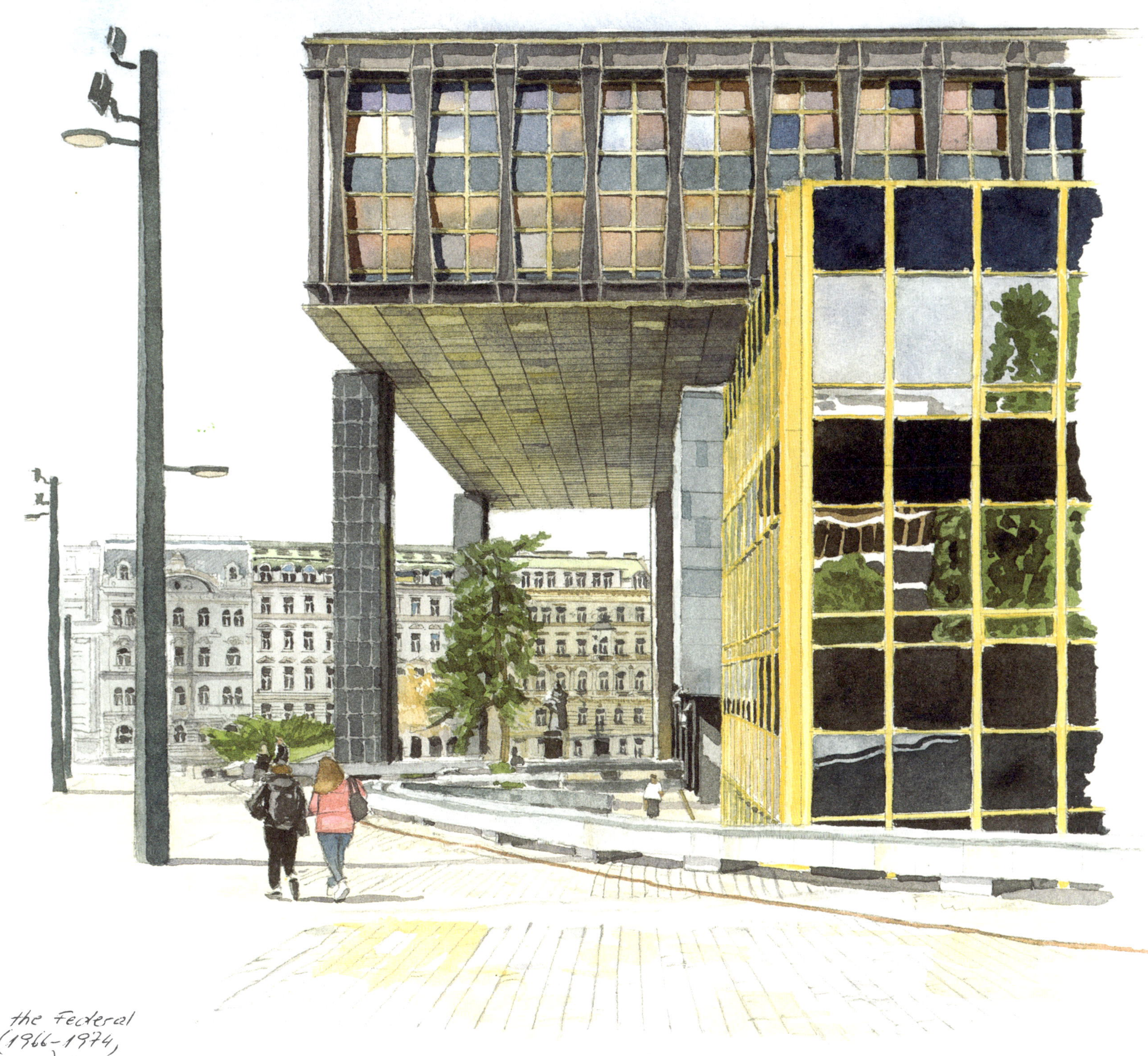

Vinohradská 52/1, the Federal
Assembly Building (1966–1974,
architect Karel Prager) is one
of the landmarks of the Velvet Revolution.
Later given over to Radio Free Europe,
it is now part of the National Museum.

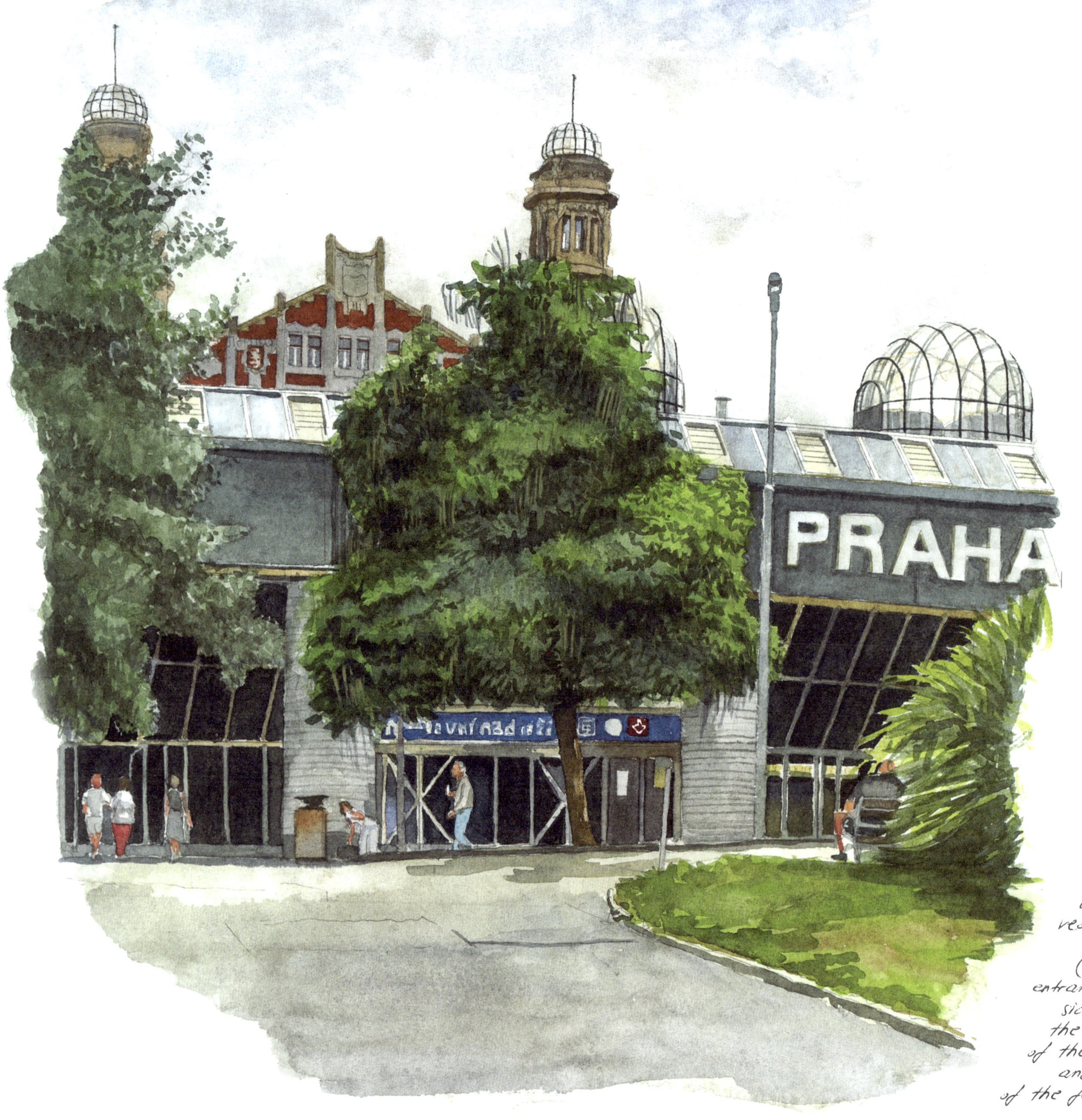

Prague Central Station (1901–1909, architect Josef Fanta), where the superb vestiges of Fanta's masterpiece (in particular the entrance dome) stand side by side with the garish confusion of the station's interior and the melancholy of the forecourt's lawns.

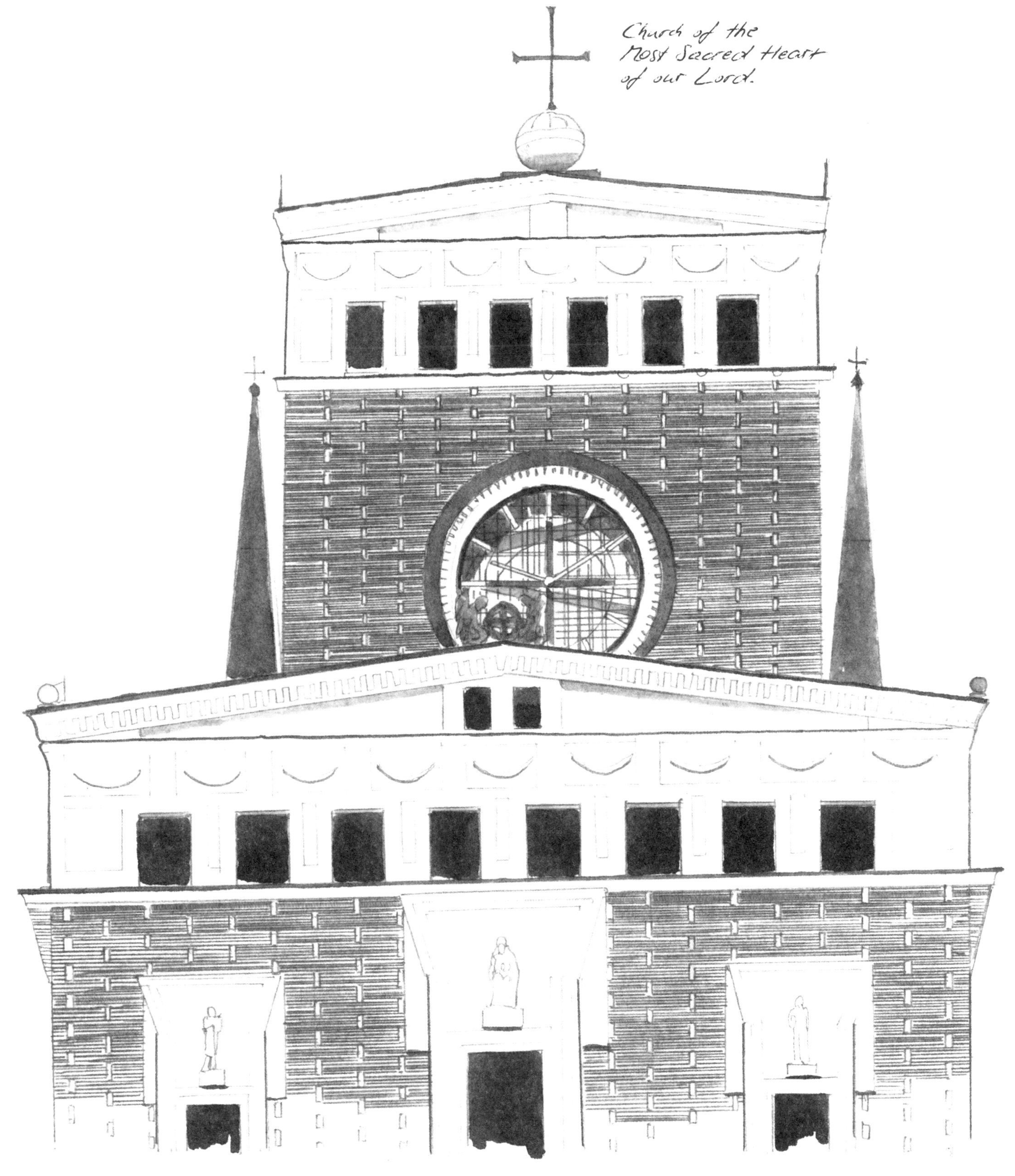

Church of the
Most Sacred Heart
of our Lord.

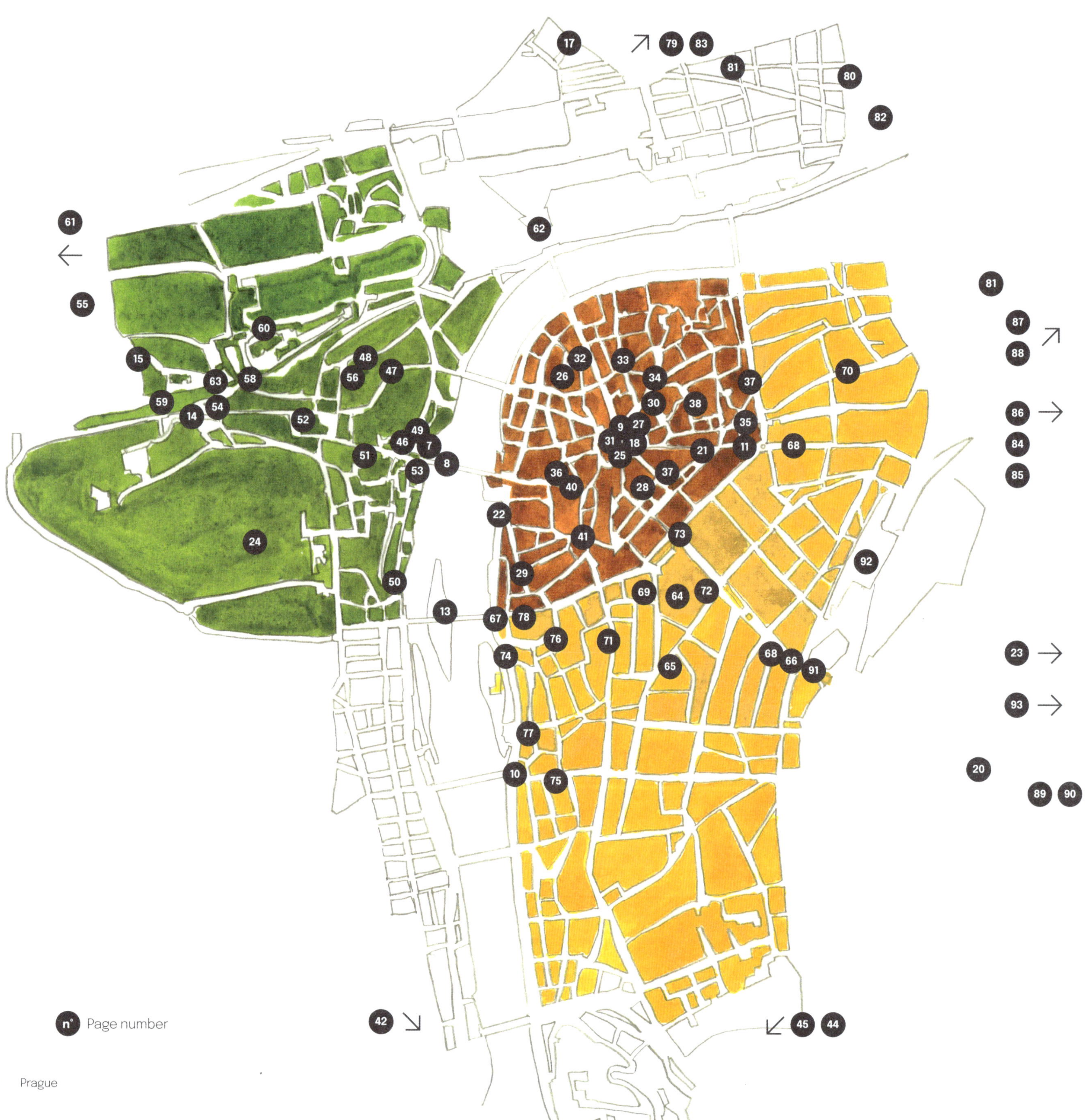

n° Page number

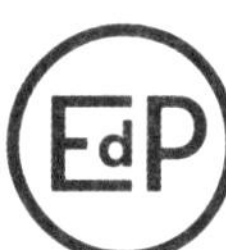

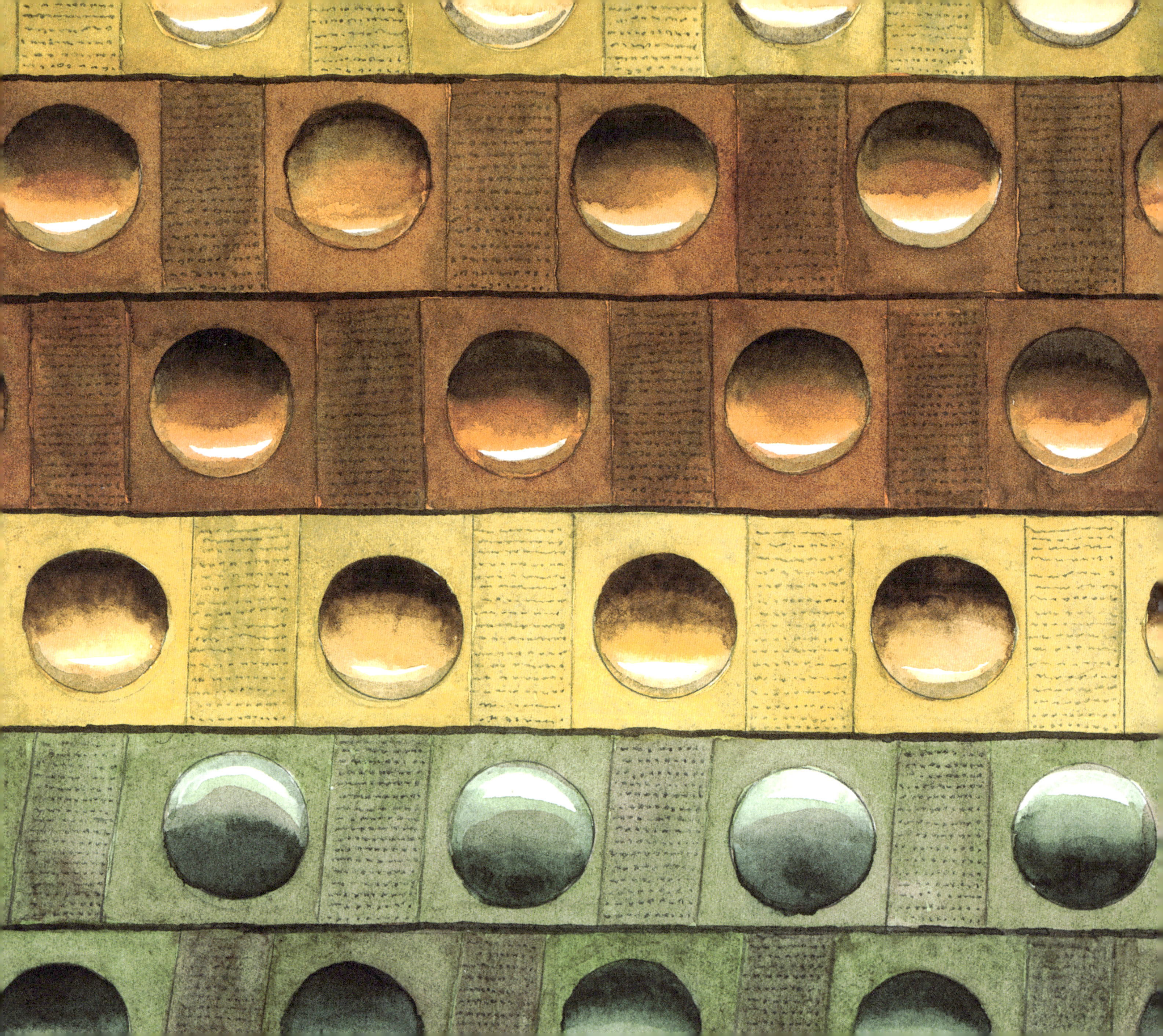